WITHOUT SIN

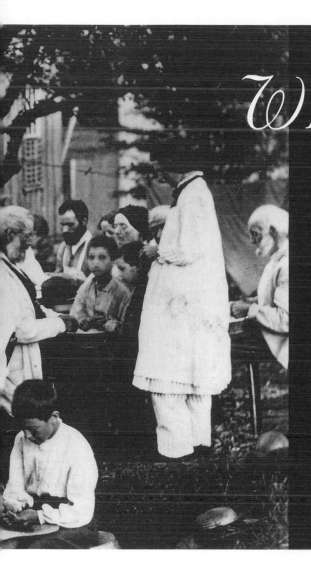

Without Sin

THE LIFE AND DEATH OF THE ONEIDA COMMUNITY

Spencer Klaw

ALLEN LANE
THE PENGUIN PRESS

ALLEN LANE
THE PENGUIN PRESS
Published by the Penguin Group
Penguin Books USA Inc., 375 Hudson Street,
New York, New York 10014, U.S.A.
Penguin Books Ltd, 27 Wrights Lane, London W8 5TZ, England
Penguin Books Australia Ltd, Ringwood, Victoria, Australia
Penguin Books Canada Ltd, 10 Alcorn Avenue, Toronto, Ontario, Canada M4V 3B2
Penguin Books (N.Z.) Ltd, 182–190 Wairau Road, Auckland 10, New Zealand

Penguin Books Ltd, Registered Offices: Harmondsworth, Middlesex, England

First published in 1993 by Viking Penguin,
a division of Penguin Books USA Inc.

1 3 5 7 9 10 8 6 4 2

The photograph that appears on the title page shows Oneidans shelling peas for canning and is reproduced courtesy of the Oneida Community Mansion House.

In the photographic insert following page 178, plates II, VIII, IX, X, and XII are reproduced courtesy of the Oneida Community Collection, Syracuse University Library. All other photos reproduced courtesy of the Oneida Community Mansion House.

LIBRARY OF CONGRESS CATALOGING IN PUBLICATION DATA
Klaw, Spencer, 1920–
Without sin: the life and death of the Oneida community/ by
Spencer Klaw.
p.   cm.
Includes index.
ISBN 0-7139-9091-0
1. Oneida Community—History.   2. Noyes, John Humphrey,
1811–1886.   I. Title.
HX656.O5K58   1993
335'.9747'64—dc20   93–7231

Printed in the United States of America
Set in Galliard   Designed by Brian Mulligan

For Bobby

Acknowledgments

Much of the most important research material on which this book is based would surely have eluded me if it had not been for the generous help of certain individuals connected in one way or another with the old Oneida Community. These are the people who steered me to letters, memoirs, and other documents tucked away in cupboards and filing cabinets and cardboard boxes in the Community's old home, the Mansion House, in Oneida, New York. I am also deeply grateful to those who shared with me documents in their own possession. Many who so kindly came to my assistance were descendants of the old Community; almost all of them lived within a three-minute walk of the Mansion House, or in the Mansion House itself.

I am particularly indebted to Judith O. Noyes, who at the time I began my research was chairperson of the Oneida Community Historical Committee. Her patient guidance and unstinting hospitality made my many trips to Oneida thoroughly pleasant as well as productive. I also want to especially thank her then-husband, Paul V. Noyes, for his persuasive intercession on my behalf with other Community descendants; his help was particularly important because many people with key documents in their possession were understandably wary of writers who might, they feared, be motivated solely by a prurient interest in the Community's peculiar sexual arrangements. One of those with whom he interceded was the late Imogen Noyes Stone, to whom I am profoundly grateful for allowing me to make use of the vast collection of documents amassed and collated by her father, George Wallingford Noyes—documents without which a comprehensive account of the Oneida Community could not have been written.

Other people for whose generosity and help I am most appreciative are May Beagle; P. Geoffrey Noyes; J. Langford Hatcher, president of the board of trustees of the Oneida Community Mansion House; and Jane Kinsley Rich, who permitted me to draw on the then-unpublished recollections of her grandmother, Jessie Catherine Kinsley, who had grown up at Oneida. I also want to thank two people whose links to the Oneida Community are professional rather than familial: Gail Doering Weimer, curator of collections at the Mansion House, and her husband, Mark F. Weimer, curator of special collections at the Syracuse University Library in Syracuse, New York.

Finally, I am more grateful than I can possibly say to my wife, Bobby, for her help with the final stages of research, for her expert editing of the manuscript, and, perhaps most important, for her sympathy and encouragement during the long gestation that preceded the birth of this book.

Contents

List of Illustrations

ILLUSTRATIONS APPEAR FOLLOWING PAGE 178

WITHOUT SIN

*I*n the early summer of 1879 the members of the Oneida Community, a tightly knit and thriving society of some three hundred Christian communists living in upper New York State, received a startling and, to many, troubling piece of news. It concerned their sixty-seven-year-old leader, John Humphrey Noyes, who had founded the Community in 1848 as a bridgehead over which, he was convinced, the armies of Christ would soon advance to establish God's kingdom on earth. If that heavenly invasion now seemed less imminent to Noyes than it had thirty years before, there was still no reason, as far as an outside observer could see, why he should feel his experiment had failed. On the contrary, the imposing brick mansion in which Noyes and his followers lived, the handsome lawns and gardens by which it was surrounded, the bustling factories and workshops that the Oneidans ran, the glowing health of their children, all bore testimony that communism could be made to work—a communism so complete that for a time even watches were owned by the Community rather than by the men who carried them in their pockets. Indeed, as Noyes had recently noted with justifiable

Spencer Klaw

pride in his widely praised *History of American Socialisms*, the Oneida Community had proved to be much the most durable, and by that token the most successful, of the forty-odd utopian communities that had been planted on American soil with such high hopes in the first half of the century. Nevertheless, on June 23, 1879, Noyes effectively abdicated the throne from which, for nearly half his life, he had ruled over the Oneida Community with what he believed to be divine authority. That he had indeed abdicated was at the time clear neither to Noyes nor to his followers. All that was known at Oneida was that he had slipped away during the night without leaving word as to where he was going or when he might return, and without appointing a deputy to rule in his—and God's—name during his absence.

As the Oneidans subsequently learned, some time after midnight Noyes had left his sparsely furnished bedroom on the second floor of the Mansion House, as the Community called its home, and had crept downstairs in his stocking feet. Outside the building he had stopped to pull on his boots and had then walked a short distance to where two men, both members of the Community, were waiting with a carriage. The three of them had then driven twenty-five miles to a railroad station in the out-of-the-way village of Holland Patent, where Noyes and one of his companions bought tickets for Ogdensburg, New York, intending to catch a ferry there that would take them across the St. Lawrence River into Canada.

Noyes later recalled the fears that had tortured him on his journey. "The omnipresence of the telegraph system, and the probability of being pursued or intercepted by that means, was always before my imagination," he wrote, "and beyond that was the shadow of a life and perhaps a death in the State Prison." To foil pursuers who might learn of his destination by questioning the station agent at Holland Patent, Noyes decided not to go all the way to Ogdensburg. Instead he and his fellow traveler got off the train at an earlier stop, Morristown, from which they could also reach Canada by ferry. "After a delay . . . which seemed to me merciless, endless," Noyes wrote, "but which was really only half an hour of ordinary life to other people, we moved out into the broad St. Lawrence, and the agony was over."

The immediate occasion of Noyes's fearful flight from Oneida was a newspaper report that a group of Presbyterian clergymen were bent on having him haled into court on criminal charges. The precise nature of the charges had not been disclosed. But, given the highly unconventional sexual arrangements that distinguished Oneida from Brook Farm and other experiments in communal living, it was easy to guess what the ministers had in mind. Noyes and his followers believed that, in a community of true Christians, God did not intend that love between men and women should be confined to the narrow channels of conventional matrimony. All the men at Oneida were therefore considered to be married to all the women. Within certain limitations—protracted love affairs, for example, were prohibited as obstructions to the free flow of love—any man was at liberty to have sexual relations with any woman who consented to be his partner. Noyes and his followers thus routinely, and as a matter of religious principle, violated the outside world's laws against adultery and fornication. A greater threat was posed by the fact—as yet apparently unknown to the authorities—that boys and girls were expected to join in the sexual life of the Community while in their early teens, and that the girls were ordinarily introduced to sex, usually by Noyes himself, as soon as they reached puberty.

Not all of Noyes's followers were convinced that the danger of prosecution for playing the role of "first husband" to twelve- and thirteen-year-old girls was grave enough to justify or explain his precipitous flight to Canada. There would have to be a complaining witness, and in view of the love and respect in which Noyes was held by the young women who had grown up at Oneida, it was almost unthinkable that any would come forward.

But fear of prosecution was not the only reason, or the most important, why Noyes left Oneida on that summer night in 1879—and why, as it turned out, he chose never to return. For some time he had been depressed by a serious challenge to his leadership. More and more Oneidans were questioning his claim to have been authorized directly by God to rule over them. The march of science; the appeal of positivism, with its rejection of all knowledge not founded on science; the Darwinian theory of evolution, which Noyes himself had studied with great excitement—all these had caused defections from the faith in Noyes's divine inspiration that for so many years had united all Oneidans. Some Community members, including Noyes's son Theodore, a Yale-educated physician whom Noyes had tried but failed to install as his successor, were no longer sure that they believed in God at all. Months before his flight to Canada Noyes had dismayed one of his lieutenants by suggesting that perhaps it was time for the Community to disband. He had then added, in an uncharacteristic burst of self-pity, "I shall have to ask the Community to dismiss me. They evidently want and need a new leader. I shall have to go somewhere else and take with me all who want to live as I do."

Noyes's departure from Oneida did nothing to heal the breach that had opened between his loyal followers and a group of disaffected critics. Their disagreement was mainly over the regulation of sex. In the past, Noyes himself, together with his wife and sisters and other so-called central members of the Community, had routinely headed off, or broken up, liaisons that they considered inappropriate. The rules, though unwritten, were well understood. Young people, for example, were not permitted to pair up exclusively with other young people; in conformity with the principle of "ascending fellowship," the young were expected at least some of the time to choose (or accept) as sexual partners older members from whose example and company they might reap spiritual benefits. At the same time, older members who failed by too wide a margin to live up to what Noyes expected of true Christians were disciplined by having their choice of sexual partners severely limited. By 1879, however, even though Noyes had wielded his power over his followers' sex lives with great tact and shrewdness, many Oneidans were demanding more freedom in sexual matters. They argued that young people should be free not to have sexual relations with older people, however uplifting their company, if they didn't want to; and they insisted that adults should be at liberty to choose their sexual partners without having to take up the matter with Noyes or anyone else. But this was unacceptable to the loyalists, and in the end all that the two parties could agree on was that even conventional marriage would be preferable to the sexual anarchy into which they were drifting. And so, two months after Noyes had fled to Canada, the Oneidans sadly voted, at the urging of their absent leader, to end their thirty-one-year experiment with what they called complex marriage.

Even though couples who now wished to get married would be free to do so, and even though there would now be no sex outside of marriage, it was hoped that the Community could carry on in other respects much as before. But as Noyes had often argued, marriage and communism were not to be reconciled, and it was communism that gave way. The old unity was shattered. Loyalty to self and family—the selfishness, as Noyes saw it, that was inherent in ordinary marriage—triumphed over loyalty to the Community. There were bitter arguments over who was to fill which jobs, over who was pulling his weight in the Community and who wasn't, and over the education of the children. God, like Noyes, seemed to have abandoned Oneida, and in 1880 communism went the way of complex marriage. The Community's property, including a spoon factory that was to grow in time into one of the world's leading manufacturers of flatware, was transferred to a corporation, Oneida Community, Ltd., the stock in which was parceled out among the former communists. Supported by a generous allowance from the new company, Noyes lived on until 1886 in a rambling stone house overlooking the American Falls on the Canadian side of the Niagara River. He was comforted in his exile by a little band of supporters who preserved, as best they could, the spirit and customs (other than complex marriage) of the Oneida Community. In 1881, reflecting on the experiment that he had launched thirty-three years before, Noyes wrote, "We made a raid into an unknown country, charted it, and returned without the loss of a man, woman or child." But such brave words only emphasized the magnitude and poignancy of Noyes's loss. As one of his grandchildren wrote years later, "Could anything be more dramatic—a man now in his seventieth year, standing amid the ruins of his lifework, shouting 'Victory!' "

Even in the long years when God smiled on Oneida there were

people who joined the Community, found it not to their liking, and departed. There was no privacy at Oneida, in sex or anything else. Anyone betraying a "bad spirit"—anyone, that is, who deviated from Community norms—could expect to have his faults unsparingly tabulated and analyzed at one of the sessions of "mutual criticism" to which Oneidans were expected to submit. ("Every trait of my character that I took any pride or comfort in seemed to be cruelly discounted," one man wrote of his first criticism; "and after, as it were, being turned inside out and thoroughly inspected, I was, metaphorically, stood upon my head, and allowed to drain till all the self-righteousness had dripped out of me.") Couples who fell in love in the wrong way, and ceased to "circulate" sexually, were accused of "idolatrous love" or "the marriage spirit"; if criticism failed to bring them into line, one of the offenders was likely to be sent off to one of Oneida's outposts or satellite communities. Ambition, such as a too-evident desire to excel as a singer or musician, was seen as a dangerous trait that bore close watching. Intellectual freedom, in common with the freedom to choose one's sexual partners, was not unlimited. It is true that Oneidans were encouraged to read and study even writers like Darwin and Auguste Comte, who seemed determined to blow up the theological foundations on which Oneida had been erected. But until near the end it was not easy for a member to disagree publicly with Noyes on anything, from the proper treatment of diphtheria (ice and mutual criticism was what Noyes prescribed) to the writing of Nathaniel Hawthorne ("glorifies evil . . . vitally pernicious"). One must assume, too, that some members and prospective members squirmed at the public professions of faith in Noyes's wisdom and divine inspiration that were all but obligatory. ("Mr. Hamilton," a report of one of the Community's regular evening meetings noted, "was conscious that his unity with Mr. Noyes had made him what he is. . . . [He] said the world cried despot to Mr. Noyes, but those of us who are honest and true call him father and liberator.")

Yet over the years hundreds of people, many of them well educated and most of them from what we would now call solid middle- to upper-middle-class backgrounds, found life at Oneida immensely rich and satisfying. Oneida was perhaps the most successful attempt ever made (the Shakers excepted) to build a society in which men and women could live together as brothers and sisters, sharing with absolute equality the fruits of their common labor. In addition—and it is in this respect that the Oneidans differed most strikingly from the Shakers or members of monastic communities—they could bear and rear children. Complex marriage was an imaginative effort to liberate men and women from the narrow, and often narrowing, confines of monogamy and conventional family life. It was particularly advantageous to women. At Oneida, women had sexual relations only when and (by and large) with whom they pleased—which could not be said of numberless married women in the world outside. All men were required to practice birth control, using a technique developed by Noyes, and no woman had to bear more children than suited her. Children, once weaned, were raised communally, and men shared with women in their care and upbringing. All this, plus the relative efficiency of communal cooking and housekeeping (in which men to some extent also shared), meant that women at Oneida were spared not only constant pregnancies but also much of the lonely drudgery of housewives in families that could not afford servants.

One remarkable aspect of the Oneida Community was its repudiation of the Christian notion of life on earth as a vale of tears. Oneidans might suffer keenly at times from a sense of not being close enough to Christ, but they were taught by Noyes that unhappiness was, if not a sin, a serious deficiency. "The more we get acquainted with God," he once remarked, "the more we shall find it our special duty to be happy." In Noyes's view, the giving of pleasure through sexual intercourse should be cultivated as an art—an art that he considered to rank above music and painting and poetry. Work, too, was intended to be joyous. Oneidans were encouraged to change jobs often to prevent boredom, and whenever possible hard and monotonous work was transformed into a social occasion. On a summer evening a hundred volunteers, with the Community band at their head, might march out to pick the strawberries that Oneida shipped in huge quantities to New York and other cities. Elderly people worked as much or as little as they liked, and in their later years they spent much of their time watching and playing with the children of the Community; when they grew too old to manage on their own, they were looked after by other, not-quite-so-elderly members. There was ample time for intellectual improvement, and it often seemed to visitors that everyone at Oneida was studying astronomy or Greek or chemistry or French. There was time, too, for music and games. The Oneidans danced, sang, organized orchestras, put on plays and operettas, played croquet and chess and backgammon and baseball, went camping and on picnics, and loafed and fished at vacation cottages on Long Island Sound and on the shore of Lake Oneida.

As the years went by and the Community flourished, journalists flocked to Oneida, and many wrote admiring accounts of what they found there. Other visitors, from Europe as well as America, included writers, politicians, educational reformers, sociologists, clergymen, and philosophers. Oneida became a great tourist attraction, and on summer Sundays trainloads of visitors, often with children in tow, came to picnic on the shady lawns surrounding the Mansion House, to stare at the short hair and short skirts of the women, and to speculate on the exotic sexual life of the Community, while their hosts fed them strawberries and cream and entertained them with band music.

The inevitable frustration of elaborate schemes for making people happy and good is, of course, the stuff of comedy. But if the Oneidans were not quite so happy or so good as outsiders were given to believe, they were happy and good enough so that it is impossible, after reading their letters and diaries and recollections, to contemplate the collapse of Noyes's daring scheme for human betterment without a stabbing sense of loss. In a memoir written for her daughter many years after that collapse, a woman who grew up at Oneida undertook to describe what life there had meant for her mother and herself. For her mother, it had been "like coming into a new world, like entering college for life. . . . These communists . . . gave up everything for a cause, sought a new home in a wild place, entered into strange new ways; yet their spiritual and mental growth was accelerated by their leader, through the enthusiasm of their numbers and the constant giving and seeking of the gifts of the mind and heart." As for herself, she had been unaware, until almost the end, of the conflicts that were to break up the Community. "I lived quite down at the foot of the hill," she wrote, "where a sweet breeze of faith and contentment blew away hate and suspicion and made me believe that I was indeed living in the Kingdom of Heaven. . . . Indeed, many mistakes were made. And yet I have faith to believe that here a great example of unselfishness was set to the world for all time, and that the future will find that out."

oyes once observed that the establishment of God's kingdom on earth was destined to be preceded by "a chaos of confusion, tribulation, and war." But God, he added, "has set me to cast up a highway across this chaos, and I am gathering out the stones and grading the track as fast as possible." He was twenty-six when he wrote these words, and although at times he despaired of his ability to fathom and carry out God's intentions, he never afterward wavered in his belief that God had set him apart from, and above, other men. At Putney, Vermont, where he first tried out many of his notions of how true Christians should live, he made his followers acknowledge his divine authority by taking a formal vow of obedience. "John H. Noyes," it read, "is the father and overseer whom the Holy Ghost has set over [us]. To John H. Noyes as such we submit ourselves in all things spiritual and temporal." Later, at Oneida, no such written declarations were required. But for nearly thirty years anyone who questioned Noyes's divine inspiration was given heavy doses of corrective criticism and was liable, if he or she did not repent the apostasy, to expulsion from the Community. Noyes himself was quick to point out that anyone rejecting his divine authority was rebelling against God. Oneidans would have to realize, he said, "that I am a man of God, and that I am right whether they understand me or not."

Noyes claimed to be more than simply a divine messenger. He believed that God had made him holier than other men. When he was asked why he never offered himself up on the altar of mutual criticism, he replied that he would be happy to be criticized if and when Christ or St. Paul, or even some lowlier member of the Primitive Church, should return to earth and take on the task. But until such time he would be uncriticizable. His belief in his spiritual superiority was also reflected in his conduct of the experiment in scientific human breeding—or stirpiculture, as Noyes called it—that the Oneidans embarked on in 1869. Parents were chosen mainly on the basis of their spiritual development—that is, on their conformity to Noyes's ideas of how Christians should deal with God and one another. Not surprisingly, nine of the fifty-eight "stirpicults" born at Oneida were fathered by Noyes himself.

Noyes was a man of powerful sexual drives, and for many years he was perhaps the most active participant in the sexual life of the Community. He was a connoisseur of female sexuality, likening a follower named Fanny Leonard to "a beautiful plant . . . having no outward activity, yet throwing around a fragrance, pleasing our eyes and giving us delight for what she is, and not for what she does." His wife, Harriet, he regarded more as a colleague than a lover. "I like her very much—" he once remarked, "not as a wife; I don't care anything about her as a wife—but as a co-worker in the Kingdom of Christ." For years he had a passionate love affair with another co-worker, Mary Cragin, of whom he said admiringly, "Anybody that has ever approached her as a lover has found her spirit exceedingly intoxicating —one that will make a man crazy." He was so deeply in love with her, and for so long, as seemingly to violate his own strictures against exclusive or idolatrous attachments. But she died in 1851—a sloop in which she was sailing on the Hudson River capsized and she drowned—and from then on Noyes was, by his own standards, an exemplary lover: tender, gallant, appreciative, solicitous of his partners' pleasure, and free from the possessiveness that he condemned in others as "the claiming spirit." He never again fell victim to romantic love, which he recoiled from as "a kind of fatality—something that people *fall* into as a man walking in the dark might fall into a pit or into the jaws of a wild beast."

Noyes was tall and rather slender, with piercing blue eyes, sandy hair, a firm mouth, a jaw that jutted forward pugnaciously, and an imposing dome of a forehead over which, in his later years, wrinkles came and went like waves when he sat and thought, as he liked to do, with his eyes closed. (Children who saw him thinking in this manner were told that he was communing with St. Paul.) But if he was not handsome—as a young man, he recalled, "I looked so uncomely that I never expected to make myself agreeable to woman as a lover"—he was nevertheless extraordinarily attractive to women. He dominated them, his son Theodore wrote, "by his intellectual power and social"—that is, sexual—"magnetism, superadded to intense religious convictions to which young women are very susceptible." To many younger women at Oneida he was both lover and father. One who had been deeply troubled by doubts about Noyes's divine inspiration wrote to a friend that Noyes had sought her out and that she had found him "so kind and loving [that] my heart melted within me." Later, she continued, "I went to his room and told him I could do one thing, and that was to submit myself to him and look for his spirit to enter into me and fill me. I . . . sat down by him and unburdened myself. He is full of mercy and tenderness."

Men, too, were powerfully drawn to Noyes. James Herrick, an Episcopal minister who had left a church in New York City to join the Community, recalled him as having "a most delicate and artistic sense of others' tastes and feelings, as though he said: 'I wish to give you all the pleasure I possibly can.'" Herrick continued, "In the Community he had the queen-bee quality of attracting all to him and making them harmonious among themselves." As a young man, it is true, Noyes could be a bully. His victims included his mother, who for years resisted his claims to divine authority. He once informed her coldly—he was twenty-six at the time—that she was henceforth to regard him as her "father." He added, "I hope you will help your father . . . like a dutiful daughter, and not go about to hinder and vex him." On another occasion he advised her to pray for deliverance from her "accusing spirit and . . . licentious tongue." And all his life Noyes was very hard on people who, having come under his influence, then chose to break with him and thereby do the devil's work. He was characteristically unsparing, for example, in his denunciation of a chronic troublemaker named Mills who was expelled from Oneida in 1864. Mills, Noyes said in a soaring flight of vituperation, was "the representative of that species of parasites which works its way through the vitals of families and society by bare power of jackass-will and brazen effrontery, without lubrication of any kind except canting pretences of extraordinary piety." But with backsliders who were, in Noyes's phrase, softhearted—who believed, or *wanted* to believe, without reservation in God and John Humphrey Noyes—he was almost always patient and reassuring. His manner when he spoke to his followers, whether individually or at the Community's regular evening meetings, was informal and relaxed. Although not much of a hand himself at making jokes, he appreciated humor, and was convinced that God did, too. "If you listen to the strains which are ever sounding through creation," he wrote, "you will find that God's everlasting melody is at once full of seriousness and full of mirth." He never ranted or threatened his followers with hellfire. His method was, rather, to persuade those who wished to be true Christians that to do what God wanted them to do was the most natural and reasonable thing in the world.

Like many other Americans of his day, Noyes was excited by the great scientific discoveries of the nineteenth century. His notions about breeding a superior race of human beings were derived mainly from the writings of Darwin and Francis Galton, the founder of eugenics. Noyes's enthusiasm for science was, indeed, so great that he came to believe that virtually all human activities could be improved by a rigorous application of scientific principles. With the zeal of a convert (and autodidact) he insisted that not even art was to be excluded. He once suggested that poetry should perhaps replace music as the principal art of the Oneida Community. "What I want," he explained, "is not empirical, sporadic, baby-efforts to manufacture poems, but a school that shall master the science that underlies all poetry."

At the same time Noyes believed in an unseen world whose inhabitants were continually influencing, both for good and for evil, the lives of people dwelling in the world we know. Once, as a young man, he had a vision of a young woman with whom he was falling in love, whom he saw "standing, as it were, on the pinnacle of the universe, in the glory of an angel." Then a voice said "Satan transformed into an angel of light," and on the strength of this pronouncement he "gave her up"—temporarily, as it turned out—"as one accursed." In later years the messages he received from the other world arrived with fewer dramatic flourishes. When an idea came to him, his son Theodore recalled, "he would hold still and consult the spiritual world, not by questions, but by holding his mind passive. If the thought became clearer, and had a particular satisfaction in it . . . he concluded that the idea was inspired." He spoke often of the devil, holding him responsible for, among other things, spreading the deplorable and erroneous notion that flesh is evil. The devil, Noyes explained, was envious of the earthly pleasures, including sex, that God had given to humans for their enjoyment. He therefore tries to convince humans, in a spirit of sour grapes, that man's "body is gross and his passions vile—that it is a bad thing to eat and drink, and a shameful thing to express love." Noyes also blamed the devil, and associated "wicked spirits," for all disease and bodily distress. Thus when Noyes one day undertook to write the copy for a poster advertising an auction at Oneida and was afflicted simultaneously by a headache, a toothache, and "general nervous torment," he knew whom to hold accountable. The devil, he said, "is jealous of my getting out before the public." Noyes conceded that the sick could sometimes be helped by doctors, and he sent his oldest son, Theodore, to Yale to be trained as a physician. In later life, too, he became an enthusiast for the Turkish bath as a means of warding off disease. But he was, Theodore Noyes once explained, "a strange composite of mysticism and common sense," and he also believed in miracle cures, claiming on occasion to have worked such cures himself. Recalling how he had rid his brother-in-law of severe headaches, he said, "I laid my hand on his head, and told him to shake off the devil. He rose at once, perfectly free from pain, and has not been troubled with this disease since." He failed, however, to cure himself, by faith, of a recurring and painful throat ailment, and possibly for this reason he seemed to lose confidence in later years in his ability to heal by simple exhortation and the laying on of hands. The best way to drive the devil out of a sick person's body, he at length concluded, was to assemble an ad hoc committee and put the patient through a brisk bedside session of mutual criticism. For years Noyes was convinced that he and some of his followers were destined to triumph not only over disease, but over death as well. Those qualifying for immortality, he said, would be changed from earthly to heavenly beings without having to die first. He expected this change to take place, at least in his own case, at a face-to-face meeting with Christ.

Noyes hated priests, and there was little that was priestly about the way he ruled Oneida. He liked working with his hands, and although much of his effort went into writing for the newspaper that the Community sent out to subscribers around the country, he also laid up stone foundations, ran a printing press and a silk-winding machine, braided palm-leaf hats, forged springs for animal traps, milked cows, shoveled manure, and worked in the Community kitchen. On the theory that it was a mistake to get into a rut, because then the devil would know exactly where to find him, he was continually trying new things. He played the violin (badly) in the Community orchestra, attended classes in algebra, struggled to master the principles of musical composition, and, in his seventies, got up at four in the morning to study Hebrew. He dressed like other men in the Community, though perhaps more carelessly. A woman who grew up at Oneida remembered noticing as a child his spotted vest and "how his coat hung off rather loosely in the back, and his slippered feet scuffed under long trousers." Wherever he was in residence, whether at Oneida or one of the satellite communities where he often lived, he was easily approached. The room he lived in at Oneida was small and simply furnished, and anyone was free to drop in. One Oneidan recalled years later that people who went to his room for advice, or with plans or complaints, often "stayed to play games of cards or dominoes; sometimes went to him for love."

For all his insistence that God had given him the last word in Community affairs, Noyes was in many ways a democratic as well as an egalitarian leader. Major questions of a practical sort, such as where a new building should be located and how it should be designed, or whether to go into a new line of business, were debated at length by committees and in open meetings, and decisions were usually arrived at by consensus. Noyes's views on such matters counted heavily. But when one of his ideas met strong resistance from the central members of the Community, as his principal advisers were known, he often seems to have concluded that the idea was not, after all, divinely inspired, and that he need not insist on its adoption.

Yet he never ceased instructing his followers in how they should behave and think. Often his instructions were general, as when he called for the rejection of prevailing American notions about the virtues of individual liberty. The only worthwhile form of liberty, he declared, was "the liberty of *unity*—the liberty . . . to approach one another and love one another—the liberty of communism." At other times he was more specific. In the first year of the Oneida Community, for instance, he complained vigorously about long skirts. "Woman's dress is a standing lie," he said. "It proclaims that she is not a two-legged animal, but something like a churn standing on casters." In the interests of honesty and comfort, he suggested, women should shift to short dresses worn over trousers, or pantaloons, and this soon became the standard costume at Oneida. To simplify its care, Oneida women also wore their hair unfashionably short. Many of Noyes's admonitions and exhortations had to do with sex. He once recommended that there be less talk during sex, explaining, "I imagine that the impotence, which some of the men complain of, may be connected with over-activity of the tongue." In the early days at Oneida he called on his followers to take more advantage of the freedom of sexual choice that complex marriage offered, urging in particular that older women must not be neglected. As he put it delicately in a letter to a group of young men, "Let us also be heroes in love, and train our hearts to scale the heights above us as well as to enjoy the beauties of our own level." He once suggested to a favorite niece that it might be a good thing if couples were to have sexual intercourse in public, on the stage of the Community's meeting hall. The spectacle "would give pleasure to a great many of our older people who now have nothing to do with the matter," and would serve to emphasize that sex is an art. "There is no reason," he said, "why that should not be done in public as much as music and dancing." Since nothing more was heard from Noyes about this idea, he no doubt decided it had not been divinely inspired. On another occasion he lectured on the folly of prudery, suggesting that his hearers draw up a list of "the most savory, clean, wholesome objects to which the sexual organs can be compared." Noyes, who was not much better at metaphors than he was at playing the violin, went on to offer an example of what he had in mind. "As a man is said to know a woman in sexual intercourse," he suggested, "why not speak of the telescope with which he penetrates her heavens, and seeks the star of her heart."

From time to time Noyes invented words and phrases to help him guide his followers along the path to holiness. Oneidans spoke of prima donna fever; of body-tending (excessive concern for physical health); and of the hypo (severe depression). Other special terms were "principality," meaning a bad habit, influence, or state of mind, as in "the tobacco principality"; and "diotrephiasis," a near relative of prima donna fever that took its name from a biblical character, Diotrephes, whose great fault was his love of preeminence. In his efforts to build up a kind of common law for Oneidans to follow, Noyes also made use of the rites of mutual criticism, in which he sometimes took part as chief critic. Thus in summing up the criticism that had been meted out to his brother-in-law, John Skinner, he observed that Skinner was a poor lover, "green, deficient in skill to make himself attractive." He went on to suggest some of the particular skills that were lacking. "The compound of a perfect lover," he said, "is goodness and a musical external nature. . . . Mr. Skinner is an honest, serious, conscientious man; but these elements of his character are not sufficiently embodied in cunning, romance, and emotion. Love, perfected, is very cunning."

Noyes believed staying out of a rut was as good for others as for himself. "We take up things and suck the marrow out of them," he said, referring specifically to the Community's forms of amusement and recreation, "and then leave them and go to something else." As a rule it was Noyes himself who decided that the marrow had been sucked out of chess, or dancing, or baseball, and that it was time to move on. He repeatedly changed the style and content of the newspaper that the Community published, and right up to the end he was hopefully tinkering with the machinery of the utopia he had invented. In the spring of 1879, for example, he undertook to revamp the format of the Community's evening meetings, with the aim of making them livelier and more edifying. "He says he has learned to edit the paper and now he is going to learn how to edit the meetings," an Oneidan wrote to a friend, adding that Noyes had said he was aiming at nothing less than "the greatest scheme and system of education that we have ever yet dreamed of." But God had other plans; three months later Noyes was in Canada and his great experiment had all but ended.

reporter for the *New York World* once wrote that the Oneida Community was steeped in an atmosphere of bookish rusticity. With the addition of the word *prosperous* his phrase may stand as a description of the circumstances in which the Community's founder was reared. Born in Brattleboro, Vermont, in 1811, John Humphrey Noyes grew up in a village society that was equally removed, both geographically and culturally, from the still-raw frontier settlements across the Hudson River to the west and the literary and religious sophistication of Boston to the east. His father, John Noyes, had been a peripatetic village schoolteacher; a student and, later, a tutor at Dartmouth, where Daniel Webster was among his pupils; and then a minister. But he had found the ministry not to his liking—his health wasn't up to it, and besides, or so his son asserted, he was "too bashful for the pulpit"—and in 1799, when he was thirty-five, he had taken a job as a clerk in a Brattleboro store. Soon afterward he married Polly Hayes, a tall, red-haired, strong-minded woman whose father was a popular tavern keeper in Brattleboro, and one of whose nephews, Rutherford B. Hayes, was destined to become the nineteenth president of the United States. By the time John Humphrey was born, the elder Noyes was in business for himself as a dealer in groceries and farm commodities and had embarked on a political career that was to take him to Washington for a term as one of Vermont's two congressmen.

John Humphrey was the first boy in the family, and Polly Noyes, a deeply religious woman, prayed that he would grow up to be "a minister of the Everlasting Gospel." At her insistence he and his brothers and sisters—there were eventually seven in all—had a strict religious upbringing. At Brattleboro, and later in the big white house overlooking the village of Putney, Vermont, where the family moved when John Humphrey was ten, there were daily family prayers and daily readings from the New Testament. Once, when John Humphrey was eight, his mother took him to a revival meeting, and he was recorded as a convert. Later, when he went to Dartmouth—he would have preferred Yale, but Polly Noyes thought Dartmouth had a more wholesome moral atmosphere—he attended the twice-daily compulsory prayer meetings and, on his own, read a chapter a day from the Bible.

But any effects of his early conversion were fleeting. At Dartmouth he was more interested in poetry and history than religion, and worried less about pleasing God than pleasing girls. He told himself that even though his cheeks were "as freckled as a toad's back," he could make girls like him if he could only overcome his extreme bashfulness in their presence. "I swear by Jove, I will be impudent!" he wrote in his diary. He was seventeen when he made that vow, and it was not long before he had mastered at least the rudiments of stylized and decorous flirtation. But it was to be years before he kissed a girl, and there is no reason to doubt his claim, made shortly before his marriage at the age of twenty-seven, that he could say, in the words of John Bunyan, "I knew not whether there is a woman in the world, otherwise than by their dress and common report."

At Dartmouth Noyes was more successful as a student than with girls. He was elected to Phi Beta Kappa and chosen to give one of the commencement day orations. He had decided to become a lawyer, and after graduating he accepted an invitation from his brother-in-law, Larkin Mead, to prepare for the bar as a clerk in Mead's law office in Chesterfield, New Hampshire. He stayed there just a year. Then, in the summer of 1831, a few days after his twentieth birthday, he announced that he was giving up the law and meant to devote his life to serving God.

Such declarations were not uncommon in 1831, a year when the country was in the grip of a feverish religious excitement rivaling the Great Awakening of the 1740s. In keeping with the spirit of Jacksonian politics, itinerant evangelists were denouncing the undemocratic Calvinist view that admission to heaven was not to be won by faith or good works, but was the predestined privilege of a chosen few. Any American, they proclaimed, could get into heaven if only he would sincerely repent his sins. To encourage repentance, the evangelists labored to portray hell in such lurid terms that sinners would all but feel the scorching heat. "Look! Look!" the celebrated revivalist Charles Grandison Finney told a trembling congregation in Troy, New York. "See the millions of wretches, biting and gnawing their tongues, as they lift their scalding heads from the burning lake! See! See! how they are tossed, and how they howl. . . . Hear them groan, amidst the fiery billows." Sinners were publicly denounced—and publicly prayed for—and when a revivalist came to town, one historian has written, "meetings were held almost daily, and prolonged until the small hours of the morning, so that the ordinary business of life virtually came to a standstill and whole communities were groggy with a mixture of exaltation and sleeplessness."

One of the communities scheduled for a revival was Putney. A four-day series of meetings was held there in mid-September 1831, and among those in attendance was Noyes, who was taking a vacation from his legal studies in Chesterfield. He went only to please his mother, and in a thoroughly skeptical frame of mind, having long since decided, as he wrote later, "to indulge the lust of the eye and the pride of life . . . in short, to [forget about] the life to come." But to his surprise, his determination to "continue at war with God" was badly shaken. A day after the meetings ended, while lying in bed with a bad cold and reflecting on the uncertainty of life—Noyes was to make a lifelong habit of treating his physical ailments as high religious drama—he began to think the time for surrender had come. He read the Bible, prayed, and meditated "until I actually sweat." After two days of this, "the matters of God and of eternity seemed alone worth attention. . . . Ere the day was done I had concluded to devote myself to the service and ministry of God."

Ecstasy ensued—ecstasy tinged with the self-satisfaction of the newly converted. His journal for the days that followed reverberates with phrases like "Hitherto the world, henceforth God!" and with celebrations of the joys of holiness. A few months earlier he had copied down a love poem he had written to a girl named Caroline; he now appended a smugly regretful footnote: "These three verses cost me an hour of labor. How much better would that hour have been spent in framing a hymn of praise to God!" In a letter to Larkin Mead, who had suggested that he might be suffering from something more serious than a bad cold, Noyes acknowledged Mead's "affectionate expressions of regret for my illness." But if anyone needed sympathy, he wrote, it was the unregenerate Mead, whom Noyes called on, in Jesus' words, to "Weep not for me but weep for yourselves and for your children." As for himself, far from being mentally distressed, as Mead seemed to imagine, "I solemnly assure you that till within the last week I never had the smallest conception of true happiness. . . . I take God to witness that I find more, infinitely more, enjoyment in the exercises of religion than I ever took in the most fascinating pleasures of the world."

Converts fleeing from the hellfires ignited by incendiary preachers like Finney did not always stay converted. Mead, a kind but worldly man, may well have wondered how long his young brother-in-law, who had just turned twenty, would carry on in this fashion. The change in Noyes turned out, however, to be lasting and profound. Religious aims, as the philosopher and psychologist William James put it in generalizing on the phenomenon of religious conversion, would from then on "form the habitual center of his energy." But the happiness of which Noyes had boasted proved fragile. At the Andover

Theological Seminary in Andover, Massachusetts, where he enrolled in 1831 to study for the ministry, the mood of complacent rapture in which he had written to Mead soon gave way to the anguish and despair that, as James also observed, so often and so painfully afflict the recent convert. He accused himself of almost every sin, including hypocrisy. "I pass off for zeal that which perhaps desire of applause produces," he wrote in his diary. "Oh God! Cleanse thou me from secret faults." He went through long periods of "sorrow and inward conflict" when he felt he was a battleground on which God and Satan were locked in combat. One night he dreamed of cholera, and in the morning felt as if he had in truth been attacked by the dread disease —sure evidence, as he saw it, of his own indelible sinfulness.

In a vain effort to dispel his depression he went on eating binges that only made him loathe himself the more. He was often physically exhausted. Sometimes, "when I was ready to sink under the infirmities of flesh and spirit, and when I could find no rest for my soul either in communion with brethren, or in prayer," he conversed with Christ "by reading through all four gospels at a sitting," noting down every passage bearing on some particular trait of Christ's, or on "some vein of truth" in Christ's teachings. But the relief he got from this exercise was temporary, and soon he would once again be agonizing over his "desperate wickedness" and the feebleness of his love for Christ. He sternly resisted the temptation to comfort himself with the thought that his classmates, whom he faulted for their "levity, bickering, jealousy . . . and worldliness and pride and unholy ambition," were, for the most part, in an even more deplorable state than Noyes himself. But he did get a certain satisfaction—for which in some moods he would accuse himself of the sin of spiritual pride—from the knowledge that at least he was aware how badly off he was. "Oh, how wretched," he wrote in his diary, "is an unprayerful frame of mind joined with a wakeful conscience."

Noyes was disappointed not only in his fellow seminarians at Andover, but in a course of studies that seemed to him overly restricted and confining. So, after a year, he transferred to the Divinity School at Yale, whose less rigid curriculum would give him more time for independent study and reflection. At Yale his spiritual and physical health both gradually mended, and he became less narrowly preoccupied with his own salvation. He offered his services as a spiritual guide to members of New Haven's Negro colony, helped to found one of the earliest of the antislavery societies, and, in the summer after his first year at Yale, spent nine weeks ministering to a congregation in the village of North Salem, New York, which had no regular pastor. His sermons seemed to be hitting home—"Christians are praying, and sinners will soon lie weeping," he exulted—and he was often blissfully happy. After one particularly good day at North Salem he noted that he had "poured out my soul unto God, and wept for joy. My peace was as a river." Back in New Haven he found that he could now study intensely for twelve or even sixteen hours a day and was no longer bothered by the "inordinate alimentativeness" that had tormented him at Andover. Indeed, he seems often to have been too happy to bother eating at all. "Many times, and for days together," he recalled, "my heart was so burdened with spiritual joy that my body became weak and pined away."

◆　　◆　　◆

It was in his second year at Yale that Noyes first set his feet on the path of religious heterodoxy that was to lead to Oneida. At Andover he had had little disposition to question the orthodox Calvinism of the Congregational and Presbyterian churches that Andover served and that between them dominated the religious landscape of New England and New York. He had even worried that he might find Yale and, in particular, Yale's professor of theology, Nathaniel Taylor, too liberal for his tastes. There were conservatives at Andover and elsewhere who considered Taylor a dangerous heretic. His offense, in their eyes, was that, in his eagerness to give revivalists like Finney a theological license to save souls, he had abandoned predestination. As interpreted by some strict Calvinists, this doctrine made it the duty of a good Christian to praise God even when he had reason to think God had damned him forever—and when he knew there was nothing he could do to change God's mind. By contrast, Taylor and the revivalists insisted that God's decisions in such cases were not irrevocable; by sincere repentance and a wholehearted belief in Christ's redemptive power, even a hardened sinner could win a place in heaven. Conservative Calvinists saw this as a form of lèse-majesté, an impertinent assault on the absolute sovereignty of God.

But after attending Taylor's lectures for a year, Noyes concluded that what was wrong with his ideas was not that they were too radical, but that Taylor did not go far enough in his departure from orthodox Calvinism. Where Taylor erred, in Noyes's opinion, was in agreeing with his conservative critics that, while people might (and should) repent their sins, there was no way they could avoid all sinning. This struck Noyes as a repudiation of Christ, whose mission on earth—or so Noyes was convinced by his intensive study of the Gospel—had been to lift completely the burden of sin and guilt from those who believed in him.

This was hardly a new idea. Christian Perfectionism, the notion that at least some Christians can lead morally perfect lives, has a long history. In the twelfth and thirteenth centuries members of the French sect known as the Albigensians believed that moral perfection—that is, freedom from sin—could be attained through celibacy, poverty, abstention from wine and meat, and complete separation from the world of sinners. These measures were considered to be effective, however, only if the striver after perfection had also received a "baptism of the spirit." Indeed, as one historian has noted, Perfectionism has often "involved some sort of ecstasy . . . or emotional climax variously styled 'Fire-baptism,' 'Holy Ghost baptism,' 'Sealing by the Spirit,' etc. . . . The believer is henceforth 'filled' with his God and is held . . . to have been promoted to a higher order of being." A more tentative and lower-keyed Perfectionism was preached by John Wesley, the founder of Methodism, whose writings Noyes read closely as he was beginning his second year at Yale. In Wesley's view, Christians must try to live without sin, and he argued that some could succeed in this aim—it is not clear whether he counted himself among them —for at least short periods of time.

But Noyes went far beyond Wesley. Reading and rereading the New Testament, he became convinced that it was not enough to *try* to lead a perfect life; anyone who failed in that attempt should not be counted as a Christian at all. The inescapable conclusion was that ordinary conversion, such as Noyes had experienced at Putney two years before, could bring the sinner only to a halfway point on the road to salvation. Beyond "ordinary sinful religion" there must be a state "in which *all* the affections of the heart are given to God, and in which there is no sin." The question that "was like a barbed arrow in my heart" was how to attain this enviable state. For a week, during which he ate almost nothing, Noyes did little else but pray and read the Bible. "I loathed my life," he wrote years later in a book called *Confession of Religious Experience*, "and desired rather to die and go to judgment at once, even if I were to be damned, than go on in sin, treasuring up wrath against the day of wrath." At length the Bible came to his rescue. "As I sat brooding over my difficulties and prospects, I listlessly opened my Bible and my eye fell upon these words: 'The Holy Ghost shall come upon thee, and the power of the Highest shall overshadow thee; therefore also that holy thing which shall be born of thee shall be called the Son of God.' The words seemed to glow upon the page, and my spirit heard a voice from heaven through them promising me the baptism of the Holy Spirit and the second birth." The next evening Noyes preached at the New Haven Free Church, whose little band of members was working for a general religious awakening in the city. There he committed himself publicly to the doctrine of Perfectionism, taking as his text Christ's words that "he that committeth sin is of the devil," and arguing that anyone who sinned was by definition not a Christian. Later, lying on his bed, he experienced the ecstasy of the rebirth that he had been promised. "Three times in quick succession a stream of eternal love gushed through my heart," he wrote in *Confession*. " 'Joy unspeakable and full of glory' filled my soul. . . . I knew that my heart was clean, and that the Father and the Son had come and made it their abode."

nless he wished to keep his second conversion a secret, Noyes knew that sooner or later he must move farther out on the doctrinal limb on which his Free Church sermon had placed him. In a mood of "buoyancy and exultation," he chose to do so at the first opportunity. A student who had heard Noyes preach came to his room the next morning to ask if he had really meant to say that no one who sinned could be counted as a Christian. Noyes said he had indeed, and the student said, "Well, if this is your doctrine you unchurch yourself as well as others. Don't you commit sin?" Recalling this moment long afterward, Noyes wrote, "I knew that my answer would plunge me into the depths of contempt; but I answered deliberately and firmly 'No.' The man stared as though a thunderbolt had fallen before him."

Within a few hours, Noyes went on, "the word passed through the college and city: 'Noyes says he is perfect'; and on the heels of this went the report 'Noyes is crazy.' " In the following days "students flocked to my room—some to see the 'perfect man,' as they would go to see an elephant . . . , and others to argue me down, or puzzle me with objections." In reply to their questions Noyes pointed out that, in asserting his freedom from sin, he did not mean that he was beyond improvement, or that he would ever reach a stage where he would invariably do the morally right thing. He was simply contending that he would never again *knowingly* do wrong; as he put it, "I only claim purity of heart and the answer of a good conscience toward God." One of his visitors was so unhinged by his arguments that, as Noyes remembered it, he fainted dead away and regained his peace of mind only after a long talk with his pastor. At Yale, if not at Andover, divinity students took their religion seriously.

A few people were moved by Noyes's preaching and example to declare that they, too, had been emancipated from sin. They included James Boyle, a well-traveled evangelist who had come to New Haven at Noyes's invitation as pastor of the Free Church. Another convert was a young woman, Abigail Merwin, who Noyes came to believe had been destined by God to be his wife and spiritual helper. But most of his fellow students and professors regarded his claim to moral perfection, even as qualified by the claimant, as arrogant and foolish. When a debate was held at the Divinity School on the question of whether holiness was attainable in this life, the decision went against Noyes. Nathaniel Taylor, who liked to instruct his students "to follow the truth though it should cut your heads off," was satisfied that what Noyes was following was not truth, but error: he had, after all, in effect excommunicated Taylor and all the rest of the sinful (if repentant) Divinity School faculty. Soon after the debate Taylor came to Noyes's room to warn him that the local Congregational Association was thinking of revoking Noyes's temporary license to preach. He urged Noyes to recant before it was too late. But Noyes made it clear that, having felt the spirit of God "in every fibre of my body," he was not going to be turned from his course even by the professor of theology at Yale. Taylor left in a huff.

What mainly upset the Congregational ministers who met to consider Noyes's case, in addition to his impudence in declaring them to be non-Christians, was his heretical position on the moral law as embodied in the Ten Commandments. Whereas Wesley had held that even the most perfect Christian was still bound by the moral law, Noyes argued that by giving himself wholly up to God, and thereby freeing himself from sin, he had at the same time freed himself from the law's constraints. Like the saints in heaven, a twice-converted Christian such as Noyes would naturally—indeed, automatically—be good, and would have no need for laws whose purpose was to keep sinners in line. As Noyes explained, "Under the old covenant God said: 'Do according to all I command you, and ye shall live.' Under the new covenant . . . he may safely say: 'Do as you please; for I promise that your pleasure shall be mine. I will write my law upon your heart.' "

Such an arrangement struck many of the ministers as highly suspect, since it seemed, for example, to allow people to commit adultery with a clear conscience simply by declaring themselves to be without sin. In reply, Noyes could argue that in his (and God's) scheme, only those who had experienced a genuine second conversion, and who had in truth been born again, were released from bondage to the moral law. But the ministers were not impressed. Noting that they were "not impeaching the Christian character of Mr. Noyes," they nevertheless voted to take away his license on the ground that his views were "erroneous, unscriptural, and inconsistent with his usefulness as a preacher of the gospel." He had already been expelled from the Free Church, which had been his spiritual home in New Haven, and soon afterward he was told he would have to leave the Divinity School. "My good name in the great world was gone," he recalled years later, adding with a certain mournful relish, "My friends were fast falling away. I was beginning to be indeed an outcast."

✦   ✦   ✦

At Andover Noyes had decided he wanted to become a foreign missionary, but now he changed his mind. As he explained, "I was already on missionary ground, among a people who (though professedly Christian) needed to be converted quite as much as the heathen." While considering how to go about this task now that he had effectively been barred from preaching in New Haven, he decided to go to New York. He would be there at the time of the so-called anniversary meetings, when roving evangelists and liberal-minded Presbyterian and Congregational ministers would be gathering to discuss ways and means of promoting religious revivals, and he looked forward to getting a more sympathetic hearing for his ideas than he had had at Yale. He also hoped to find—and offer sound advice to—other Perfectionists of more or less his own radical persuasion.

For Noyes was only one of a good number of young Americans who, having been convinced at a revival meeting that they had it in their power to save their souls by faith, had seen no reason why they could not, by a similar act of faith, escape the toils of sin. By the time of Noyes's expulsion from Yale, Perfectionist groups were meeting regularly in New York City, in Albany, in western Massachusetts, and in a dozen or so towns and villages in central New York, a territory so scorched by the flames of revivalism that it was known in the trade as the burned-over district. Noyes was critical of many of his fellow Perfectionists on two counts. For one thing, most of their leaders did not go along with Noyes in his conviction that a Christian who had once been properly emancipated from sin by God could never sin again. They took the position that moral perfection was a prize that, once won, could be lost and won again. A Perfectionist could thus commit a sin, or a series of sins, and still keep his standing as a Christian—or, at any rate, regain that standing after a decent interval for repentance. In Noyes's view this was the same old system of licensing sinners that he had found intolerable in orthodox Christianity. Noyes was also disturbed by the way in which some Perfectionists were flaunting their newfound freedom from sin. Three Albany Perfectionists, for example, two young men and the sister of one of them, had been tarred and feathered after they had been discovered sleeping in the same bed. Their intention, it appeared, had been to show that the ordinary conventions governing relations between men and women could safely be disregarded in the case of men and women who had become incapable of sinning. There was no evidence that the unfortunate trio had done anything but sleep together in the literal meaning

of the phrase, but Noyes believed such irregularities, however innocent, played into the hands of clergymen who chose to regard Perfectionism as simply a cover for licentiousness.

New York proved as hostile and depressing as New Haven. The
clergymen whom Noyes managed to see were unsympathetic or indifferent. He had no better luck with the Perfectionists. Calling on
James Latourette, a principal leader of the New York school of Perfectionism, Noyes found him to be "a self-conceited, uncivilized [per-
son] of the very class against whose views and practices I determined
to protest." Noyes was invited to speak at one of Latourette's meetings, but afterward, he wrote, when he was being questioned about
his contention that genuine conversion conferred permanent immunity from sin, his host "roared upon me with a voice of thunder thus:
'Your doctrine is from hell! Get thee behind me, Satan! etc.' So I left
the meeting, overborne not by argument but by clamor."

Concluding that he might reach more people with his ideas if he
set them down on paper, Noyes retreated to his boarding house to
compose a tract on Perfectionism. But before he could start, he found
himself locked in deadly combat with the devil. The battle, which went
on intermittently for three weeks, began as Noyes was reflecting that
what frees Christians from sin is their ability, through the strength of
their belief in Christ, in effect to die with him and rise again. Might
not Christ's resurrection, he wondered, enable his believers to overcome death as well as sin? No sooner had this thought occurred to
him than, as he wrote in his *Confession of Religious Experience*, he was
assaulted by the devil. "Strange thoughts coursed through my brain,
[which] finally settled into a strong impression that I was about to
part with flesh and blood. . . . I put my room in decent order, and
lay down to die. The pressure [on my lungs] increased till my
breathing stopped and my soul seemed to turn inward for its flight."
Then suddenly the pressure was removed, and terror gave way to joy.
"To my imagination the transaction was as if I had been inclosed in
a net, and dragged down to the very borders of Hades, and then in
the last agony, had burst the net and returned to life."

But the devil soon returned to the attack. Again and again Noyes felt himself on the brink of death. He all but stopped eating, and tried not to sleep because it was in sleep that "the powers of darkness had most advantage of me." At night he walked the streets, napping in doorways or on park benches. On these excursions he went into "the vilest parts of the city," handing out Bibles and money to prostitutes, whom he beseeched to "believe on Christ that they might be saved from their sins." In an act of spiritual bravado reminiscent of the Perfectionists who had slept three in a bed, he violated the temperance pledge that he had taken. He seems to have drunk no more, however, than was required to test his sinlessness—to prove to himself "as I expected, that God is able to keep me from intemperance and all other evil, without the help of pledges."

His mind, or the devil, played strange and terrifying tricks. At one moment he was convinced the final judgment was at hand; the sky "seemed just bursting for the descent of Christ with his mighty angels, in flaming fire, to take vengeance of the world." At another moment he imagined that Copernicus had been wrong—that the earth was indeed the center of all things, and that God dwelled at the center of the earth. He imagined that Adam, Abraham, and Christ were the same being, and that this being was to appear again as the world ended. Once, as noted, he heard a voice declare authoritatively that Abigail Merwin—for it was she who appeared to him as "an angel of light"—was in reality the devil in disguise. At times he was persuaded that the Bible was "a monstrous imposition" and Christ the prince of devils, and "my belief in God was overclouded, and the darkness of atheism fell upon me."

At length the fever burned itself out. "When this spirit of darkness had done its worst," he recalled in *Confession of Religious Experience*, "I said within myself: 'If the universe is a blind chaos without a God, and the destinies of all beings are to be worked out by their own strength, I have as good a right to try what I can do for existence and happiness as anybody.'" But this uncharacteristic mood of disbelief and existential resignation soon gave way to a renewed faith in God, and in Noyes's own energy and power as a soldier of God. "The result of all my sufferings," he wrote, "was, that when I finally emerged from them, I had a satisfying consciousness that my life was 'fire-proof.' I could say, 'Hell has done its worst, and yet I live.' "

At this point, when Noyes had been in New York nearly a month, he had a visit from Everard Benjamin, a brother-in-law of Abigail Merwin and one of the few members of the New Haven Free Church, besides Abigail, who had been converted to Perfectionism. On the strength of rumors that Noyes had gone out of his mind, Benjamin had come to New York to see what he could do. He found Noyes sane enough and, after paying the bill that Noyes had run up at his boarding house, took him back to New Haven. Soon afterward Noyes went home to visit his family and think about what he should do next.

Noyes later wrote that he had emerged from his New York ordeal with a new and solid confidence in himself. But this was not apparent to an observer who saw a lot of him at this time without seeing any signs of the bubbling charismatic power Noyes was later to display. Writing to Noyes many years afterward, one of his nieces said that she remembered him as "a pale feeble sad-faced young man"—he was then nearing twenty-three—who impressed her as "living with yet apart from 'the rest of Mankind' and particularly fleeing as if from contamination from the presence of womankind." She continued, "Vividly do I remember your days of fasting and prayer—dear old Grandmother's tearful eyes and trembling lips—the silence that was imposed upon me in your presence, even to the hiring of me not to sing '*cause it was so wicked*.' " The letter concluded mockingly, "I should like to measure swords with you now . . . to see if it is possible that a natural man, with heart and soul, could be made out of a sinless saint, that would hasten to do penance if anything caused him to laugh—or even smile involuntarily. Oh poor dyspeptic!"

Chapter 5

*T*he cunning and ferocity with which the devil had fought for Noyes's soul in New York were, in a sense, gratifying, in that they confirmed the importance of the spiritual task to which Noyes had dedicated himself. While there was no pulpit available from which he could carry out his mission of liberating halfway Christians from sin, there was nothing to stop him from proselytizing in print. This way of serving God's purposes had also occurred to James Boyle, who had been dismissed as pastor of the New Haven Free Church after he had joined Noyes in proclaiming that he, too, was morally perfect. Noyes soon left Putney for New Haven, where, in partnership with Boyle, he began to put out a monthly paper called the *Perfectionist* in which he explained the biblical foundations of his beliefs. Noyes—and, in part, the paper—were supported by an allowance that his family had agreed to send him only after he had threatened, if it were not forthcoming, to throw himself on the charity of strangers.

Noyes's articles in the new paper made a few converts. They were not necessarily willing, however, to go along with his notions of how, as sin-free Christians, they should comport themselves. This posed a dilemma. On the one hand, Noyes believed that, having once tri-umphed over sin and achieved moral perfection, a twice-reborn Christian would be guided directly by God, and his or her behavior would not be subject to human correction. On the other hand, Noyes's views on sex and marriage at this time were thoroughly conventional, not to say prudish. And he was not happy about reports of blissfully sin-free young people kissing and fondling one another at Perfectionist gatherings—behavior that could, if unchecked, nullify Noyes's determination to make Perfectionism respectable.

The problem was brought disturbingly close to home in the winter of 1835, when, six months after his return to New Haven, Noyes set out to visit towns and villages in western Massachusetts where Perfectionism had taken root. His second stop was Brimfield, where he found, as he wrote in *Confession of Religious Experience*, "a group of handsome, brilliant young women" who plied him, "as preacher of the doctrine which had taken all by storm," with flattering attentions. One young woman seemed downcast, and when Noyes asked her why, she said it was because she was afraid he had no confidence in her. Noyes, whose bashfulness seems to have been dispelled by the warmth of his reception at Brimfield, goes on to say, "Thereupon I took a seat beside her and put my arm around her. As we separated she kissed me in token of recovery from her distrust."

That night Noyes lay awake worrying about the young women of Brimfield and about the intimidating power of his own sexual urges. As he put it, "I became afraid of them and of myself." The best way to cope with the peril in which he stood, he decided—as he was to decide more than once when he found himself in danger of one kind or another—was to remove himself instantly from the scene. "I left the next morning alone," he recalled, "without making known my intention to anyone; and took a bee-line on foot through snow and cold—below zero—to Putney, sixty miles distant." As it turned out, there was to be more than kissing at Brimfield. Noyes had been accompanied on his visit there by a young Perfectionist convert named Simon Lovett, who had stayed on after Noyes's sudden departure. One night two of the young women who had frightened Noyes went to Lovett's room after midnight and got into bed with him. Noyes later argued in their defense that, like the unfortunate trio of Perfectionists from Albany, they had wanted only to prove they could resist temptation. They had emerged from Lovett's room, Noyes insisted, "in the innocence of Shakerism." Even if that were the case, of course, when word of the incident got around it was certain to give aid and comfort to Perfectionism's enemies.

For the moment, however, Noyes, who remained at Putney through the early spring, found his views being treated with a new respect. Impressed by his articles in the *Perfectionist*, people made their houses available to him for meetings, and he preached almost daily in Putney and its neighboring villages. His style was relaxed, and there was no hellfire or burning lakes. He would read from the Bible, comment on what he had read, and then throw the meeting open for questions and informal discussion. Tall, broad-shouldered, with his lofty forehead and a face that "shone like an angel's," as one of his hearers recalled, he made a strong and favorable impression on people who were tired of the showmanship of conventional evangelism. Enthusiasm for his message ran high, and he made some converts. "The lord is opening before me a wide door for the preaching of the gospel," he wrote Boyle, "and is giving me power that prevails against all adversaries."

The door soon slammed shut, however, and Noyes once again found himself an outcast. News of what came to be known as the Brimfield Bundling at length reached Putney, and Noyes was pressed by his father to dissociate himself publicly from such goings-on. Instead he outraged the elder Noyes by inviting Simon Lovett to join him in conducting religious meetings in and around Putney. Father and son quarreled, and in the late spring Noyes left home, this time with no promise of an allowance, to begin a period of what he characterized as "vagabond, incoherent service" to God and Perfectionism.

✦　　✦　　✦

New Haven, to which Noyes soon returned, proved a poor refuge. He had fallen out with Boyle in a doctrinal dispute, and Boyle, who retained control of the paper they had started, seemed bent on reading Noyes out of the Perfectionist movement. Other former allies, such as Everard Benjamin and Abigail Merwin, had gone back to orthodox sinful Christianity. Once again, as in New York, Noyes was assailed by agonizing doubts about the reality of God's love and about his worthiness of that love. At times he spoke so wildly and bitterly that people wondered if he might be crazy. An older sister, Joanna, who saw him in New Haven, wrote back to Putney, "He would not reason at all, but denounced everything and everybody. He looked haggard and careworn, and I felt positive . . . that he was deranged." He was, she wrote a few weeks later, "a homeless wanderer . . . entirely dependent upon charity."

He worked briefly as a bill collector, helped to map the town of Milford, Connecticut, and then went to New York to look for work. He was unsuccessful, and when his money ran out he walked the seventy-five miles back to New Haven, going without food, he recalled, for the three days it took to make the trip. A few weeks later, with winter coming on, he went home to Putney by stagecoach, his mother having sent him money for the fare. But when the snow melted in the spring he left again. For a time he wandered about New England, traveling mostly on foot, living on borrowed money, and thinking about how he could rescue Perfectionism from the disarray into which it had fallen. Reflecting on his quarrel with Boyle, who had by then closed down the *Perfectionist* and gone to work in a machine shop, he came to an important conclusion: in whatever he should now attempt, he must be the unquestioned leader. Accordingly, as he wrote later, he decided to stop trying to organize and discipline the "broken and corrupted regiments" of Perfectionism. Instead, he would start afresh "by devoting myself to the patient instruction of a few, simple-minded, unpretending believers, chiefly belonging to my father's family." Returning to Putney, he set to work to convert his mother, spending long evenings in her room reading and discussing the Bible with her. But she was not yet ready to accept her son as her spiritual director, and held out stubbornly against what she complained of as his bullying. Noyes was more successful with his younger sisters Charlotte and Harriet, and with his brother George, all of whom publicly proclaimed that, through Christ, they had been forever saved from sin.

Noyes was not content for long, however, to give himself up exclusively to the cultivation of so small a garden. He was determined eventually to stand at the head of a great religious movement and soon he left Putney to place his ideas before social reformers and liberal clergymen—there was a considerable overlap between the two groups—in Boston, New York, and other cities. His aim was to get from them testimonials that would lend respectability to Perfectionism as he preached and practiced it.

In recent months a striking change had taken place in Noyes. It was perhaps induced by his mounting conviction that God had chosen him as his principal collaborator in establishing his kingdom on earth. Whatever the reason, he spoke with a new calmness and authority that impressed the men to whom he now presented himself. They included William Lloyd Garrison, with whom he had a long talk at the offices of Garrison's magazine, the *Liberator*, in Boston. "He spoke with great interest of the *Perfectionist*," Noyes reported back to Putney, "said his mind was heaving on the subject of holiness and the kingdom of heaven and he would devote himself to them as soon as he could get anti-slavery off his hands." (This was not just a polite brush-off; Garrison was in fact much taken with Noyes's ideas, and later declared his opinion that "total abstinence from sin in this life is not only commanded but . . . obtainable.") In New York Noyes spent several hours with the great revivalist Charles Grandison Finney. Finney was soon afterward, as president of Oberlin, to promote his own milder brand of Perfectionism, and his warm interest in what Noyes had to say filled his visitor's breast with "a reanimated hope" of building public confidence in himself and in "the gospel which I preach."

Thus encouraged, Noyes decided to start a new newspaper, this time making sure that it would be completely under his control. He had no money, but he was sure God would provide it, and in the

summer of 1837 he set off from Kingston, New York, where he had
been staying with a friend, to walk to Ithaca, New York, 140 miles
away, with the intention of publishing his newspaper there.

✦   ✦   ✦

Noyes's reason for choosing Ithaca was that Abigail Merwin was there.
Although he had seen her only twice after she had abandoned Perfectionism, he had come to believe that God had forged an imperishable
bond between them. A year or so before his trip to Ithaca, on hearing
that she was to be married, he had written her a rambling letter in
which he tried to explain the nature of that bond. The terrible vision
he had had of her in New York, he wrote, had turned out to be the
work of the devil. A year later, "in the midst of another series of
sufferings . . . I saw you again clothed in white robes, and by the word
of the Lord you were given to me." Noyes was vague about the exact
terms of the gift, noting only that since this second vision "I have
been with you in spirit, not doubting that you will ere long return to
your first love and dwell with me in the bosom of God." Conceding
that Abigail might be unaware of what was in store for her, he assured
her that in due course God would "make you know that he has joined
us in immortal marriage."

The notion that God had given Abigail to him exclusively and
forever seems inconsistent with ideas already taking shape in Noyes's
mind about love and sex in God's kingdom on earth. In this kingdom,
he had begun to think, there would be no indissoluble unions, no
marriage as the world knew it. Noyes himself, long afterward, wondered if he would have led his followers into the verdant pastures of
complex marriage if Abigail Merwin had agreed to be his wife. As
Noyes had surmised, however, God's plans for Abigail were not so
clear to her as they were to her lover. She did not answer his letter,
and when Noyes arrived in Ithaca, where she was living with her
schoolteacher husband, she seems to have refused to see him.

But if Noyes's journey to Ithaca failed to advance his cause with
Abigail, it was successful in another way. In Genoa, New York, on his

way from Kingston, he had raised $40 from former subscribers to the *Perfectionist*. With this sum, together with credit supplied by a sympathetic printer, he put out in Ithaca the first issue of a fortnightly paper called the *Witness*. In it Noyes stated his belief, from which he was never to depart, that the word of God could most effectively be transmitted in a journal that ranged widely over the entire field of human knowledge and experience. As he explained it, rather grandiloquently—he had not yet developed the more relaxed and conversational style that he was to employ in his later writings—"I shall therefore pass and repass as I please the usual boundaries of technical theology, knowing that the theology of heaven includes every other science." The first number included, among other items not ordinarily to be found in religious periodicals, a phrenological analysis of Noyes's character. Prophetically, it read, in part, "Amativeness, large; Philoprogenitiveness, very large."

Although subscriptions came in at an encouraging rate, the *Witness* sank almost before it was launched. It was wrecked by the unauthorized publication, in a Philadelphia religious magazine, of a letter Noyes had written to a friend, David Harrison, in which he had set down for the first time his ideas about sex in the kingdom of heaven. These ideas were closely bound up with Noyes's refusal to accept the orthodox view that the second coming of Christ was yet to occur. Noting Christ's hint (as reported by St. John) that he would return to earth within the lifetime of his disciples, Noyes insisted that the second coming had, in fact, already taken place, in semi-secrecy, in the year A.D. 70.

At that time, Noyes contended, the early Christian believers, having achieved a state of sinlessness as members of the so-called Primitive Church, had passed "into the invisible world." In the centuries that followed, later Christians had, indeed, as Christian theologians had almost unanimously insisted, been condemned to lead lives of sin, however often—and sincerely—they might repent. But it was now God's intention to extend his sway over earth. And to that end, Noyes argued, God had ordained that a new church should arise whose members, like the members of the Primitive Church, would be perfectly holy; and who, once the kingdom of heaven should have been established on earth, would be united with those early Christians who had attained heaven eighteen hundred years before.

Christ's statement that "in the resurrection [the saved] neither marry nor are given in marriage" has ordinarily—and not surprisingly—been taken to mean that there is no sex in heaven. But Noyes, for reasons that he would later set forth at great length, had been convinced by his reading of the Bible that what had been done away with in heaven was not sex, but only marriage and monogamy. "In a holy community," he had observed in his letter to Harrison, "there is no more reason why sexual intercourse should be restrained by law, than why eating and drinking should be—and there is as little reason for shame in the one case as in the other." Noyes went on to note that God had put up a "wall of partition" between men and women during the apostasy—that is, during the long years when even the best Christians were in bondage to sin—and "woe to him who abolishes the law of the apostasy before he stands in the holiness of resurrection." But in the time of resurrection, now fast approaching, there would be no need for such a partition. In the new heaven on earth, as in heaven itself, the "jealousy of exclusiveness" would be unknown. "I call a certain woman my wife—she is yours, she is Christ's, and in him she is the bride of all saints," he exulted. "She is dear in the hand of a stranger, and . . . I rejoice. My claim upon her cuts directly across the marriage covenant of this world, and God knows the end."

This was too much for many Perfectionists and Perfectionist sympathizers, even if they had managed to take incidents like the Brimfield Bundling in their stride. Thus, the editor of a journal called the *Advocate of Moral Reform*, whose Perfectionist leanings had previously been tolerated by her employers, was now dismissed from her job, and her successor editorially denounced Noyes's scheme of sex without marriage as a "master stroke of satanic policy" that "by a refinement of wickedness . . . sanctifies the very incarnation of impurity." Even before this and other similar attacks appeared in print, the flow of subscription orders for the *Witness* stopped, and Noyes had to suspend

publication after three issues. With the fortuitous help of an unsolicited gift of $80, sent by an admirer in Vermont, he paid off the
printer (along with his boarding-house keeper) and retreated to the
farm near Kingston from which he had set out for Ithaca. For a time
his disappointment was mitigated by the hope that he might yet claim
Abigail as his earthly bride. That hope was based on a report that she
had left her husband and was living with her father outside New Haven. Noyes wrote to his friend Harrison, saying "I love her more and
more" and asking Harrison to see Abigail and plead with her on his
behalf. Harrison did this, but had nothing encouraging to report. A
few weeks later Noyes composed and copied into his journal a "Farewell Lay to Abigail." Its final stanza read:

> We'll meet again, be sure of that,
>> Some time 'twixt now and never.
>> An age or two I well may wait,
>> Since we are one forever.

Noyes now took a step that was to secure him the money he needed
to start up the *Witness* again and to end his years of homeless wandering. Having concluded that there was nothing to be done about
Abigail Merwin until the establishment of the new post-resurrection
sexual order of which he had written to Harrison, Noyes proposed
marriage—of the conventional variety—to another woman. Her name
was Harriet Holton, and it was she who had sent him the $80 with
which he had paid off his debts in Ithaca.

Harriet Holton was now thirty, three years older than Noyes. Or-
phaned as a young child, she had grown up in Westminster, Vermont,
not far from Putney, in the home of her grandfather, Mark Richards,
a well-to-do lawyer who, like Noyes's father, had represented Vermont
in Congress, and whose money Harriet stood to inherit. According to
a biographical sketch printed years later in the Oneida Community's
newspaper, she was a shy and serious girl, endowed with "a good
mind, not brilliant, but plodding and thorough," who spent most of
her allowance on books. As a young woman she attended dances and

card parties, went for boat rides on the Connecticut River, and generally joined "in the gayety and pleasure-seeking common to that age." But she told her biographer she had always been "cramped by bashfulness," adding, "I never felt at ease away from home. I was too self-conscious, felt small, and always thought I did not look well."

In 1831 Harriet, like Noyes, went to a revival meeting and was converted. For three years she busied herself with church and charitable work. In 1834, when she was twenty-six, she became engaged to a widower living in Mississippi. At the same time she informally adopted a ten-year-old girl whom she intended to take with her when she moved south. Although in later years she was much loved by children, she was a poor foster mother, repeatedly flying into rages at her ward and punishing her severely. Overcome with guilt, "she condemned herself for something every day, and longed for a new grace." While in this despairing mood she read an article by Noyes in the *Perfectionist* and announced that she had been permanently freed from the clutches of sin. Turning her ward over to another foster mother —or so one may assume, since her biographer says nothing more about the girl—she informed her intended husband that if their engagement was to continue, it would have to be on a different basis. Her heart, she explained, had been "cleared of all special attachments to persons; she loved everybody . . . she wished him to understand she had no special love for him." Her fiancé, understandably jolted by this turn of events, came north to plead with her. But she was adamant, and at length he "withdrew his suit . . . and [Harriet] renounced marriage forever."

The following spring she heard Noyes preach in a nearby village, and later, on her invitation, he preached at East Westminster, where she lived, and was a guest at her grandfather's house. There is no evidence that this diffident and homely young woman, with her deep-set eyes and rather grim, turned-down mouth, made much impression on Noyes. But three years later, when he composed his farewell lay to Abigail, Harriet's loyalty and generosity to his cause, not to mention the wealth that had made her generosity possible, were much on his mind. After his retreat from Ithaca he saw Harriet at Putney. And while, as he once said, "There was no particular love of the sentimental kind between us," he soon afterward sent her a letter of proposal.

The tone of this extraordinary document is totally at variance with the passionate extravagance of Noyes's letters to Abigail Merwin. "After a deliberation of more than a year in patient waiting and watching for indications of the Lord's will," he wrote, managing to sound at once pious and businesslike, "I am now permitted, and indeed happily constrained . . . to propose to you a partnership which I will not call marriage till I have defined it." He reminded her that "as believers we are already one with each other and with all saints." Therefore, he continued, getting to the crux of his proposal, "we can enter into no engagements with each other which shall limit the range of our affections as they are limited in matrimonial engagements by the fashion of this world. I desire and expect my yoke-fellow will love all who love God . . . as freely as if she stood in no particular connection with me." Noyes left no doubt that he expected his yoke-fellow to grant him the same freedom.

Noyes went on to explain, sounding rather like a cattle judge ticking off the good points of a prize guernsey, why he wished to form a partnership with Harriet. "In the plain speech of a witness and not a flatterer," he wrote, "I respect and love you for many desirable qualities, spiritual, intellectual, moral, personal, especially your faith, kindness, simplicity and modesty." Noyes was aware that Harriet had been told by their mutual friend, David Harrison, about the quite different feeling he had for Abigail Merwin, and he assured her that this was no obstacle to the union he was proposing: "I still believe her to be a child of God and therefore love her. Yet I am as free as if I had never seen her." In conclusion, addressing his words as much to Harriet's grandfather as to Harriet herself, he said that despite the past "irregularity and seeming instability of my character and fortune," he was now ready to settle down and fulfill the responsibilities of domestic life.

Harriet replied at once, and with gratitude. She said she had long thought of Noyes as a morning star in the theological heavens, and it was reason enough for her to accept his offer that he believed, as he had said in his letter, that their marriage would promote his "happiness and improvement" and "increase our means of usefulness to the people of God." In gladly accepting Noyes's proposal, she continued, attempting to match his lawyerlike tone, "I agree with you that it will not 'limit the range of our affections.' " She added humbly, "I only expect . . . to be placed in a situation where I can enjoy what Harriet and Charlotte [Noyes's younger sisters] and your mother are now blessed with, your society and instruction as long as the Lord pleases and when he pleases."

Mark Richards predictably wondered how Noyes planned to support a wife. But when Noyes undertook to reassure him by pointing out that he was now in a position to make money by preaching, and, more important, that he stood to inherit substantial property from his father, Richards made such considerations irrelevant by giving the couple not only his blessing but the promise of a handsome allowance.

There remained one matter to be settled. A week or so after accepting Noyes as her future husband, Harriet hinted that she might prefer to live with him as a sister rather than a wife. From the tone of his proposal, at once lofty and utilitarian, she might well have inferred that he, too, would prefer such an arrangement. But Noyes, who was counting on marriage to shield him from temptation of the kind he had been exposed to at Brimfield, replied sternly that abstinence from sex was not at all in accord with either his or God's wishes. "I know not how far you may have imbibed the spirit of Shakerism," he wrote, "but I will say frankly, that there may be no mistake between us, that so far from regarding the act of sexual enjoyment as in itself unholy, I am sure that there is no sacrifice except that of the heart, that is more acceptable to God." This seems to have ended the discussion, and three days later, on June 28, 1838, the couple were married in Chesterfield, New Hampshire, by Noyes's brother-in-law, Larkin Mead.

Chapter 6

W hen an English journalist years later accused Noyes of having married Harriet Holton for her money, he replied indignantly that "it was not the love of money but the love of truth that drew us together." While there is perhaps more to this defense than a cynic might allow, Harriet's dowry did enable Noyes to put the spiritual enterprise to which he was committed on an entirely new and more comfortable footing. Within days after bringing his bride home to his parents' house in Putney, where they were to live while building a house of their own, he had bought a secondhand printing press and installed it in the loft of a sawmill belonging to a Putney Perfectionist named Cutler. His plan was to operate the press himself, with the help of his wife, his younger sisters Harriet and Charlotte, and his fifteen-year-old brother George, who had worked briefly for a printer and was the only one of the group with any real notion of how printing was done. To develop their proficiency, Noyes decided to print up a book consisting of the articles he had written for the *Perfectionist* explaining the theological basis for his beliefs. All five took turns at setting type, and when the forms were ready, Noyes worked the hand lever on the press while his wife manipulated the ink roller. It was slow work, and four months passed before the book, *The Way of Holiness*, was off the press and Noyes felt ready to resume publication of the *Witness*.

For nine years, at the end of which they were forced to leave Putney, Noyes and his family, who were soon joined by other helpers, published a newspaper that went out every month—later, every fortnight—to everyone who asked for it, whether they could afford to pay for it or not. Toward the end of this period, when its name was changed to the *Perfectionist* and, later, to the *Perfectionist and Theocratic Watchman*, the paper's contents were animated and varied. They included, for example, reports on life among the faithful at Putney, lively discussions of the vogue for community-building inspired by the utopian schemes of the French writer Charles Fourier, and—in serial form—Noyes's own spiritual autobiography. But in the earlier years readers had to get along on a diet consisting mainly of biblical exegesis ("Paul's Views of the Law"), theological arguments ("The Two-Fold Nature of the Second Birth"), and testimonials by converts to Perfectionism.

The *Witness* also ran a series of articles called "Secret History of Perfectionism," in which Noyes denounced the treachery of former allies such as James Boyle. These were maneuvers in a renewed campaign by Noyes to seize command of the "broken and corrupted regiments" of Perfectionism. From one point of view, these regiments had no need for a commander, since true Christians should get their orders directly from God. But reports continued to reach Noyes of Perfectionists who, without waiting for the establishment of God's kingdom on earth, were violating the country's laws against extramarital sex. The offenders, if they were not simply false Christians, must be misreading God's messages, and he concluded that it was up to him, as the one true prophet of Perfectionism, to straighten them out.

This claim, which Noyes pressed not only in the *Witness* but on visits to New Haven, Hartford, and other places where there were Perfectionist colonies, was often strenuously resisted. When an emissary from Putney, disturbed by the carryings-on of Perfectionists in Newark, New Jersey, suggested that they should spend more time reading the *Witness*, he was told that this was quite unnecessary since everybody at Newark was "taught by God." Noyes's advice was also breezily rejected by a Perfectionist leader named Josiah Gridley. Gridley, a physician once characterized by Noyes as "a pill-vendor, brassy, smart, witty and licentious," liked to boast that Christianity had armored him so effectively against temptation that he "could carry a virgin in each hand without the least stir of unholy passion." When Noyes accused him of encouraging loose sexual behavior—by precept and perhaps by example—among a group of Perfectionists living in the village of Belchertown, Massachusetts, Gridley counterattacked vigorously. It was true, he wrote Noyes, that at one time "the Devil [had] pressed hard upon our sails, and thus drove some of us beyond the sea of discretion." But he went on to note slyly that several of the Perfectionists thus driven "have declared most emphatically that they received their first lessons, in theory at least, directly from yourself; that it was not superior grace but your natural timidity of women that saved you." As for the alleged irregularities in Belchertown, Gridley dismissed these as harmless frailties, and warned Noyes that "if you assume the spirit of a leader, you will lose the spirit of Christ."

Such rebuffs failed to weaken Noyes's conviction that he had been appointed God's first deputy in the work of establishing the kingdom of heaven on earth. But he came to believe that the best way to prepare for the coming of that kingdom was to concentrate on gathering around him a group of followers whose perfect obedience to the will of God would be assured by their obedience (and physical proximity) to God's deputy. At first the followers were all members of his family: his wife, his two younger sisters, his brother George, his invalid father, and, finally, his mother. They were soon joined by other converts to Perfectionism who were prepared to accept Noyes's interpretation of God's commands. Among them were several who would later, like his wife and sisters, serve as cabinet ministers in the government of the Oneida Community. They included John L. Skinner, a young teacher of Quaker parentage who came to Putney to help on the *Witness* and soon married Noyes's sister Harriet; and John R. Miller, a former Putney storekeeper who married Charlotte Noyes. Both marriages seem to have been arranged by Noyes.

Another recruit was Mary Cragin, who was destined to take the place that Noyes had reserved for Abigail Merwin when the resurrection should be attained. A former schoolteacher, she had been converted to Perfectionism in New York and had persuaded her husband, George, the business manager of the *Advocate of Moral Reform*, to join her in declaring his freedom from sin. He was thereupon fired for embracing a doctrine that the *Advocate*'s new anti-Perfectionist editor had just denounced as the work of the devil. Soon afterward he and his wife went to visit an old friend of Noyes, Abram Smith, on whose farm—at Rondout, New York, near Kingston—Noyes had spent the winter before his marriage. At Rondout, Smith seduced Mary Cragin by assuring her that theirs was a holy love of exactly the kind Noyes approved, and by persuading her husband that any objections on his part to their intimacy would prove that he was no Christian. When this came to Noyes's attention, and when Smith continued the liaison after promising to break it off, Noyes in effect excommunicated him as a Perfectionist for his "works of evil and concupiscence." But while recognizing that Mary Cragin, a woman as highly sexed as Noyes himself, was partly to blame for what had happened, Noyes was much easier on her. She reminded him, he said, of Mary Magdalene, and he invited her to come to Putney with her husband and their two young children to live with him and his wife and study the Bible.

Bible study by this time had become one of the principal occupations of Noyes's followers at Putney. It was the only religious exercise of which he approved. Public prayer and other traditional rites of Christianity were, in his view, quite unnecessary for people who already had God's absolute assurance of salvation. But being relieved of the burden of sin did not rule out all moral error, and it was the duty of Christians to work incessantly to improve their capacity for love and for dealing justly with their fellows. Christians must think hard about what God wanted them to do, and Noyes had concluded that the best way to search out God's intentions was to study the Bible and discuss it with other believers. He considered this particularly important for the believers at Putney, who had undertaken to help him set an example to the world of how to achieve "present and eternal salvation."

Accordingly, in 1840, soon after Noyes and his wife had moved into the new house they had built, they began holding Sunday meetings there. Biblical evidence for the main tenets of Perfectionism was closely examined, and Noyes led discussions of such topics as the relation between human and divine will, and the meaning of Christian suffering. Soon there were sessions on Wednesday and Thursday evenings as well, and Noyes began calling his extended family of believers the Putney Bible School. Early in 1841 Noyes's father divided his estate among his eight children; the portion that fell to the four who were members of the Bible School included two farms and other property worth, all told, nearly $20,000. Perfectionists who had wanted to join Noyes and his followers but who had been unable to do so because there were no jobs for them in Putney could now get work on the two farms. During the next two years enrollment in the Bible School, or the Society of Inquiry, as the group also designated itself, rose to thirty-five.

Life at Putney took on a strong monastic flavor. The believers rose at five, read the Bible for half an hour, and spent the morning working at the print shop or on one of the farms. In the afternoons they met for three hours to read and discuss not only the Bible but works on the history and archaeology of the Holy Land. (Many of the students had so much trouble staying awake after their hard morning's work, however, that the study sessions were eventually shifted to the morning hours.) Women were expected to take part, and so that they would be free to do so, only one meal a day—breakfast—was prepared and served. A printed card with the heading "HEALTH, COMFORT, ECONOMY, AND WOMAN'S RIGHTS" was posted on the door to the pantry in the Noyeses' kitchen. It explained that the custom of providing three hot meals a day had the drawback of "subjecting females almost universally to the worst of slavery" and invited members of the Bible School and guests in search of dinner or supper to help themselves from a variety of cold foods set out on the pantry shelves. The study hours were inviolate, and when George Cragin, who was in charge of the community's farms, hinted that everyone would be better off if they spent more time farming and less time reading the Bible, Noyes quickly set him straight: "If the growth of our faith and the improvement of your mind require you to sit still half the time, freely obey that instinct. I would much rather our land should run to waste than that you should fail of a spiritual harvest." This policy, however good for the community's soul, was hard on its finances. At the end of 1845 money was so scarce that publication of the *Perfectionist* had to be suspended. Everyone was on short rations until the next summer, when Harriet's grandfather, Mark Richards, died, leaving her $9,000. This relieved the family, as they ordinarily referred to themselves, of further financial difficulties for some years to come.

In the mid-1840s the terms on which the Putney Perfectionists lived together underwent a gradual but fundamental change. What had begun as an informal family association evolved into a socialist commune in which all adult members of the Putney Corporation, as the Bible School was now designated, shared equally—or according to need— in the income produced by their labors.

This transformation took place some fifteen years after the failure of one of the century's most ambitious social experiments: the community of New Harmony, Indiana, established by the Scottish industrialist and reformer Robert Owen. New Harmony had expired in 1830, a victim of its founder's naïveté and of the laziness and rapacity of many who answered his call to help him build a "new empire of peace and good will." But its demise, and that of several smaller associated communities, was followed, ten years later, by a sudden surge of enthusiasm for communal living. "We are a little wild here with numberless projects of social reform," Ralph Waldo Emerson reported in a letter to Thomas Carlyle in 1840. "Not a reading man but has a draft of a new community in his waistcoat pocket." Over the next ten years more than forty utopian communities were founded in America.

The aim of most of Emerson's reading men was to show that people's lives could be dramatically improved without the violence and terror that had attended the French Revolution or the reaction that had followed it. They believed the horrors of industrialism and capitalism could be done away with piecemeal, as it were, by setting up communities in which cooperation would replace exploitation and men and women would find it easy and natural to live together in harmony.

Most of the communities founded in the 1840s were inspired by Charles Fourier. In Fourier's view the world was approaching an age of harmony that would last thirty-five thousand years, during which, in conformity with a plan drawn up by God and revealed to Fourier, the world's inhabitants would be grouped in self-contained cooperative units called phalanxes, each having between 1,620 and 1,820 members. These phalanxes would spread over the globe until there were exactly 2,985,984 of them, uniting the entire human race in a brotherhood with a single language and a single uniform mode of life. In this golden age the sea would lose its saltiness and turn to lemonade, and the world would be governed, from Constantinople, by a supreme ruler called an Oniarch, assisted by 3 Augusts, 12 Caesarians, 46 Empresses, 144 Kalifs, and 576 Sultans.

But for all the baroque extravagance and lunatic precision of his visions, Fourier had interesting and original ideas about the organization of work. In 1840, three years after his death, a young American named Albert Brisbane published a book called *Social Destiny of Man* in which he set forth the most sensible of Fourier's notions. These added up to a detailed prospectus for cooperative associations that would be at once industrial and agricultural and that would be quite free—or so Brisbane persuasively argued—of the wastefulness, exploitation, and periodic unemployment inherent in capitalism. In these associations, or phalanxes, moreover, jobs would be assigned and rotated in such a way as to eliminate boredom and drudgery from the working day.

Brisbane's book made a strong and favorable impression on many Americans. They included Horace Greeley, who gave Brisbane a column in his New York *Tribune* in which to propagate Fourier's ideas. Greeley himself wrote editorials and made speeches on behalf of the associationists, as Brisbane and his followers were called, and invested his own time and money in the founding of Fourierist associations. Another prominent convert was George Ripley, the founder of Brook Farm. In 1844, when Brook Farm was three years old, it was reorganized along modified Fourierist lines, and for the remaining three years of its life it was known as the Brook Farm Phalanx.

Brisbane and Greeley had no illusions about the high cost of starting up a Fourierist community. But their warnings on that score were widely ignored. Poorly financed bands of enthusiasts, lacking money to buy good land, set out to erect their phalansteries, or communal homes, on remote and barren sites or in malarial swamps. "Think of the great hope at the beginning; the bitterness at the end," Noyes wrote twenty years later in his *History of American Socialisms.* "Plodding on their weary march of life, Association rises before them like the mirage of the desert. They see in the vague distance magnificent palaces, green fields, golden harvests, sparkling fountains, abundance of rest and romance; in one word HOME—which is also HEAVEN. They rush like the thirsty caravan to realise their vision. And [then] the scene changes." Even associations that were adequately financed tended to break up in ugly disputes over money and property, and only three of the Fourierist communities lasted more than two years. One of these was the North American Phalanx, in Monmouth County, New Jersey, whose imposing phalanstery and beautiful orchards made it for twelve years the showplace of Fourierism. But in 1854, after a religious quarrel that led to the withdrawal of many of its members and stockholders, and after a fire destroyed its mills and workshops, it, too, expired.

In the mid-1840s, however, when Noyes was working out at Putney the principles of Bible Communism, as he was to call the social and religious system embodied in the Oneida Community, the collapse of Fourierism was still in the future. Noyes followed the associationist movement with keen interest, and in later years acknowledged Oneida's debt to Fourier and his American disciples for the notion that work could be made much more rewarding by allowing workers to change jobs at frequent intervals. He was also impressed by the Fourierists' insistence that manual labor should be regarded—and rewarded—just like any other kind of work.

But Noyes was at pains to point out that, in forming their little communist society in Vermont, he and his followers had been driven by motives quite different from those of the phalanx builders. Although Noyes was a close and admiring reader of the Fourierist paper the *Phalanx* and its successor, the *Harbinger*, which he praised for their "comprehensiveness of view" and "conservative moderation," he pointed out that the Fourierists had things backward in their insistence on the possibility of "regenerating and perfecting human nature by improving its external conditions." In Noyes's view, a new and more perfect society could come into being only if its members had undergone a radical spiritual change. "The trouble is that what the world needs is good *men*, not good institutions," he argued, adding that only Christianity could produce good men. The sole purpose of such a community as had taken shape at Putney was to make it easier for its members to live a true Christian life and to spread the truth about God's intentions for the world. "Formal community of property is not regarded by us as obligatory on principle," he observed, "but as an expedient. . . . We are attempting no scientific experiments in political economy, or in social science, and beg to be excused from association in the public mind with those who are making such experiments."

✦   ✦   ✦

Noyes liked to emphasize the informality of the arrangements by which the believers at Putney were bound together. "A few families of the same religious faith," he explained to readers of the *Perfection-ist*, "without any formal scheme or written laws, have agreed to regard themselves as one family." This was not strictly true. As early as 1841 Noyes had proposed, and his followers at Putney had adopted, a written constitution. Four years later it was superseded by a more elaborate instrument amounting to a contract between the Putney Corporation and its members. By its terms, the corporation was required to provide its members with food, shelter, and pocket money, while the members were to be governed in all their "expenses, labors and domestic arrangements" by the officers of the corporation. This constitution was soon forgotten, however, since it later became a central tenet of Bible Communism that Christians should look to God, not laws, to guide them in their conduct.

As far as the Christians at Putney were concerned, however, it would be more accurate to say that it was Noyes, not God, who kept them on the path of righteousness. "I shall watch and admonish all with whom I am associated until they are without fault," he thundered at an erring follower, and anyone at Putney who challenged Noyes's right to tell them what to do did so at his or her peril. Any doubt on this score was dispelled when two members, John Lyvere and Almira Edson, got married in defiance of Noyes's wishes. Noyes had at first looked favorably on their engagement. But after they had scandalized the neighbors by their constant hugging and kissing in public, he concluded that they had been attracted to one another only by "the blind instinct of brutes" and changed his mind. "Knowing that neither of them had any good ground of confidence in the other I opposed the marriage," he recalled. "They however were in a hurry, and on the first occasion of my absence from home stole away like thieves in the night . . . and were married." Noyes, outraged, drew up a resolution charging the couple with "an act of gross and deliberate insubordination" and formally expelling them from the Putney community. The resolution was approved by all "responsible" members of the Putney Corporation—that is, by everybody but the two offenders—and the Lyveres left Putney.

As this incident suggests, while written laws and constitutions might violate Noyes's sense of theological fitness, he was not loath, at least at this stage of his career, to have his authority spelled out. Accordingly, soon after the expulsion of the disobedient Lyveres, he introduced at a meeting of the corporation a paper headed "First Principles." In it, Noyes argued that the Putney Corporation, like a cotton factory, must have a foreman armed with strong disciplinary powers; otherwise "we cannot act as one man or protect ourselves from the disorderly doings of individual members." Noting that it was up to God to decide "who is the right man for foreman," Noyes reasserted his conviction that God had already made his choice. When he formally posed the question "Is John H. Noyes the man for president [of the corporation]?" the members unanimously answered yes.

But not everyone who joined the Putney community was prepared to tolerate the jolts of criticism and reproof to which Noyes regularly subjected them. He insisted on conformity in matters of belief as well as conduct, advising one member, for example, whose daughter had trouble accepting Noyes's theory about the second coming of Christ, that unless she fell in line, "I should openly hold her as a heathen and a publican." While there were no further expulsions after the departure of the Lyveres, a number of members left of their own accord, put off by what one young man described as Noyes's "studied effort . . . to reprove, or rather to reproach me before others." But the defections did not make Noyes any more tolerant of the shortcomings of those who remained at Putney. By 1846 he had come to believe that the establishment of God's kingdom on earth was very near, and if he was to prepare his followers to be, as it were, the advance settlers of that kingdom, there was little time to lose.

Chapter 7

*I*n July 1845 Noyes, not for the first time, warned readers of the *Perfectionist* that until the final resurrection God would tolerate no departure from the sexual code promulgated by Moses three thousand years before. Perfectionists, Noyes cautioned, should be wary of religious leaders who hugged and kissed their female followers, and should believe "no one who professes to have attained the resurrection of the body." Yet less than a year later he secretly informed a few of his closest disciples at Putney that he had misunderstood God's intentions. There was no reason, he now said, why Christians in an advanced state of holiness, and acting under inspired leadership—that is, the leadership of Noyes himself—should not enter at once into the arrangement that Noyes's critics were later to describe as free love, but that Noyes preferred to speak of as complex marriage. To break free from the bonds of conventional matrimony, he asserted, was not only permissible, but a spiritual duty: by freeing sexual love from the taint of selfishness and from narrow exclusivity, he and his followers would hasten the day of resurrection and the establishment of God's kingdom on earth.

At the same time, Noyes instructed his confidants in a technique that would allow them to enjoy the freedom of complex marriage without fear of bringing into the world children whom the world would brand as illegitimate. The secret was coitus reservatus, or, as Noyes called it, male continence—intercourse without ejaculation. Harriet Noyes had had a series of hard pregnancies ending in still-births, and Noyes, determined to spare her further suffering and disappointment, had hit on this method of contraception as an alternative to celibacy. He assured his possibly skeptical listeners that it entailed no loss of pleasure—on the contrary, he said, he and Harriet now found sex more joyful than ever before—and that the necessary self-restraint was not hard to acquire. Years later, in a pamphlet published at Oneida, Noyes evoked vividly, and with unintended comic effect, the chief danger confronting the would-be practitioner of male continence, and the appropriate strategy for overcoming it. "The situation," he wrote,

> may be compared to a stream in the three conditions of a fall, a course of rapids above the fall, and still water above the rapids. . . . There is a point on the verge of the fall where [the oarsman] has no control over his course; and just above that there is a point where he will have to struggle with the current in a way which will give his nerves a severe trial, even though he may escape the fall. If he is willing to learn, experience will teach him the wisdom of confining his excursions to the region of easy rowing.

Noyes once said that the discovery of male continence was a necessary condition for the inauguration of complex marriage. But it was not, as he had previously viewed the matter, a sufficient one. There is no explanation by Noyes—or none that has survived—of why he now concluded that there was, after all, no need to wait for the resurrection. But there is persuasive evidence that he was impelled less by theological considerations than by his own experience of the awesome power of sexual desire. In their years at Putney the families who formed the nucleus of the community—John and Harriet Noyes; the Cragins; John's sisters, Charlotte and Harriet; and their husbands— had been drawn very close to one another. In this intimacy, it was natural to dwell in imagination on that future time when, as Noyes once put it, "sexual intercourse [will become] a purely social affair, the same in kind with other modes of kindly communion, differing only by its superior intensity and beauty." It was also natural to feel increasingly impatient for the resurrection to arrive.

Noyes himself was perhaps the most impatient, having fallen help- lessly in love with Mary Cragin. She was then thirty-five, a year older than Noyes, a moody and deeply religious woman who at times since coming to Putney had felt so remote from God, and so unworthy of his love, that she had considered suicide. "Indeed, every evil passion was very strong in me from my childhood, sexual desire, love of dress and *admiration, deceit, anger, pride*," she once wrote, adding that, to her dismay, even after declaring her freedom from sin she had found "these former lusts returning." In the only portrait of her that sur- vives, she looks tense, melancholy, timid, and far from beautiful. But by all accounts she was a woman of great warmth and vivacity, with a huge capacity for loving. "Her only ambition was to be the servant of love," a eulogist wrote after her death in 1851, "and she was beau- tifully and wonderfully made for this office." Noyes once said that her "wisdom, the whole of it, is the wisdom of love; her virtue is the virtue of love." She was not only irresistible to men, but physically passionate as well. As Noyes often observed, there is a close relation- ship between sexual and religious ecstasy;* in Mary Cragin's case they seem to have melted into one another. This fusion is strikingly sug- gested by a passage from a notebook recovered from the sloop in which she drowned. "In view of [God's] goodness to me and of his desire that I should let him fill me with himself," she had written, "I

---

* "Religious love," Noyes once explained to an English journalist, "is very near neighbor to sexual love, and they always get mixed in the intimacies and social excitements of Revivals. The next thing a man wants, after he has found the sal- vation of his soul, is to find his Eve and his Paradise."

yield and offer myself, to be penetrated by his spirit, and desire that love and gratitude may inspire my heart so that I shall sympathize with his pleasure in the thing, before my personal pleasure begins, knowing that it will increase my capability for happiness."

In an atmosphere so highly charged with sex, waiting was not easy. Noyes's brother-in-law, John Miller, was also in love with Mary Cragin, and, in her words, "some trifling familiarities took place." Strains were developing within the little inner circle of believers, and in March 1846 Noyes found it advisable to reassure them—and, no doubt, himself—by hinting that the time for a "community of hearts" was fast approaching.

It came two months later, on a warm evening in May, when Noyes was seized by a desire for Mary Cragin so urgent, and so unadulterated by any feeling of guilt, that he concluded it must be inspired by God. In a paper titled "My First Act in Sexual Freedom" he described how he and Mary, out for a walk, had sat down on a rock by the roadside to talk. "All circumstances invited advance in freedom," he recalled, "and yielding to the impulse upon me I took some personal liberties. But at this point came serious thoughts. I said to myself, *I will not steal!* I revolved in my mind, as before God, what to do, and when I thought of going home for confession and consultation with those who had rights in the case, I got a signal that that was the true thing to do."

On their way home, Noyes continues, "we stopped once and took some liberty of embracing, and Mrs. Cragin distinctly gave me to understand that she was ready for the full consummation." Noyes insisted, however, that they must first get permission from their spouses. Leading Mary home, he called a meeting of the two couples. At first George Cragin was upset, accusing Noyes of doing exactly what Mary's seducer Abram Smith had done. But he was soon won over, and Harriet Noyes, too, gave her consent. "The upshot of the conference," Noyes's account concludes, "was that we gave each other full liberty all around, and so entered into complex marriage in the quartette form. The last part of the interview was as amicable and happy as a wedding, and a full consummation soon followed."

The arrangement into which the two couples had entered was for many months a closely guarded secret. But the following year, after Noyes's two sisters and their husbands had moved in with the Noyeses and the Cragins, they, too, began to experiment cautiously with the new freedom of complex marriage. These experiments were closely supervised by Noyes, who required the others to acknowledge in writing his authority to act on God's behalf as "the director of our combinations"—another instance of Noyes's belief that there were times when the rule of grace needed to be buttressed by the rule of law. Noyes taught his followers that sexual love, within the sheltering confines of complex marriage, was a holy ordinance—a means of bringing the lovers closer to God. He insisted that no one was fit to enter into complex marriage who still felt any guilt about committing what the world would regard as the sin of adultery. He was very slow to admit John Miller, for instance, to the rites of the new dispensation. "He stands opposing my theory," Noyes complained to his sister Harriet Skinner. "Yet he is availing himself of [its] privileges." Noting that Miller had "embraced Mrs. Cragin last evening," Noyes instructed his sister—who was to become his chief deputy for the regulation of sexual affairs at Oneida—to tell Miller that "you will not allow him to do anything which he thinks is wrong and will be ashamed of afterwards . . . I cannot go along with him until he has decisively adopted our principles." It was six months before Miller could convince Noyes that he at last truly believed that it was God, not the devil, who was propelling him into the arms of Mary Cragin.

Noyes tried to prevent jealousy by requiring that sexual liaisons—or partnerships, as they were often called—must not only have his sanction, but must be discussed and agreed to by all others concerned. Thus the question of whether John Miller was at last ready for complex marriage was talked over at length at a meeting of the Cragins, the Noyeses, and Miller and his wife, Charlotte. An account of that meeting in Mary Cragin's journal suggests the strange and daunting emotional terrain onto which they were all venturing. "I told [John Miller]," she wrote, "that I was desirous of entering into partnership with him upon certain conditions, which were these: his full and hearty consent that Mr. Noyes should be a third party to our union, that we should keep in open and direct communication with him, relying on his honor and generosity to teach us how to love each other in that way which would be the most improving to our characters and tend to make us the happiest."

✦   ✦   ✦

About a year after complex marriage had been secretly inaugurated at Putney, Noyes was struck with the thought that perhaps the establishment of the kingdom of heaven on earth would not happen all at once, like a clap of thunder. Almost surely its arrival would be gradual, like the coming of the spring after winter. That process, he came to believe, was already under way. There was, to begin with, the evidence offered by the faith cures that had been effected at Putney. Two years before, Noyes himself had been brought to the brink of death, or so he had been convinced, by a painful throat ailment that for months had made it all but impossible for him to speak above a whisper. But when the symptoms were at their worst, Christ had advised him "to neglect my disease and I did so, and entered upon a course of new and severe labors with my voice in meetings and conversation." Since then he had been "substantially well." Recently, too, Mary Cragin, through faith in Christ and with Noyes's help, had recovered from a prostrating illness without the aid of doctors or medicines. The holiness of the believers at Putney and the unselfish and saintly love that united them were further and even more significant indications that God's reign on earth had already begun. On June 1, 1847, Noyes put these thoughts before his followers, and "it was unanimously adopted as the declaration of the believers assembled that *The Kingdom of God Has Come.*"

Later, as the years went by at Oneida, it became clear to Noyes that the extension of God's rule to the earth was going forward at an all but imperceptible pace. Certainly, Noyes's decision in 1869 to set in motion the long, slow process of creating a spiritually superior race by scientific human breeding was a tacit admission that God had no plans for an immediate takeover. But in the summer of 1847 immortality and union with the saints in heaven seemed just ahead. Noyes's belief in the imminence of resurrection was fortified when, in collaboration with Mary Cragin, he succeeded in effecting a faith cure far more spectacular than any that had preceded it. The patient was Mrs. Harriet Hall, a Perfectionist of some years' standing—though not a member of the inner circle at Putney—who was then in her late twenties. She had long been an invalid, and at the time Noyes and Mary Cragin came to see her, she was bedridden, almost blind, and, by her own account, "unable to move or be moved without excruciating pain."

Mary Cragin began to tell the invalid how faith in God had enabled her to regain her health. As she talked, she felt herself inexplicably "sinking lower and lower into a dreadful, dark abyss," and lost consciousness. But when Noyes commanded her to look at him, she obeyed and instantly came to herself. "I arose and walked the room astonished and delighted at the power which I felt diffusing itself through my veins," she remembered. "I said to Mrs. Hall, 'This is the most effectual preaching you can have; I have tasted of death, and behold the power of resurrection.' " The invalid replied that she had felt "something good" happening to her during her visitor's fainting spell, and when Noyes now told her to get out of bed, she did so. "Mrs. Cragin raised the curtain and let in the blaze of day," she recalled a few days later. "My eyes were perfectly well, and drank in the beauty of a world all new to me with wonderful pleasure. All pain had vanished. . . . I can honestly say that, whereas for eight years I have been a miserable, bedridden, half-dead victim of disease, I am now well."

The miraculous recovery of Harriet Hall, the most convincing sign yet that the kingdom of heaven had indeed arrived at Putney, was a blow to those Perfectionists who had persisted in rejecting Noyes's claim to divine inspiration. George Cragin, who had been sent to scout the religious terrain of central New York, where Perfectionists were now most heavily concentrated, gleefully reported back to Putney how a Perfectionist leader named William Gould had reacted to a letter from Noyes to Cragin describing Mrs. Hall's cure. "When I read it to Gould," Cragin wrote, "it knocked concave for the time being his eternally doubting, damning spirit that is always pushing its horns against faith." Not long afterward Noyes himself attended a Perfectionist convention in Geneva, New York, at which his claim to leadership of the movement, which he had once again been pressing, was implicitly recognized. Before adjourning, the convention voted to form a second "heavenly association" modeled on Putney; it was to be located in central New York, and one of its missions would be to help finance the publication, at Putney, of Noyes's newspaper. But in October 1847 Noyes was arrested on a charge of adultery—his alleged partner was Fanny Leonard, the woman he had once compared to a beautiful and fragrant plant—and this plan had to be drastically modified.

Chapter 8

*F*or more than a year Noyes and those of his disciples who had been granted the privileges of complex marriage had kept their bold experiment a secret even from most other members of the Putney community. In the fall of 1847, however, Noyes had told the secret to Harriet Hall's husband, Daniel. His aim was to draw Hall, a trusted convert to Perfectionism, into full membership in the community, and Noyes seems to have given him a detailed account of the new sexual freedom he and some of his followers now enjoyed. But he had misjudged his man. After a few days' reflection, without saying anything to Noyes, Hall went to the state's attorney in the nearby town of Brattleboro. Soon afterward the county sheriff was at Noyes's door with a warrant for his arrest.

Noyes's immediate reaction was to welcome the chance to expound and defend in open court his views on sex and marriage. Indeed, as his sister Harriet reported to their mother, who was visiting in Connecticut, Noyes's mood when he returned to his anxious family after posting bail was positively jubilant. "If you have ever seen him with a radiant countenance, walking with elastic buoyancy, his cane raised in flourish, relating some glorious adventure midst shout and laughter, you have some idea of the scene," she wrote. "He was in duress about four hours, and had opportunity to parry wit with the lawyers. He told them that they would have the first picking of this affair, but that it was a controversy of principles, and would have to be settled at last by priests and philosophers."

It quickly appeared, however, that the community was in deeper trouble than Noyes at first realized. Even before his arrest, as a result of an incident having nothing to do with the community's as yet unrevealed offenses against sexual morality, he had made enemies of some influential townspeople. Soon after the seemingly miraculous cure of Harriet Hall, a Putney man named Knight had pleaded with Noyes to do what he could to save his daughter, Mary, who was in the final stages of consumption. She had thereupon been moved into one of the community's houses, where, after taking a brief turn for the better, she had died. This had persuaded some Putneyites, already skeptical of Noyes's ability to heal by faith, that he was a dangerous quack. Noyes's critics included the local Methodist minister, Hubbard Eastman, and a prominent local physician, Dr. John Campbell, neither of whom was impressed by Noyes's claim that Mary Knight would have recovered if her worldly friends had not at the end undermined her faith in Christ.

Thus predisposed to think the worst of Noyes, his enemies now seized on his arrest as ground for declaring open war on the Putney community and its leader. Noyes was denounced, in the words of the Reverend Eastman, as a "hydra-headed monster of iniquity" whose sexual doctrines were "as fatal to the moral principles of those who are brought *fully* under [their] power, as the deadly *Simoom** is to the hapless wanderer who may chance to fall in its way." Meetings were held to consider how to go about breaking up the community or, failing that, how to neutralize it as a source of deadly moral contagion.

Noyes was at first inclined to let the storm blow itself out. But a month after his arrest, while awaiting trial, he received a disquieting

---

*   A strong, hot, sand-laden wind of the Sahara and Arabian deserts.

message. It was from his brother-in-law and former legal mentor, Larkin Mead, who was now practicing law in Brattleboro. When Mead had heard of Noyes's arrest he had made no effort to hide his bafflement. "To all I hear of Putney affairs," he had written to John Miller, "I have only to say, I am not able yet to associate in my mind the names of my dear family friends there with—adultery." He added that if Noyes was bent on putting into actual practice in Putney or anywhere else his theories about sexual relations among the saints, "the sooner he is shut up in some kind of a prison the better for all concerned."

But Mead had not let his distaste for the new sexual order at Putney keep him from acting as Noyes's legal adviser in his present difficulties. The message he sent to Noyes was that there was ugly talk of mob action against the community; Dr. Campbell had been heard to say that if "there is no law that will break them up, the people of Putney will make law for the occasion." Noyes went at once to Brattleboro, where he told Mead that he was prepared to forgo bail and go to jail at once if his enemies would undertake to let his followers live in peace. But Mead, who did not really want to see his wife's brother in prison, had a different plan. The best way to cool things down, he suggested, might be for Noyes and certain other leading members of the Putney community—he specifically named George and Mary Cragin, who he said he had reason to think were facing imminent arrest—to leave the state at once. This proposed retreat, to which Noyes readily agreed, might well have been viewed by him as a major setback to the Perfectionist cause. But once again, as on the occasion of his arrest, Noyes succeeded in persuading himself that what might seem to others to be defeat was, in truth, a glorious victory. John Miller, who had gone with Noyes to Brattleboro, recalled the scene when arrangements for the flight from Putney had been completed: "Mr. Noyes danced across the room and snapping his fingers and laughing heartily said: 'We shall beat the Devil at this game.' It tried Mr. Mead exceedingly to see him feel so well in such awful circumstances."

Without returning to Putney, Noyes left at once for Hamden,

Connecticut, where his mother was staying with friends. The Cragins left Putney secretly at two o'clock the next morning and joined him there. They had left their three older children behind in Putney, but had brought with them a baby, Victor, to whom Mary Cragin had given birth two months before, and whose paternity Noyes was later to acknowledge. No testimony survives as to whether his conception was deliberate or whether, in the first surge of Noyes's passion for Mary Cragin, he had imprudently paddled into the rapids and been swept over the waterfall.

✦   ✦   ✦

While there was no further talk of mob action in Putney, Noyes's departure did not make things easier for his followers there. On the contrary, John Miller reported to his absent leader, "The moment the people here found that we were on the retreat their wrath was excited to the highest pitch. The situation has been ten times as bad as before you left." More indignation meetings were held, and a citizens' committee called on the community to sign what Miller described as "the most outrageous document ever written, saying that we had broken the laws of God and man, had become convinced of our errors, and promised to abandon our pernicious practices." The citizens also demanded that the community halt publication of the *Spiritual Magazine*, which had succeeded the *Perfectionist* as Noyes's medium for the propagation of his ideas.

Miller and Noyes's brother George, who was the editor of the magazine, refused to sign the paper that was handed to them. They did promise, however, that members of the community would in the future abide strictly by the laws governing sexual practices and would publish nothing in the *Spiritual Magazine* that readers might construe as suggesting any "violation of the laws of the land." Noyes, who had left Hamden to stay with friends in New York City, assured Miller that he was taking the right line in "yielding to public opinion" to the extent of agreeing not to break the law. But there would be no retreat on the theological front: "As to abandoning the testimony that the Kingdom of God has commenced, or acknowledging that we have done wrong, that is out of the question with me." Recognizing, perhaps, that such an attitude was a lot easier to strike in New York than in Putney, Noyes went on to justify as best he could his having left his followers to fend for themselves. "It seemed hardly right that I should be free and comfortable while you were battling with the storms of Putney," he wrote. "But then I thought that my presence with you would only increase the fury of the storm, and that it would do you no good to see me imprisoned or"—he added melodramatically—"assassinated." There are hints that some of the storm battlers at Putney were not altogether convinced by such arguments— "We must laugh at you a little for getting out of scrapes," Harriet Skinner wrote her brother, doubtless having in mind his precipitous cross-country flight from the compliant young ladies of Brimfield— but, in any case, they were too loyal to complain.

As the weeks went on, the storm abated. Business at the general store that the community operated in Putney, which had fallen almost to zero, picked up again. "Those even who have . . . said much to injure us began to show themselves," Miller reported to Noyes. "It has been amusing. Ladies would come into the store with faces as long as a yardstick, and leave with their prettiest smile. . . . Last Saturday, the store being open in the evening so that the ladies could come in under cover of night, we had our store full all evening."

Still, there were threats of further legal action. Larkin Mead reported a plan to prosecute all male members of the Putney Corporation for gross lewdness and other "offenses against chastity, morality, and decency." Even if nothing came of this (as it turned out, nothing did), and even if Noyes could straighten out his own legal difficulties, it was obvious that he and his followers could stay in Putney only at the cost of indefinitely putting aside the task God had set for them. God had commanded them, Noyes wrote Miller, "to live in the social state of heaven"—in Noyes's vocabulary, *social* often meant *sexual*— and if they were to obey his commands they would have to find another home. Toward the end of January 1848, two and a half months after his flight from Putney, Noyes was convinced he had discovered the right place.

◆   ◆   ◆

The place was Oneida, New York, where an early Perfectionist convert named Jonathan Burt had recently bought some land and a sawmill on the Oneida Indian Reserve, land that had formerly been held by the Oneida Tribe but that had been bought back by the state of New York and then offered to white settlers on easy terms. In the fall of 1847, Burt had offered to make his land available for the "heavenly association" whose establishment had been called for by the Perfectionist convention held the previous summer in Geneva, New York. By the end of the year three families of Perfectionists, who had been living in the nearby village of Beaver Meadow, had joined Burt, and the men in the group were working with him in his lumber business. In January, Burt had written to Noyes in New York City, inviting him to visit the embryonic community. Struck by the potential advantages of bringing the New York State Perfectionists under his direct leadership, while at the same time finding a new home for himself and his Putney followers, Noyes set off at once for Oneida.

He was pleased with what he found, even though it was obvious that Oneida could offer few of the amenities of Putney. Besides the sawmill, Burt's property consisted of forty acres of woodlot, a hastily built shanty in which some of the recent arrivals from Beaver Meadow had been installed, and the modest farmhouse in which Burt and his wife were living. But two farms, with substantial houses and other buildings, were for sale in the immediate vicinity, and Noyes was confident that enough money could be found, in addition to what remained in the Putney Corporation's treasury, to make the necessary down payments.

First, however, he had to deal with a challenge to his leadership of the new community. The challenger was William Gould, an Oneida physician who had been for years a mover and shaker in New York

Perfectionist circles. In the fall of 1847, before Noyes's arrest, Gould had visited Putney and apparently liked what he saw. He had seemed put out when Noyes, having revealed to Gould that complex marriage had been instituted at Putney, refused to admit him at once to its privileges. But on returning to Oneida he had announced his intention of selling his house and joining the group at the old Indian sawmill, and when the possibility was raised of Noyes moving to Oneida with his Putney followers, Gould had seemed delighted. Writing to Noyes, who was then in New York City, he addressed him as "J.H.N., Commander-in-chief" and, throwing in a playful reference to the commander's legal difficulties, promised that any orders Noyes might care to give him would be "as promptly executed when issued from the Tombs of New York as from the White House at the Capital."

But by the time Noyes got to Oneida, Gould had changed his mind about enlisting under Noyes's banner. He told Burt that Noyes had shown himself at Putney to be a mean-minded despot, and that if Noyes were to settle in Oneida it should be as a follower, not a leader. When Noyes went to see him, Gould threatened to discredit the projected community with other Perfectionists, or so Noyes reported to Burt, unless Noyes stopped claiming that he had been divinely ordained to regulate the flow of love in complex marriage. In a holy community such as was contemplated at Oneida, Gould argued, people should be free to choose sexual partners without having to get Noyes's approval. This was a freedom Noyes had no intention of granting to Gould or anyone else, and he told Burt so, emphasizing that if he were to come to Oneida to stay he would insist, as he had at Putney, on absolute obedience to his wishes in anything having to do with Perfectionist doctrine and its application. The two men talked for an hour, during which, Burt recalled, "there was a great flow of heart between us. . . . and I gave in my adherence to him as an inspired leader. At the close of our talk Mr. Noyes took from his pocket a small bag which contained five hundred dollars in ten dollar gold pieces, and gave it a whirl upon the bed, saying, 'There, Mr. Burt, if that will help you in any way, it is at your service. I offer it as my first contribution to a New York community.'"

Burt told Gould that he would have nothing more to do with him, and invited Noyes to move in with him and his wife. The next day Noyes did so, and began making plans for the new community. "Everything conspires to bring about concentration here," he wrote exultantly to George Cragin. "I have the confidence of all now on the ground.* They see for themselves and by sure tokens, that I am as hostile as ever to licentious spirits, and that my 'tyranny' instead of being an annoyance is highly useful in protecting them from the wolves."

Turning to practical matters, Noyes proposed that the Cragins come to Oneida and settle on a twenty-three-acre farm across the road from the Burts' house. This property, he noted, included a barn, a small shoemaker's shop, and a log house built by the Oneida Indians, and could be secured for a down payment of $500. With Burt's help, Noyes wrote, Cragin could farm this land while keeping the books and handling the business side of Burt's lumbering operations. "I think you can live at least as comfortably there with your children as the Beaver Meadow folks live in their shanty (and I assure you they are happy) until we can build a Chateau," Noyes concluded. "There is some romance in beginning our community in the log huts of the Indians. But your house, though built of hewed logs and by the Indians, is well plastered and papered, warm and pleasant."

The Cragins readily agreed to this plan, and it was arranged that Noyes and his wife, and their seven-year-old son Theodore, would for the time being share the log house with them. At the end of February Harriet Noyes left Putney with Theodore and the three Cragin children and traveled by coach and train to Springfield, Massachusetts, where they were joined by George and Mary Cragin and the baby Victor. On the afternoon of March 1, 1848, the travelers got off the

---

* Not quite all. Burt's wife, Lorinda, who at first welcomed Noyes as a house-guest, later changed her mind. If she could not get rid of Noyes in any other way, she told her husband, she would burn the house down over their heads. But after reading Noyes's *Confession of Religious Experience* she was won over and, in her husband's words, "came out with an open confession of Christ as a savior from sin and had a bright spiritual experience."

train at Oneida Depot, three miles north of Burt's sawmill. Sleighs had been sent to meet them, and they drove across a flat and snowy plain, dotted with black-looking tree stumps, into what Harriet Noyes recalled as "almost a howling wilderness," to take up again, this time on a much larger scale than at Putney, the task of establishing God's kingdom on earth.

◆　　　◆　　　◆

The little group at Oneida grew rapidly, and by the end of the year the Oneida Association, as the new community was formally designated, had eighty-seven members, including children. Besides the believers who had formerly been gathered at Putney, they included many Perfectionists from other Vermont villages, as well as from central New York. None were poor, but most had grown up in much harder circumstances than the Noyeses and the Cragins. Several of the new recruits had been farmers. Among the others were a printer, a trap maker, two carpenters, an architect, a wagon maker, a gunsmith, two shoemakers, two cabinet makers, and a former Methodist minister. Most of the adults were married couples in their twenties and thirties, and many had been Perfectionists for years. A few may have been drawn to the new community by the hope of enjoying greater sexual freedom. But the great majority who came to Oneida from other villages than Putney had no notion of the new sexual order that had been inaugurated there. Many, indeed, found the prospect of having many different sexual partners—and of having to accept the fact that their husbands or wives would be free to have other partners too—more threatening than enticing.

For the most part people had sold their farms and homes and come to Oneida because, as one of them said, they were "ready to commit their all to the service of God." At Oneida they would be able to live the life that God had ordained for those whose belief in Christ had freed them from sin—and from the grim theological confines of Calvinism—and raised them to a state of near-holiness. The most essential element of a holy life, Noyes had instructed them in the pages of the *Perfectionist* and the *Spiritual Magazine*, was the absolute communism of property foreshadowed by the Holy Spirit's descent on the day of Pentecost, when "all that believed were together and had all things in common; and sold their possessions and goods, and parted them to all, as every man had need." At Oneida, Perfectionists could purge themselves of the selfishness inherent in private ownership. In this connection the Oneidans, many of whom (like their leader) had a weakness for ornate metaphors, were fond of quoting a contributor to the Community's newspaper who, after noting that grapes have to be crushed to make wine and flowers to make perfume, went on to say that "all that is beautiful in our life and atmosphere is the wine and perfume of crushed selfishness—the aroma of natures that have known the cross of Christ, and its sufferings and losses."

While Noyes and his followers were feeling their way into their new life, they undertook, as their first major piece of practical business, to build a home for themselves. The buildings already standing on the Association's property were soon filled to overflowing, and more living space was urgently needed. Noyes was determined that all members of the new community should live together as one family—it was as "the family" rather than "the Association" or "the Community" that the Oneidans customarily referred to themselves—and that they should all live under one roof. As a site for the family home he settled on a broad, flattop knoll, half encircled by the same rushing creek from which Burt's sawmill got its motive power. One of the family's new members contributed $800 for a down payment on the eighty-acre farm within whose boundaries the knoll was situated. There being little cash left in the family treasury, George Cragin was sent out to raise money with which to build a home there for "the cause of God and of humanity." His goal was to raise $1,500, but he ended up with nearly twice that sum, much of it contributed by Perfectionists hoping to move to Oneida as soon as there was room for them.

One moonlit night in the early summer of 1848, Noyes and Erastus Hamilton, an experienced builder and architect who had just joined the Community, staked out the foundation of the new building, and work began the next day. Most of the work was done by the

Community itself. Noyes laid up stones for the foundation, and when the building's frame was up, Harriet Noyes, Mary Cragin, and other women nailed on the laths on which plaster would be applied for the interior walls. The Mansion House, as it was called, was three stories high and contained a kitchen, dining room, meeting room, sitting rooms, laundry, and other necessities for communal living. Unmarried men and boys were to sleep in a garret dormitory, while the third floor was to be divided into small sleeping rooms for unmarried women and married couples. (Later, married couples would be separated, and all adults, as far as accommodations permitted, would sleep alone.) But when the cold weather came, the necessary partitioning had not yet begun, and some other arrangement had to be devised to give the sleepers a little privacy. The solution was to turn most of the third floor into what was called the tent room. Cotton curtains were hung on wires to form twelve small sleeping compartments. These compartments, or tents, were grouped around a big open space, containing a stove, that served as a sitting room, and the curtains were arranged so that they could be drawn back and the whole area made into one large room. The tent room was formally dedicated on Christmas Eve, when the entire family gathered there, including the children, who from then on were to live by themselves, with appointed "parents," in the larger of the two farmhouses. Husbands and wives sat in the doors of their tents, which were trimmed with evergreen boughs, while Noyes read to the company from the Old Testament.

✦　　✦　　✦

In keeping with Noyes's dislike of laws and written constitutions, there was no blueprint for the Oneida Community except as it existed in his head. But by the close of 1848 the general features of that plan were clear enough. Members had begun experimenting, albeit timidly, with complex marriage. Children were being cared for communally. Mutual criticism was in force, and a committee consisting of four of the family's "most spiritual and discerning judges," having had their faults and virtues tallied up by Noyes, had given everyone else in the

Community at least one good lick of criticism. The women had begun to wear short skirts and pantaloons, and to cut their hair short. Each evening there were meetings in the parlor of the Mansion House; members were at liberty to speak their minds on religious or other matters, and when nobody had anything more to say, there were scheduled activities. On Monday evenings someone read aloud from the newspapers. On Tuesdays Noyes lectured on "the social theory" of Bible Communism—that is, on love, sex, and the etiquette of complex marriage. Wednesday evenings there were classes in "phonography," as shorthand was then known. (The Oneidans needed skilled phonographers to carry out their intention of recording and preserving for posterity everything that was said at their meetings.) Thursday evenings were devoted to musical practice, Friday evenings to dancing, and Saturday evenings to readings from Perfectionist publications. Although the Oneidans did not hold with public prayer or formal religious ceremonies, Sunday evenings were reserved, possibly out of deference to conventional views of what was appropriate on the Sabbath, for lectures by Noyes on the Bible.

It was a time when, for all the hardships the Oneidans had to put up with in their new home, the joy and excitement of building a new life were most intense. Or so it seemed to many Oneidans when, in their later years of affluence and ease, they sang the Community hymn, written by Noyes and set to an old Scottish air, "The Braes o' Balquither." The final stanza went:

> Now love's sunshine's begun
> And the spirit-flowers are blooming;
> And the feeling that we're one
> All our hearts is perfuming;
> Towards *one home* let us all
> Set our faces together
> Where true love shall dwell
> In peace and joy forever.
> Let us go, brothers, go!

question that was as yet unsettled as 1848 ended, and that would remain unsettled for years to come, was how the Oneidans were to support themselves. It was a help that, if they managed their affairs properly, they would have little need for cash. There was no shortage of farmers and skilled craftsmen at Oneida, as there had been at Brook Farm, and the Oneidans could count on growing most of their food and making their own shoes, clothing, and furniture. But at this time the Community was taking in almost any applicant who claimed adherence to Perfectionist doctrines, and as more and more people joined—by the end of the second year membership was nearing two hundred—it became obvious that no matter how frugally the Oneidans might choose to live, they would have to have more money than they could earn by selling lumber and shingles from the Community's sawmill.

The scheme on which they settled was to raise and sell fruit. This plan was agreed to in the face of warnings by a Community member named Henry Thacker, an experienced horticulturist, who cautioned that the climate at Oneida was as bad for growing fruit as any he had encountered. But the Oneidans, like the Fourierists, were bent on creating a new Eden, and the notion of living amid vast plantations of fruit trees, from which they would derive their livelihood, had an irresistible appeal. And so, in 1849 and 1850, they hopefully set out acre after acre of young peach, plum, pear, and cherry trees, relying on divine providence to temper the icy northern winds that swept across the Oneida plain. As one Community member observed, Christ would surely give Oneida "a genial climate, outwardly as well as inwardly," thereby enabling the Community "to carry fruit culture to a development and perfection that the world has no conception of."

But even with Christ's cooperation it would be years before the newly planted fruit trees could be counted on to bring in much money. And while the Community had some capital, consisting mainly of money that members had realized from the sale of homes or farms and had contributed to the common treasury, most of this capital was promptly invested in land and in additional buildings that the growing membership required. To help cover expenses while waiting for their fruit trees to bear, Oneidans tried their hands at a variety of money-making schemes. For a time they made gold chains. When this proved unprofitable, as well as hard on the eyes, they shifted to another home industry: stitching together precut carpet bags. At the same time, men were sent out on the road to peddle silk thread, needles, buttons, pins, and other notions. When this plan was first proposed, a member noted, it "cut across the pride of some." But members were soon vying for the privilege of going out as peddlers, one man declaring that he would "shoulder a razor-grinder, and joyfully too," if it would help the Community. At first the peddlers went on foot or drove out in wagons. Later they traveled by rail and were away for weeks at a time. When a peddler returned to Oneida he was routinely immersed in a bath of criticism intended to wash away such spiritual grime as might have rubbed off on him on his travels.

None of these ventures was very profitable, however. Noyes's brother-in-law, John Miller, the Community's financial manager, was often hard-pressed to find money for such necessities as lamp oil and shoe leather. Once—or so the Oneidans liked to recall in their later years of prosperity—the Community gave the last dollar in its treasury to a visitor who needed it to pay his way home. On another occasion forty members turned in their watches to be sold for cash with which to settle the Community's accounts. To save money, people went without butter and other table luxuries, subsisting on a diet made up largely of brown bread, milk, bean porridge, and potatoes with milk gravy.

Noyes, too, lived quite simply in these years, but not so simply as his followers. Later he was to make a point of living like everybody else, taking his regular turn in the kitchen and the cow barns. At this time, however, he seems to have seen nothing wrong in claiming certain special and relatively costly privileges. In 1849, for example, he took Mary Cragin to Niagara Falls for a week. True, it was a working vacation. Noyes was planning to write a detailed account, or "confession," of his sexual experiences—he later abandoned the project—and Mary was instructed to "provide herself with a full set of our publications, a polyglot Bible, a Shakespeare, inkstand . . . etc." But other members of the Community who had writing to do did it at Oneida, not at Niagara Falls. Later Noyes drew a large sum from the treasury to finance a visit to the great industrial exhibition that opened in London's newly built Crystal Palace in the spring of 1851.

Noyes's bland detachment from the economic difficulties of his disciples was made easier by his decision to leave Oneida, after some eighteen months there, and take up residence at a distant outpost. There were several such colonies or satellites in the Community's early years—in Cambridge, Vermont; in Newark, New Jersey; at Wallingford, Connecticut, and at Putney, where a group of Oneidans, after satisfying themselves that Noyes's old enemies were no longer bent on harassing his followers, reopened, in 1851, the gristmill that the Putney Corporation had formerly operated there. There was also a colony in Brooklyn, where, some years before, Mary Cragin's old seducer, Abram Smith, had bought a comfortable house on Brooklyn Heights. In 1849, having been forgiven by Noyes for his sins, Smith joined the Oneida Community and turned over to it the deed to his house. A few months later Noyes moved in, together with his wife, the Cragins, and a few other followers. He was apparently persuaded that he was no longer needed at Oneida, that God now wanted him to work on winning the world over to Bible Communism, and that he was entitled to the tranquillity he would gain for writing and re-flection by removing himself from Oneida's ceaseless ditch digging and carpentry, and from the day-to-day management of its affairs. He left no doubt, however, as to who was ultimately in charge, advising his followers at Oneida "not to get into a quarrel with God or with him." God, he said sternly, "would defend whatever course he took, and whoever undertook to judge him would find in the end that he"—Noyes—"was their judge." This admonition was heeded, and during the five years that Noyes lived in Brooklyn his advice on what should be done at Oneida was faithfully followed.

Noyes had long believed that the most efficient way to gain con-verts to Perfectionism was to put out a newspaper devoted to the service of Christ and "divorced from Mammon"—by which he meant that payment by subscribers should be voluntary. Publishing such a paper, he said, should be the chief business of the Oneida Community, and when the Community could furnish the necessary men and money, it should be published every day of the year. Encouraged by the way Bible Communism was taking hold at Oneida, by the time he moved to Brooklyn Noyes looked forward confidently to the im-minent establishment of other Perfectionist communities all over the United States and the rest of the world. When they came into being, he explained on an occasion when his and God's work seemed to be going particularly well, the "mighty engine of a free daily omnipresent Press" would serve as a super-government and spiritual regulator, "combining and harmonizing the local Communities, and distributing the bread of life to all."

For the moment, a daily newspaper was out of the question. But as a first step Noyes had arranged for the old hand press that he had bought with Harriet's dowry to be moved from Putney to Oneida, and publication of the *Spiritual Magazine* was resumed on an irregular schedule. After Noyes moved to Brooklyn its name was changed to the *Free Church Circular*—in the matter of naming his newspaper, as in most other things, Noyes seemed to believe in change for change's sake—and it began to appear fortnightly, its contents consisting largely of articles and essays by Noyes, and the texts of the "Home Talks" that he gave to his followers in Brooklyn and that were taken down in shorthand by Mary Cragin. In 1851, after a fire destroyed the newly built printing office in which the press was housed at Oneida, Noyes, who may have been feeling underemployed and at loose ends, took over the editorship of the paper himself. A steam-powered press was bought and installed in a building adjoining the house on Brooklyn Heights, and with the help of a crew of writers, editors, and typesetters who moved to Brooklyn from Oneida he began to get out an expanded version of the *Free Church Circular*, now called simply the *Circular*, which was soon coming out three times a week.

But in 1854 Noyes found himself confronting some discouraging realities. Bible Communism still existed only at Oneida and its outposts, and God seemed in no hurry to extend his earthly beachhead. It struck Noyes that perhaps what God wanted him to do was to return to Oneida and concentrate on perfecting—if such a term can be applied to people who were in a narrow theological sense already perfect—the social arrangements and spiritual life of the little world he had created there. It had also become obvious that something must be done quickly to put the Community on a sounder economic footing. Despite repeated appeals for donations, most of the *Circular*'s subscribers were exercising their option to take the paper free, and putting out a paper three times a week was not only taking up the working hours of a great many people, but was siphoning large sums of cash out of the Community treasury. The death of John Miller in 1854 forced Noyes to face up to the dangers of this situation, and on examining the books he concluded that the only way to avoid bankruptcy was to find some other source of income than fruit. As a Community historian wrote sadly some years later, "Mr. Thacker was a true prophet, and our frostbitten and blighted orchards were turned into brush heaps for the fire."

Steps were taken at once to conserve the Community's dwindling capital. The Brooklyn property was sold, and Noyes and the others who had been living there moved to Oneida, taking the press with them. Publication of the *Circular* was resumed after a brief hiatus, but in a less ambitious format and on a once-a-week schedule. Other branch communities besides Brooklyn were shut down to save money, with the notable exception of the colony at Wallingford. There was not enough room at Oneida to house all Community members, and it was thought that some could support themselves at Wallingford, where the Community owned a farm well suited to market gardening, by growing peas, cabbage, spinach, and other vegetables.

Noyes himself joined enthusiastically in the search for new money-making schemes, and soon after his return to Oneida he was deeply involved in a project that was to become the chief source of Oneida's later prosperity. The key to this venture was an improved animal trap invented by a Community member named Sewall Newhouse. A black-smith as well as an experienced hunter and trapper, Newhouse had for years forged his traps by hand in his shop in the nearby village of Oneida Castle, and he continued to do so after joining the Community in 1848. By 1854, with part-time help, he was turning out two to four hundred traps a month and shipping them to dealers as far away as Chicago.

When the moneymaking potential of the Newhouse trap had earlier been called to Noyes's attention, he had not been impressed. "Our horticultural flag had been nailed to the mast," one of his followers later explained, "and, sink or swim, we were going to do our best to make a success of fruit growing." But in everything but fundamental matters of religious belief Noyes was reasonably flexible, and by 1854 he had second thoughts. Newhouse did not like people poking into his business, but by offering his services as a forge hand, Noyes succeeded in getting Newhouse to let him in on the secrets of the trap and its manufacture. Newhouse was still making his traps laboriously by hand and could not nearly keep up with the orders that were pouring in. It seemed to Noyes, and the Community's businessmen, that making traps could be a highly profitable business if a way could be found to make them more efficiently.

Among the Community's members was an inventive machinist named William Inslee. At Noyes's urging, Newhouse agreed to let Inslee see what he could do to mechanize the trap business. With the help of some young apprentices, Inslee built water-driven machinery to punch out certain parts and to form the springs of the traps—a task that had previously entailed pounding a bar of steel one hundred and twenty times with a two-handed sledge. Newhouse had been making his traps in just one size, but an Oneidan named John Hutchins, who had earned a living both as an itinerant Baptist preacher and as a trapper, now helped Newhouse design specialized traps for otters, beavers, black bears, grizzly bears, and moose.

By the late 1850s the Community was selling more than 100,000 traps a year to, among other customers, the Hudson's Bay Company. New mechanical devices were introduced in the trap shop. These included a revolving oven, capable of tempering up to 5,000 trap springs at a time, invented by a young machinist who later became the Community's dentist. (The Oneidans were great believers in versatility.) Profits soared, and in 1865, after a year in which production of traps reached a new high of 275,000, the trap business was moved into a new brick building a mile or so north of the Mansion House. The Oneidans, having cheerfully abandoned their dreams of a purely pastoral existence, took enormous interest and pride in the new factory, where, according to an article in the *Circular*, "fine mechanical skills and inventive genius are [developing] curious and wonderful machines which do their work rapidly and in the most perfect manner."

✦   ✦   ✦

The *Circular*'s glowing tribute to the new trap shop was only one instance of the delight the Oneidans took in thinking up and turning out new products and mechanical devices. It was not just that mechanical ingenuity and resourcefulness could contribute importantly to their comfort and prosperity. The Oneidans also assigned great spiritual significance to achievements like the new trap-shop machinery. For they believed that the better they could make things work in the world they had created, the more certain they could be that God was pleased with them.

The Oneidans' bent for invention was not limited to the devising of new and better factory machines. The first lazy Susan was invented and put into service at Oneida, along with other useful domestic items such as a mechanical mop wringer, a mechanical potato peeler, and a washing machine. This last "was an amazing object," one of Noyes's grandchildren recalled. "Attached to a revolving rod near the ceiling were what seemed like two long, ungainly but powerful legs shod by big, clumsy overshoes which sloshed back and forth in a large trough full of deliciously foaming suds." Oneida women, dissatisfied with high-heeled and high-laced boots, invented a low, laceless shoe, with an elastic insert to make it fit snugly, which they hopefully called the "final shoe." An Oneida woman also invented a forerunner of the garter belt, which was thought to be much healthier than the conventional round garter because it didn't restrict circulation in the legs. Noyes himself designed an ingeniously appointed lunch box to add to the Community's line of traveling bags.

Machines did not have to be invented by Oneidans to be appreciated by them. They shared the country's enthusiasm for material progress, and its reverence for the wonders of the age of steam. "Why," Noyes asked at an evening meeting, "cannot someone celebrate the clang of railroads and machinery in high-flown language like that we have been reading from Ossian?" Taking their cue from their leader, writers for Oneida publications rhapsodically described the workings of the Community's water wheels, steam cookers, caloric engines, and silk-spinning machinery, and marveled at newly installed dumbwaiters and Turkish baths. "Good-bye woodsheds," the *Circular* apostrophized when central steam heating was introduced at Oneida in 1869, "good-bye stoves, good-bye coal scuttles, good-bye pokers, good-bye ash-sifters, good-bye stove dust, and good-bye coal gas! Hail to the one-fire millennium!" Oneidans were as fascinated with the process of making mechanical improvements as they were with its results, seeing that process as an analogue of their efforts at spiritual perfection. "If we compare the form of a [primitive] machine with the perfect type of the same instrument," a Community writer asserted, "we observe as we trace it through the phases of improvement, how weight is shaken off where strength is less needed . . . how the straight becomes curved and curve is straightened, till the struggling and cumbersome machine becomes the compact, effective, and beautiful engine."

The Oneidans also worked constantly, as a religious obligation, to improve the comfort, efficiency, and beauty of their Community home. They believed its design should both reflect and facilitate the complex harmony for which they were striving in Community life, and they gave a lot of thought to architecture and landscaping. They read and discussed the work of Andrew Jackson Downing, Capability Brown, and other leading landscape architects of the time, and studied Frederick Law Olmsted's plans for New York's Central Park. Under the direction of their resident horticulturist, Henry Thacker, they laid out the grounds around the Mansion House with shaded walks, hedges, a formal garden, and an avenue of elms. Their guiding aesthetic principle, in landscaping and architecture as well as in the design of machines, was that beauty was inseparable from utility. "We are convinced," the *Circular* noted, "that simplicity, absence of pretension, and the straightforward adaption of means to end, will ultimately prove, in architecture as well as in all things else, to be the truest standard of taste."

Since the Community was constantly changing—the decision to hire outside workers, for example, and the later decision to begin the systematic production of babies, both altered drastically the character of life at Oneida—adherence to this principle required a pragmatic and flexible approach to design. Whenever possible the Oneidans proceeded tentatively and by experiment. In the summer of 1866, for instance, the *Daily Journal*, the miniature newspaper that the Oneidans had begun to publish for their own edification, reported that a path was being cut across the oval green in front of the Mansion House portico. "A kind of contest has been going on in the minds of a good many between the taste that preferred to keep the oval intact and the necessity that demanded the path," the *Journal* reported;

"but it may be assumed as a safe principle that beauty and utility are never truly antagonistic. At some future time the paths and grass plots may be entirely re-arranged in conformity with new requirements and new ideas." In landscaping, as in the improvement of their spiritual lives, the Oneidans saw perfection as an unending process rather than a settled state.

◆   ◆   ◆

During the years when the trap business was being mechanized and expanded, the Oneidans experimented with other ventures. They made mop handles and hoes and rustic outdoor furniture designed by a Community member named Charles Ellis. This furniture, no two pieces of which were alike, was constructed of gnarled and twisted white-cedar crooks cut from nearby swamps. When the Community ran out of cedar the business was discontinued, but Ellis left his mark on Oneida. "Our lawns," a Community historian noted, "were . . . adorned with seats of every description, artistic and fantastic: seats with arms, seats with rockers, double or tête-à-tête seats; arbors, trellises, corner seats." Ellis also built a summer house for the Community, a rustic Gothic structure whose conical thatched roof supported, at its apex, what looks in old photographs like a gigantic birdhouse. The Oneidans also launched cottage industries at which everyone, including children, could work. Besides making traveling bags, they braided palm-leaf hats, embroidered men's slippers, made brooms from broom corn that they grew themselves, and sewed "satin-sprung cravats." All these businesses were soon dropped except bag making, which in the 1860s was partially mechanized and transferred to a small factory building.

There were other Community businesses besides these. Thacker pointed out that while the climate might be wrong for fruit trees, there was no reason why the Community couldn't profitably raise corn, peas, tomatoes, and other vegetables and can them for the market. When Thacker and his associates got the hang of canning, they began putting up not only home-grown produce, including jams and jellies made from the Community's grapes and strawberries—both of which did very well at Oneida—but large quantities of peaches and other fruit imported by rail from areas with milder climates. The Community also sold silk thread purchased from a New York manufacturer. At first it was sold door-to-door by Community men working as foot-peddlers. Later it was sold wholesale by half a dozen members assigned to travel around the country by train calling on dry-goods stores. Then, in 1866, the Community began buying raw silk and making its own silk thread on water-powered spinning and winding machines built by William Inslee and his assistants and installed in a wing of the new trap factory.

✦   ✦   ✦

In the early 1850s Noyes had declared war on the wage system, calling on employers to make full partners of their workers. This partnership was not to be confined to the factory or shop; employer and employees, he wrote, should live together as one family, striving jointly for spiritual improvement. But Noyes the businessman was capable of overriding Noyes the reformer, and in 1862, with the trap business booming, the Community began hiring outside workers without any thought of having them join the Oneida family. Workers were taken on not only as factory hands—by 1867 thirty-one women and girls, some only ten years old, were working in the silk mill—but to dig ditches, handle the farm teams, and help out in the laundry and kitchen. By 1870 more than two hundred employees were on the Community payroll.

Judged by contemporary standards the Oneidans were good employers. They saw to it that their workers had decent housing, furnished many of them with free transportation to and from work, organized evening classes for the boys and girls who worked in their factories, paid good wages, and, at least once, gave their employees an unsolicited raise. Workers and their families were also on occasion entertained at lawn parties at which they were invited to eat their fill of strawberry shortcake and listen to music by the Community orchestra.

But paternalism did not imply intimacy. Children were forbidden to speak to the hired men, and fraternization by older people could get the fraternizer into trouble. Until the final days of the Community, when discipline grew slack, a Community man caught flirting with one of the girls in the silk mill could count on having to swallow a deep and bracing draft of mutual criticism.

One aim of this enforced separation was to protect Oneidans from spiritual contamination. But there was also a fear that intimacy between the Oneidans and their employees might, in a sense, contaminate the employees, too. To a large extent the Oneidans chose the jobs they worked at, and in many instances decided for themselves how long and hard they would work. Any extension of these "free habits" to the hired workers, Noyes the businessman warned, would play the devil with industrial efficiency at Oneida.

Three years after Noyes's return to Oneida from Brooklyn, the Community was in the black, and during the boom years of the Civil War profits rose steeply. In 1864 alone the Community made enough money ($61,000) to increase its net worth by more than one third. After the Civil War the Oneidans gave up bag making—it didn't pay enough—and expanded their other businesses. They built a new cannery and opened a second silk mill at Wallingford, using water power from the Quinnipiac River, on which the Community's property bordered. In the early 1870s they built a new dam on the Quinnipiac to furnish power for further expansion of the silk business and of the job-printing business that had been carried on at Wallingford on a modest scale at a time when the *Circular* was being published there. In 1877 the Community also began manufacturing tin-plated spoons at Wallingford. Profits continued to run almost as high as in the fat Civil War years, and until 1878, when dissension and discontent began to sap the vitality of the Community's business ventures, the Oneidans could count on enough money flowing into the treasury to let them live pretty much as they liked.

♦   ♦   ♦

While Noyes in later years worried that a growing preoccupation with making money was stunting the spiritual growth of his followers, he saw no virtue in poverty. God, he told the Community in a talk titled "Asceticism Not Christianity" and later printed in the *Circular*, chose to surround Adam and Eve "with the greatest means of enjoyment," and this enjoyment was *"the very business that [God] set Adam and Eve about*, AND NO OTHER." Despite occasional twinges of nostalgia for the austerity of their early years—every society has its golden age of salutary poverty—Noyes and his followers considered wealth a blessing, and they used their profits, apart from what they put back into the Community's businesses, to improve themselves and to make life easier and pleasanter at Oneida. They sent promising young men to college (most of them to Yale) at Community expense. They bought books for the Community's excellent library and built vacation retreats on Lake Oneida and on Long Island Sound. As time went on, Oneidans tended to work fewer hours and to leave the most menial, exhausting, and boring jobs to outside workers.

The most visible manifestation of their prosperity, and the one in which they took perhaps the greatest pride, was the new Mansion House, for which ground was broken in 1861. An imposing three-story structure, built of brick that the Oneidans themselves made, its design was the product of years of discussion and debate at evening meetings. The bedrooms were small, in line with Noyes's belief that men and women should only share a bed, and a bedroom, during sexual encounters, or interviews, as they were commonly called at Oneida. (Noyes disapproved of using bedrooms for social gatherings, on the theory that this could lead to cliquishness and unhealthy attachments.) But there were a number of pleasant common rooms—some big, others small and cozy—where people could gather. There was also the family hall, a generously proportioned chamber with a twenty-one-foot ceiling on which were painted allegorical figures representing Justice, Music, Astronomy, and History. At one end was a large stage, framed by a frescoed proscenium arch; a balcony, or gallery, ran around the other three sides of the room. When benches were set out on the main floor, the hall could comfortably seat more than seven hundred, and it was there that the Oneidans held their evening meetings, watched theatrical performances, listened to music, and danced.

In 1869 a new wing was added to the building, big enough to accommodate those adults who had had to go on living in the original Mansion House, as well as the children of the Community, who had been housed in a separate building. A third wing was added in 1878, just before the Community broke up. The new Mansion House's most striking features were two square towers, one with a handsome arched doorway and a mansard roof, the other a simpler structure with an open parapeted roof from which visitors were sometimes invited to view the Community's domain. "On reaching the top," one viewer reported, "a landscape of unspeakable beauty lies before us. At our feet, the lawn with its neatly-trimmed paths, the flower gardens with their brilliant colors, and the rustic seats and arbors, half concealed in shady nooks, entice the eye with their quiet loveliness."

The Mansion House still stands, looking from the outside very much as it did when it was completed in 1878. Inside, groups of the tiny bedrooms have been thrown together to form larger rooms and apartments, some of them occupied by descendants of the stirpicults—the products of the Oneida Community's experiment in scientific human breeding. The walls of the old common rooms are hung with portraits of John and Harriet Noyes, of their son Theodore, of Harriet Skinner and Mary Cragin and other leading Community figures. There are photographs of children hoeing weeds, of adults stitching up traveling bags while a bearded man reads to them from a book, of Oneidans posing stiffly with croquet mallets on the lawn outside the old Mansion House.

The most evocative of these photographs shows a group of perhaps fifty men, women, and children sitting under a tree. The women are in trousers and short skirts; many of the men are wearing long, smock-like white coats. They are all shelling peas, but their rapt and solemn faces suggest that they are taking part in a ceremonial rite—a form of worship, perhaps, or meditation. This may be no more than a result of their having been instructed to hold absolutely still so as not to blur the photographer's plate. But to a viewer familiar with the Community's history, the picture is a moving reminder that work at Oneida, like every other activity, from playing croquet to making love, was meant to be a holy ordinance, a conscious submission to the will of God and a celebration of his goodness.

oyes often pointed out to his followers that it was their duty to God to get all the pleasure they could from the world in which God had placed them. True Christians would, of course, always act so as to make other people happy, too. And they would never forget that happiness came from God. But Christians who abided by these principles could count on pleasing God by pleasing themselves, and it was doing God an injustice, Noyes once declared, to suppose that weeding strawberries was any more meritorious in God's eyes than eating and enjoying them. In truth, Noyes said, God *wanted* his children to enjoy eating strawberries, since it was "the main focus and center of all duty to 'eat the fat and drink the sweet' and enjoy God and his works."*

---

* In one of his talks Noyes made the same point in another way: "There is no sight in this world more melancholy than that of a man who has worked all appetite out of himself and is sick of everything. He is weary of the sun, and has no pleasure in the singing of the birds, in the flowers of the field, nor in anything else that is naturally pleasant to man. He has burned his appetite out, and is in a sense dead while he lives, and damned."

Such teachings did not eliminate unhappiness at Oneida. Noyes himself conceded that the "deep kind of discipline of spirit by which God is refining, purifying and perfecting our characters" was bound to cause suffering. Some people found this discipline so painful that they left the Community. Others left because they felt stifled by the pressure to believe just what Noyes believed. Some who stayed were tortured by doubt and alienation from God. "I know what it is," a young woman wrote a friend, "to doubt the existence of God and to struggle day and night for months, and years even, with the powers of darkness." Love, too, could be painful at Oneida. "I hope your love for Beulah has been satisfactory," Harriet Noyes wrote from Oneida to a friend living at the Wallingford branch. "I sympathize with any love that does not bring torment with it. I think sometimes we have had a kind of love going in the Community that was a source of torment." But the Oneidans were in general energetic in their pursuit of happiness and reasonably successful in catching up with it. Their tastes in pleasure were simple and Arcadian, and they aimed to give free play to what one Community writer called "the sportive, spontaneous action of life." A report in the *Circular* in August 1855 gave readers a good notion of the kind of spontaneous action the Oneidans particularly liked: "These are nights to suggest serenades and all kinds of romance. The moon shines on nature, now in all the exuberance of its summer beauty, and an enchanting mystery is added to the scene. . . . Last night, after the watch had retired and most of the family were fallen into peaceful slumbers, some who were yet wakeful heard music in the distance, sweet voices and a song. We knew it was a band of screnaders, discoursing love to the sleepers. . . . [Then] after a little silence the same music was heard on the lawn before the Mansion, now near enough to gently wake the slumberers within or mingle pleasantly with their dreams. This company of 'intriguants' was composed of ten or twelve of the best singers of the Commune. They sang last night, besides two familiar songs, one that was new here and very beautiful, we thought, 'The Guardian Angel.' " Another article in the *Circular* catalogued the sounds heard on the Mansion House lawn after supper on a July evening in 1872: "The

click of mallets and balls on the croquet ground . . . the music of
piano, clarinet, and cello playing in the Hall; a quartet singing in the
cottage at the foot of the hill; children's voices laughing; boys playing
horse; cows lowing at the barn; sheep bells tinkling; lambs bleating;
frogs peeping in the pond below the gardens . . . the ringing of the
car bell which announces the arrival of our friends from Joppa"—
Joppa was the Community's vacation lodge on Lake Oneida—"a
merry meeting of the newly arrived; the high note of the whistle which
calls us together for an hour in the Hall."

The Oneidans loved elaborate family parties. "A cooking stove
which sent the steam and smoke up through the trees and served to
bake potatoes, etc., made the scene seem gypsyish and camp-like," a
Community reporter noted after a festive Saturday afternoon in the
woods. "We had music—songs of praise and instrumental music.
There was some laughing too, to make the woods echo." When it
was too cold for picnics there were parties in the Mansion House to
celebrate birthdays or to honor individuals or groups. One December
evening, for instance, there was a party for the boys whose job it had
been during the fall months to drive the cows to and from pasture. A
special supper was served in the schoolroom, which had been deco-
rated with a banner proclaiming "Honor to the Youthful Heroes,
who, in loyal obedience to the Association . . . quit their beds in the
dark hours of the morning." At times parties were gotten up at a
moment's notice just for the sake of having a party. On one occasion,
reported in the "Oneida Journal" column of the *Circular*, the pretext
for a celebration was simply that it was a pleasant Saturday evening
and the week was ending. "Now what shall we have?" the columnist
inquired. "A march, a game of ball in the meadow, or a Community
dance in the broad garden walk under the plum and cherry trees? The
young people show a bright-eyed alacrity at the last suggestion, and
a dance it is. The supper things are cleared away, violins, flutes and
bass viol form the orchestra and lead into the garden, figures are
formed, and the hour's dance in the cool summer gracefully completes
the week's drama and sweetens the succeeding repose."

The Oneidans swam, fished, skated, hiked, went sleigh riding, and camped out. They loved croquet, which they played even in winter, wearing overcoats and gloves. When they first took up the game they worried about the combativeness that it brought out in the players: if one truly loved one's opponent, wasn't it wrong to get pleasure out of knocking his ball away? This dilemma was resolved when Noyes, who was almost always able to enlist God in support of what he wanted to do, announced, "after playing a fine game of croquet," that he had "got a new view on the subject of competition." God, he explained, was on both sides in any game. And as long as it was recognized "that he controls the result and gives the victory to whom he pleases, we may enter into [a game] heartily and exercise our utmost skill and power to win." He went on to say, sounding like the famous schoolmaster Dr. Thomas Arnold of Rugby, that games were good for developing character, and that "competition, instead of being a mere exhibition of antagonism, becomes a harmonic cooperation with God." The Oneidans also played baseball, chess, dominoes, and a forerunner of tiddlywinks called squails. For many years, however, they did not play card games—not because they thought cards inherently wicked, but because of their unsavory connotations. "They put us in rapport . . . with a diabolical sphere," a Community writer warned.

Noyes and his followers had no such reservations about the theater. They entertained themselves with dramatic readings from *Pickwick Papers* and the novels of Harriet Beecher Stowe, with performances of farces written by Community humorists, and with plays by Sheridan and Shakespeare. Between plays they mounted and applauded elaborate dramatic tableaux. A granddaughter of Noyes, recalling what it was like to grow up at Oneida, noted that tableaux were "great favorites, since those who had beauty but could not act could yet know the joys of the limelight for a brief period." Her description of a production called *Cleopatra's Barge* pokes gentle—very gentle—fun at the rustic innocence and naive enthusiasm that animated so many of the Oneidans' undertakings. "The carpenters and painters," she writes, "had produced from a drawing the semblance of a royal barge which, being set up on the stage, was then filled with six of our most beautiful girls dressed in fluffy, white tarlatan, their short hair covered with wigs of jute ringlets. Mrs. Helen Noyes"—the wife of Noyes's brother George—"at least a mature forty, as Cleopatra, in regal robes of white, sat on a dais in the gilded prow. It was a breathtaking sight for the whole audience."

The Oneidans went in for music even more enthusiastically than they did for dramatics.* In this, as in other things, they took their lead from Noyes, who once wrote a poem characterizing music as one of God's "three sacred gifts" to humankind, the other two being work and love. (On another occasion he described music as a form of worship, though ranking it below "a still higher form of worship, which is sexual love.") At one time Noyes threw himself into the study of harmony and counterpoint, and he liked to play the violin. But by most accounts he played it terribly, and his use of phrases like "social music" and "the music of work" suggests he may have been fascinated by music mainly as a metaphor.† It was easy to see in a composer's willing submission to the laws of harmony a paradigm of the submission to God that was, in Noyes's view, the only basis of genuine human freedom. He may also have been struck by the ways in which the Oneida Community resembled—or should resemble—an orchestra, whose members, in the service of art, must subordinate themselves to

---

* In the early days, when the Oneidans were too poor to buy musical instruments, some of the violinists performed on homemade instruments fashioned by two skilled cabinetmakers who were members of the Community. "At least one could play upon them," a Community historian, George Cragin (who was himself a violinist), recalled, adding that even though "the tops or bellies . . . were made of basswood, a totally unfit wood for this purpose, they actually gave a muffled tone that was not half bad." This had one advantage, Cragin noted: "In private practice with these homemade affairs it was hardly necessary to close your door to avoid annoying your neighbors."
† In Noyes's mind, music and sex were closely intertwined. He told his favorite niece, Tirzah Miller—who was also one of his favorite sexual partners—that "there is as much difference between women in respect to ability to make social music as there is between a grand piano and a tenpenny whistle." Making it clear that Tirzah was a grand piano, he added, "I always expect something sublime when I sleep with you."

the intentions of the composer and the commands of the conductor.

In any case, music was queen of the arts at Oneida. So many people played and sang that before the new Mansion House was built they were hard-pressed to find room to practice and rehearse. "Where shall we go to scrape our first lesson on the fiddle, or to bolt our first brayings on the horn?" a Community journalist inquired, adding, "If we have any proper Academy of Music it is the dairy house! Quartet clubs and amateur violinists find a retreat there, and our parlor performances are often importations from that quarter." A musical census in 1864 revealed that twenty-one of the forty-four people living at the Wallingford branch were taking lessons on the harmonium, while Oneida boasted two orchestras (one with twenty-two pieces), a brass band, a choir of twenty-five singers, two male quartets, and a "club of eight male voices." Later there were string quartets and a girls' glee club. Music was considered so important that the conductor of the Community's principal orchestra, a young, self-taught musician named Charles Joslyn, was allowed to reserve half of each working day for study and composition. One year four of the Community's best singers were sent off for several months to study music in New York.

The Oneidans played and sang overtures and choruses from operas by Mozart, Handel, Meyerbeer, and Rossini; waltzes by Strauss; English glees; military marches; and homegrown products such as Joslyn's "Oneida Quickstep." There were informal concerts during and after midday dinner, and formal evening concerts in the hall of the new Mansion House. The Community's workmen and people living in nearby villages were often invited, free of charge, to these concerts, and even though the hall could hold nine hundred people in a pinch there was not always room for everyone who came. The last and perhaps the most ambitious of the Community's musical ventures was a production of *H.M.S. Pinafore* in the winter of 1879–80, when people badly needed a diversion from the fierce quarrels that were by then ripping the Community apart.

✦　　✦　　✦

The Oneidans also spent a lot of time taking courses from other Oneidans in subjects such as algebra and Greek. They sometimes explained their passion for study on the ground that it better equipped them for the task that God had set them—that is, to bring the world around to Bible Communism and thereby prepare the way for the rapid expansion of God's kingdom on earth. But they seemed to have looked on learning mainly as a form of pleasure that, like music, was at the same time a form of worship, celebrating God's goodness in endowing his children with the capacity to solve quadratic equations and plot the orbits of the planets.

Besides algebra and Greek and astronomy, the Oneidans taught one another arithmetic, grammar, Latin, French, physics and mechanics, geometry, chemistry, musical theory, Hebrew, theology, spelling, trigonometry, geography, elocution, rhetoric, English composition, and shorthand. "There is scarcely a person who does not belong to one of these classes—most persons are members of two," the *Circular* reported in 1864. "The enthusiasm is intense." At another time when the passion for study was at one of its periodic peaks, trap-shop hands took to memorizing irregular French verbs in the intervals of work. One Oneidan reported that he studied Greek while he was out on the road selling Community products—an occupation that had the advantage of serving as a protective shield against the worldly temptations that beset the Community's traveling men.

In 1869 an embryo college, as Noyes called it, was established at Oneida. Its faculty consisted of two young Oneidans who had recently graduated from Yale, and its mission was to furnish a college education to any Community member who wanted one. It opened with an enrollment of sixty-five students, who were to be given half of each day to study and attend classes. The plan was dropped when the Community decided it could not afford to have so many people taking so much time off from work. But Oneidans could still take spare-time college-level courses in such subjects as chemistry and physics. Community members, whether at Oneida or one of its branches, were faithful attendants at evening lectures on such topics as new discoveries in geology or the history of the Medo-Persian Empire, and they listened to readings from works like Jonathan Dwight's biography of Jonathan Edwards and Pope's translation of *The Odyssey.*

✦   ✦   ✦

It was not only in their leisure hours that Oneidans were expected to cultivate the art of happiness. They might have to work for a living, but in a community like theirs, Noyes had predicted, work would "become sport, as it would have been in the original Eden state." And to a degree that never ceased to astonish and delight them, the Oneidans in fact contrived to make work joyful and exhilarating.

One way they eased the burden of labor was by allowing people, as far as was practical, to pick their own jobs and to change them frequently. A woman named Jessie Kinsley, who was born and grew up in the Community, recalled with pleasure how varied her work had been:

> Waiting on table, dish-washing and wiping, dining-room work, kitchen work, sweeping and dusting and bed-making, filling lamps—hundreds of lamps—and cleaning their wicks and chimneys . . . working in the sewing-room on children's clothes, helping in the dairy, helping in the laundry, sometimes helping as nurses for the sick, making chains in the chainroom, making boxes in the Arcade, helping in the Fruit Canning House, working out-of-doors . . . caring for children in the Children's House—all these labors and others not remembered came and went and came again as time passed by.

She went on to say that people who liked and were good at particular jobs were usually allowed to stay with them. "When bookkeeping or typesetting proved to be someone's *special province*," she wrote, "or gardening and the care of plants seemed someone's *positive gift*, or business leadership or other leadership was immediately evident, then such people, as gifted, were left to use their highest, best talents, but the usual plan was a changing round of duties, and I took the circuit year by year."

Hard or monotonous work was broken up with short periods of recreation. In 1855, the typesetters regularly paused to play games, talk, or take a run over to the Community shoe shop and back. "And again," the *Circular* reported, "a dance in the unoccupied garret is tripped off—all with their inky, sooty hands—then all return immediately to their different employments, and again the music of labor is heard throughout the building." Oneidans were encouraged to combine, or alternate between, physical and mental work. "I have been here a few days at work in the machine shop," one of the *Circular*'s regular contributors wrote. "I find when I get nervous or worn out by literary confinement, that to come over here and go to chiseling and filing black and dirty iron, in the midst of the rattle of machinery, is better than going to the Springs [a nearby spa]. I have more good and refreshing thoughts while working at the vise in one day, than I should have in a week if I had nothing else to do but think."

Not only were jobs changed frequently, but work was arranged so that few had to labor all day long at a single task. In an account of how she had spent her day, one woman reported that she rose at quarter to six, ate breakfast, helped serve breakfast to the children, milked three cows, sang for half an hour with two other women, and then went to the trap shop to spend the rest of the morning there working at the forge. "At noon waited on the first table," her log continued; "sewed from one till two. At two joined [in] braiding palm-leaf hats. I usually spend from three to four o'clock in a kind of school with the girls; but today, as they had a lesson to study, I braided till half past three. At half past four went to milking again. After milking sewed till supper time, then helped serve the supper in the parlor. . . . After supper helped J. study his Greek."

Some jobs, such as kitchen work, were understandably less popular than others, and no one was required to do them for more than a few weeks at a stretch. But it was the style at Oneida, set by Noyes, to discover deep satisfaction in even routine tasks. At an evening meeting in the fall of 1857, at a time when volunteers were being sought for the job of milking the Community cows, a woman spoke at length about how bracing it was to milk in cold weather. "Instead of curling up over the register, she liked to straighten herself up in the frosty morning air—it put courage into her for all day," the official reporter noted. "If a woman wants to slip out of her effeminacy, one cannot take a more effectual way than to milk in the winter." Noyes himself liked physical labor, and encouraged his followers to view it in a romantic light, as a form of spiritual combat against an enemy—the devil—bent on proving that Bible Communism was incompatible with hard work. He elaborated this metaphor at length, and with characteristic literary bravura, in an 1856 article titled "Voice from the Trap-Shop." "I enjoyed in the midst of swinging hammers, flights of fire, and noisy confusion the excitement and sublimity of battle," he wrote. "We had the rattle of small hammers at the vises for pistol shots, the steady clank of anvils for the rolling fire of musketry, and now and then the thunder of the trip-hammer for a big battery of cannon. Thank God for a place in the front rank of this work-battle!"

✦　　✦　　✦

Whenever possible, Oneidans tackled work in the spirit of a husking bee. If there were apples to be picked or strawberries to be weeded, a storming company, as they called it, would be assembled. On a spring or summer evening as many as seventy-five or a hundred volunteers—men, women, and children might gather after supper under a big butternut tree outside the Mansion House and march out to the fields. Sometimes they marched to the music of a fife and drum, an idea that the Oneidans got, like many of their notions of how to make work pleasant, from Fourier. Bees were religious as well as social occasions, at which the Community joyfully affirmed its success, with God's help, in triumphing over selfish individualism. "We have never seen anything so brilliant," the *Circular* reported after a bee in which 171 persons had assembled to prepare a shipment of peaches for canning. "It was perfectly electric. The condensation of magnetic life produced a general sparkle and flash of mirth and humor." When peas were to be shelled, or other sit-down work was to be done, a member of the work party might read aloud, often from a novel by Scott or Dickens or the then-popular Edward Bulwer Lytton. Sometimes the workers sang, or were entertained by songs and comic recitations. Outdoor bees were often held just after sunrise when the workers could breathe "the purest and sweetest of morning air." A call for volunteers having been issued the evening before, the organizer of the bee would rap on everybody's door at dawn and then ring a big bell. Like many other Community rites, the early-morning bee was commemorated in verse, in a parody of Longfellow's "Excelsior" titled "String Beans":

> The streaks of light were coming fast
> As through the [building] slowly passed
> A youth who bawled at every door,
> These words not often heard before,
>   String Beans!

> "O stop that noise" the maiden said,
> "A half hour more I'll lie in bed."
> The youth passed on; his head was bent,
> But still he shouted as he went,
>   String Beans!

There were regular as well as ad hoc bees. There were periods when people gathered daily to sew traveling bags, braid hats, or make trap chains.* Before help was hired to do the washing, there was also a laundry bee each Sunday morning, when a crew of twelve men and twelve women, whose names had been drawn from a hat the evening before, would be wakened at four-thirty to labor in the laundry until breakfast, after which another crew would take over. In its later years the *Circular* was filled with nostalgic recollections of Oneida's early days, and among these was an account of how the Community washed its clothes that evokes in Breughel-like detail the atmosphere of an Oneida bee:

Ah! our old washing days—the whole scene comes up before me as I write. . . . An odor of soap suds, emanating from two large caldrons of boiling clothes, fills the atmosphere. One by one the washers come in, some looking rather sleepy. . . . Finally, the wash-boxes are surrounded, the partners standing vis-à-vis. In a few minutes all are busily washing—a pleasant hum of voices can be heard, despite the thumping of the one

---

* The discontinuation of bag making, in 1868, was marked by funeral rites that included the singing of an elegy, "The Bag-man's Lament," said to have been "written in a deserted bag-shop." The concluding stanzas went:

Gone, gone those bags, so wide and deep,
Those satchels great and small;
Friend, drop a tear, help me to weep,
Gone, gone are one and all.

Ye Gods! What mem'ries I recall,
Of love, of love tales read,
Of bright-eyed maidens short and tall,
Who lined, and stitched, and bled!

But words are weak, they cannot tell
One half my heartfelt grief.
My speaking tears in torrents fall,
Where *is* my handkerchief?

washing-machine in the corner. . . . Anon, the whole group are formed into a grand musical chorus; now singing snatches of an old anthem, and now divided into sections, the air is soon resonant with such rounds as "Scotland's Burning," "Merrily, Merrily Greet the Morn," "Glide Along my Bobby Boat," etc. Tired of this, all is quiet until Mr. T____ is prevailed upon to sing "Dearest Mae," which he alone can render to suit this audience. He is loudly applauded, and before another song can be produced the breakfast bell sounds, announcing to the astonished company that they have washed an hour and a half.

All work at Oneida was equally rewarded; that is, it was not re-warded at all. All Oneidans, no matter what jobs they did or how well they did them, had an equal claim on the Community for food, cloth-ing, and shelter. For most of the Community's life, members simply applied to a clothing committee when they needed new clothes, or checked off on a printed form the items they would require during the coming year. "If you need a new window curtain, stand-spread, an easy chair, a footstool, a different bedstead, a looking glass, or a larger bureau," the *Circular* explained, "just apply to Mrs. S., who has charge of the furniture, and she will be sure to do her best to accommodate you. When the carpet in your room grows threadbare and shabby, let Miss K. know of it and she will provide you with a better one." It was not until 1862, after a long period when many Oneidans had not handled money from one year to the next, that allowances were instituted: twenty-five cents every three months for each adult, twelve and a half cents for each child. In 1875 the system was changed, each adult being given an annual sum for clothing and incidentals. But everybody got the same amount: that is, the men got $75, while the women, who were expected to make most of their own clothes, got $40.

When visitors were informed of these facts they were often curious to know what was done with people who didn't want to work. The standard reply was a bland assertion that the problem really didn't exist at Oneida because such persons simply "cannot live under our system of religious influence, criticism, and education." Noyes and his followers were not above stretching things a bit when describing their system to outsiders—love and sex were never quite as free of conflict and frustration at Oneida as the world was asked to believe—and now and again someone had to be rebuked for trying to get out of menial jobs. William Inslee, the Community's chief machinist, was once publicly criticized for "daintiness about work," having given the impression that he was too proud to do unskilled work in the trap shop even though more hands were urgently needed there. But, in general, Oneidans willingly took their turns at washing dishes and mucking out the cow barns, and until the very last years, when Noyes and his chief lieutenants worried that the will to work had been sapped by too great a reliance on hired help, laziness was not really a problem. One powerful deterrent to shirking was fear of penalties that could include, besides public criticism, severe restrictions on the shirker's choice of sexual partners. "There is a strong current here which favors activity; and it is easier, I find, to go with the current than against it," an Oneidan observed mildly. "So if I wanted to be lazy I should choose some other place."

Actually, Noyes worried less about shirkers than about people who worked too hard or in the wrong spirit. In his view, work should develop the worker's understanding and love of God and of his fellows, and he insisted that this was more important than mere efficiency. Work was to be seen as a school in which the young and the spiritually laggard would learn from their elders and betters. Noyes and his lieutenants repeatedly reminded the Oneidans that work was a form of service to God, and that it must not be tainted by the selfishness in which work and business in the world outside were so firmly rooted. In 1856, the foremen of the trap shop were sharply criticized for driving their workers too hard and paying too little attention to their spiritual formation. When the foremen failed to respond to this treatment, a different remedy was prescribed. It was decided to stop the machinery three times a week for shop meetings whose chief object would be "to promote spiritual improvement and the acknowledgement of the presence and spirit of Christ in the business."

✦   ✦   ✦

"We believe," the *Circular* proclaimed in 1853, "that the great secret of securing enthusiasm in labor and producing a free, healthy, social equilibrium, is contained in the proposition, 'loving companionship and labor, and especially the mingling of the sexes, makes labor attractive.' " The *Circular*'s message, freely translated, was that mixing up men and women at work not only made work pleasanter, but helped people to find new partners in the dance of complex marriage. Men and women at Oneida worked together not only in doing the laundry, but in getting out the *Circular*, sewing traveling bags, and hoeing corn. In the years when the Oneidans did their housework without hired help, two men were regularly assigned to the kitchen crew, together with five women. Men helped wash dishes, men and women both milked cows, and men and women worked together in the Children's House. On occasion men even took a hand in the delivery of babies.

For a long time, women worked alongside men in the trap shop. In a letter written in 1867, not long before she became editor-in-chief of the *Circular*, a young woman named Harriet Worden recalled her days as a trap-shop hand many years before. The letter was addressed to "Father Noyes," as he was often called, who was then living at Wallingford, and it is a declaration of love from a woman who, three years later, was to have a child by Noyes. But it also suggests the loving companionship, to use the *Circular*'s phrase, that could develop when men and women worked together, and when there was a lowering of the barriers that conventionally separated the worlds of work, love, religion, and the nurturing of the young. She wrote:

> Last evening there was a call for volunteers to give a little extra help in the trap shop . . . and as I used to work at that, I thought I would volunteer. . . . My work, the noises and the

odors of the shop—everything around me—reminded me of old times; and when not looking up, I could almost imagine that you were standing at the bench with me.

And so my thoughts went gliding down the "gulf of time," and I saw myself at your side, heating springs for you to hammer out, a girl of fifteen just waking up to the idea that this world contained many things not dreamed of at the children's house. Then I found myself weighing steel for you, and could see your every attention to detail, and myself grown a little older . . . confiding in you for guidance, yet wayward and thoughtless. . . . With every improvement and incident in the trap shop, my own life seemed intertwined, for thinking of one brought up the other; and at this stage, I could see myself with youthful excitement—having seen the end of several youthful flirtations, but under new fascinations, and still clinging to you as my guide and refuge.

Chapter 11

*I*n Noyes's theology, the achievement of moral perfection was a beginning, not an end. An ex-sinner might never again do anything his conscience told him was wrong, but this did not mean that he would never again displease God. He must still emancipate himself from subservience to the devil and to his own "corrupted propensities." And while Noyes assured prospective converts that genuine acceptance of Christ as one's savior from sin was a guarantee of eternal salvation, there was a catch. Although Noyes never said so in so many words, it was clear that a person who proclaimed his or her freedom from sin but who then failed to lead a moral life—or, at least, to try his best to lead one—might not after all have freed himself from sin, and so might not after all be saved.

Thus perfection was likely to be a lifelong process of learning how better to understand, love, and please God. As Noyes put it, "Conversion is but an entrance into a school in which [the converts] will be required to advance steadily and patiently from truth to truth till they overcome ALL SIN." Self-improvement was the central purpose of life at Oneida, and powerful sanctions were invoked against anyone who did not struggle fiercely enough to escape the fell embraces of the devil and his loyal allies, selfishness and egotism. "Egotism is tormented here, and harassed like a toad under a harrow," an editorial in the *Spiritual Magazine* proclaimed near the end of the Community's second year; "it is stuck full of pine-knots, burned at the stake, and tortured to death." Some forty years later one of Noyes's disciples made the same point in less lurid and more elegiac terms. The Oneidans, he said, had "regarded themselves as a peculiar people, chosen by God to do a certain work. All selfishness must, therefore, be put away, and every heart made pure. [Oneida] was a school for the discipline and refinement of character."

To crush the toad of egotism, and to prune and shape the characters and spiritual lives of his followers, Noyes relied in part on familiar techniques of religious persuasion. He did so even though he had little use for the rituals and symbolism of the churches in which he and his followers had been raised. There were no crosses at Oneida, no communion, no formal prayers or invocations. While the Community did shut down its shops and mills on Sundays, it did so only out of regard for the feelings of its employees and neighbors. Oneidans were not expected to spend any more time thinking about God on Sunday than on any other day. Sunday, a writer observed in the *Circular*, was "a day of books and pens, of music and meetings, and sometimes of industrious committees."

But at Oneida, and at each of its branches, people gathered every evening for the purpose, among others, of reflecting on their duties to God and discussing the strategy and tactics of moral improvement. At Oneida these meetings were held in the family hall of the Mansion House. A designated leader, usually one of the Community's central members, sat at one side of a table placed just in front of the stage. Noyes, when he was living at Oneida, sat at the other side. Other tables were scattered about the room, some holding reading lamps for the convenience of women who wished to bring their sewing or knitting.

Noyes's dislike of fixed routines, which he saw as blocking the flow of divine inspiration in the Community, was reflected in frequent changes in the format of the meetings. One evening in 1864, for example, the leader failed to call for a song to open the meeting, as had been the custom for some time. Instead he remarked that doing things the same way day after day led to stagnation and spiritual death, and sat down. Thereupon, according to an item in the next week's *Circular*, "there entered upon the stage a trio with *fife and drums*, which filled the room with the rhythmical vibrations of martial music." The next evening, the report continued, "C. gave us on the tenor drum a representation of a battle, with its confused noises of musketry, roar of cannon, and battery broadsides. Friday evening Mr. A. opened with a declamation, and Saturday evening Mr. C. gave us an oratorical impromptu."

But the essential character of the evening meeting changed little over the years. It was an occasion for listening to newspaper articles, books, and letters from branch communities; for considering applications to join the Community; for discussing hygiene, finances, the rearing of children, and the design of a new building; for deciding whether to install a new floor in the kitchen, to auction off some heifers, or to close down the bag business. It was an occasion for listening to, and discussing, lectures on topics that included, in one four-week period, German philosophy, the theory of storms, "Poor Cheese and its Consequences," and "The Philosophy of Dominoes."

Ordinarily the latter part of the evening was given over to religion. If Noyes was present he might deliver a short, extemporaneous sermon, or home talk, to use the term he preferred. An Oneidan who began going to evening meetings when Noyes was in his sixties recalled her impressions of him. Often, she wrote, he sat through the earlier part of a meeting "with eyes closed, and rolled his thumbs and wrinkled his great forehead." Then "he would rise to speak . . . and again he appeared tall and large, well formed. I saw the brightness of his blue eyes, the sometimes firm mouth with its jutting jaw, and again the kindliness of his smile, and his pleasing gestures and rapid changes of expression." Noyes's talks were almost conversational in their informality, and varied enormously in content, touching on such matters as the devilishness of slander, the virtue of patience, the nature of false love ("no . . . links connecting it with God"), the importance of getting in touch with God by quiet meditation, the practical advantages of being humble ("I know if I am [proud]," he said. "God will not let me have anything to be proud of"), and the merits of praying while lying down, the position that Noyes himself preferred. When Noyes was at Brooklyn or Wallingford, or in New York City, where he once stayed for a year or so when the Community had a big sales office there, his talks were taken down stenographically to be read later at Oneida.

On evenings when there was no new home talk to be delivered or read, the leader might read an old talk, or an article Noyes had written for the *Circular*, or else bring up for discussion a remark Noyes had made in conversation. Or there might be a discussion of the moral deficiencies of a particular individual, or of some spiritual disorder—coldness toward God, vanity, carelessness in replacing borrowed tools—that the devil had loosed on the Community. Meetings often ended with professions (or confessions, as the Oneidans called them) of faith in Christ. "We expressed our desires and emotions in confessing Christ in us a guide and leader," a memoir writer noted in recalling the meetings she had attended as a girl. "It meant a tremendous screwing up of courage for me to speak aloud in meeting. But occasionally when I heard my dearest [friend] say quite loudly, 'I confess Christ in me a soft heart,' then I would follow with the same prayer, or 'I confess Christ in me a *good spirit*,' or 'I confess Christ my *helper* neither to give or take offense.' A warm glow would follow this effort and a sense of being able to be a better girl."

There were other occasions as well when Oneidans were supposed to think about their relation to God. They were expected to spend some time each day in meditation and, in addition, to seek out their spiritual betters for the purpose of getting private lessons, as it were, in religion and the principles of Christian conduct. Sometimes, too, small groups would get together to help one another along with the endless work of self-improvement. One such group, made up of young women, met regularly at Wallingford in the late 1860s, and a letter from a member to a friend at Oneida suggests the often excruciating intensity of religious life under Bible Communism. The writer was Noyes's niece, Tirzah Miller, who was later, like Harriet Worden, to serve a term as editor of the *Circular.* "We made another vigorous thrust at the spirit of unbelief which oppresses us so much here," she wrote, "& at least got our tongues free on the subject, & testified strongly in favor of faith, inspiration and the power of God in us. . . . I found my heart a good deal lightened afterward, for which I felt thankful, because all the week I had felt almost overwhelmed by the dark, unbelieving suggestions which the devil raises every opportunity to tempt us with."

✦   ✦   ✦

Sermons and confessions of faith and earnest discussion were not the only tools on which Noyes depended, as he once put it, to make crooked sticks straight and smooth. There was also the ordeal of mutual criticism, to which every Oneidan was expected to submit from time to time, and which converted the struggle for self-improvement at Oneida into a species of theater. Mutual criticism may have had its roots in the Chapter of Faults, a Benedictine ordinance inspired by St. Paul's injunction that Christians should "admonish," "rebuke," and "reprove" one another. Noyes had become acquainted with this technique for the force-feeding of spiritual growth at Andover Theological Seminary, when he joined a secret society of seminarians who intended, like himself, to become foreign missionaries. It was a rule of the society that each member, in turn, must sit quietly while "the other members, one by one, told him his faults in the plainest way possible." Years later, Noyes introduced this absorbing and harrowing game at Putney and Oneida.

At Putney the entire community had sat in judgment on each of its members. At Oneida, too, members were sometimes criticized, at their own request, by the whole family. But in general, criticism was meted out by a small standing committee, or by an ad hoc committee most or all of whose members had been designated by the person to be criticized. At one time there were also clubs whose members, like the Andover seminarians, took turns criticizing one another. However the critics might be chosen, they were required to file detailed reports on each person they criticized, and these were open to inspection by other members of the Community.

In theory it was up to Oneidans to decide for themselves when they needed criticism. But Noyes or one of the central members might point out to someone that he was overdue for a treatment, and anyone who ignored the hint—or who, after being criticized, customarily rejected the critics' advice—could be punished by a drastic restriction on his or her choice of sexual partners. From time to time an evening meeting would be largely given over to criticism of a member who hadn't asked for it, but whose behavior struck the central members as so disruptive that he or she should be called to account before the whole family.

Criticism, the *Circular* once noted, could be "as soothing as a mother's touch," and critics took pains to praise as well as blame. One committee, after accusing a young woman of vanity and disrespect for her elders, added that "her wonderful exuberance of life, gayety, and impetuosity of temper [are] her gift . . . and no one would have it changed." An older woman, criticized for being "incautious in her dealings with young men," was commended for "large-heartedness, loyalty, and general kindness of disposition." James Herrick, the former Episcopal minister, got a light tap on the wrist from Noyes for occasionally talking too much and for telling irrelevant anecdotes— "not an artistic method of conversation"—but otherwise drew extravagant praise from his leader. Noyes said he had never met a man "who seemed to have a more rapid and adroit mind in the reception of ideas from me." Perhaps aware that this might sound condescending, Noyes improved matters—somewhat—by adding generously, "He is also full of ideas of his own and manifests an originality of inspiration that surprises me from time to time."

But critics were unsparing in their delineation of faults. Oneidans were criticized for insincerity, egotism, obstinacy, self-righteousness, frivolity, pride, excessive concern with bodily health—the Oneidans called this "body tending"—and failing to open their hearts up to

God. (Sitting in judgment on the Community's dentist, Frederick Norton, a critic observed that "what Frederick needs, in order to do justice to God, is to have his heart all broken to pieces under the sense of God's goodness.") Critics also paid close attention to defects in manners and social bearing. A man identified as "A" was urged to improve his conversational style. "He takes a position that you are not prepared for," his critics reported, "and announces it with such flat assurance that it gives you a *jolt*." His critics added that even when "A" seemed to be in the right, his manner was so abrupt and positive that his hearers "naturally resist being *jerked* into the admission of it." A young woman was said to be "gross in her alimentiveness," and to spend too much time reading novels. A young man was reproved for affectation: "He talks for effect and walks for effect, he flourishes his handkerchief for effect; takes out his letters and watch for effect." A young woman at Wallingford was said to have "a way of showing her foot as though it was very pretty and she wanted others to notice it." She was also faulted for talking too much about former lovers, a habit her committee described—somewhat surprisingly, given the rules of complex marriage—as "not virgin-like." A man named Henry Clarke, who had taken advantage of a trip to New York "to post himself up in comic performances," was advised "to leave off his attentions to the comic as an actor, & give himself to serious reflection & religious culture." An elderly man, a native of Vermont, was told that his chief faults included "stiffness of character, too much gravity and not enough vivacity; an over-estimation of New England men and too frequent mention of Vermont." Oneidans were criticized for being slovenly, foppish, tactless, argumentative, and sexually awkward.

Noyes insisted that having one's faults pointed out need not be painful. Criticism, he said, "takes effect on only the external character, and that we can bear to have washed, as we do our clothes, without feeling ashamed." But this blandly offered advice, given more than forty years after its author had last experienced in person the rigors of criticism, was not easy to follow. While Community publications were filled with testimonials to the immediate spiritual lift that criticism provided, there were people who hated it so much that they quit the

Community. Even those who believed that criticism did them a world of good could be painfully shaken up. One woman recalled "the mental chaos in which I, after a criticism, would leave the friendly group of critics . . . and go away by myself to take thought and cry a little. . . . 'Oh! how glad I am George M. said that there was no lack of *desire in me to do right*. Yet how *can* I be as good as I want to be!' "

✦   ✦   ✦

The Oneidans prided themselves on their emancipation from what they called legality. By this they meant subservience to the laws and regulations necessary to curb the evil impulses of people who, unlike themselves, were mired in sin. Thus, at an evening meeting in 1867, Noyes proposed that Graham bread be banished from the Community table because it stood for slavery to the laws laid down by the dietary reformer Sylvester Graham. Graham bread was tainted by "a poisonous spirit—a principality of dyspepsia and legality," Noyes explained, adding dramatically, "I feel that I eat damnation in meddling with it." Although Oneidans had been meddling with Graham bread for some time without noticeable impairment of their physical or spiritual health, they were quick to agree with their leader. "There is a terrible bondage of the flesh in these hygienic and dietetic systems," one man observed sententiously, and after a brief discussion Graham bread was voted out by acclamation.

But release from the shackles of legality did not mean that the Oneidans were free to act and think and feel in ways that Noyes would not approve. Although Christians should ideally be guided only by the voice of God, they were likely at times not to hear, or to misunderstand, what God was telling them—or to mistake the voice of the devil for the voice of God. The only way to be sure of doing what God wanted was to do what Noyes wanted, and affirmations of belief in his God-given authority to mold the character and conduct of his followers were a frequent feature of the evening meetings. An 1867 report noted, for example, that "Mr. Hamilton was conscious that his unity with Mr. Noyes had made him what he is. . . . Mr. Hamilton said the world cried despot to Mr. Noyes, but those of us who are honest and true call him father and liberator." A declaration of faith in Noyes's divine mission, and a pledge of obedience to him, were the minimum price of readmission for an Oneidan who had left the Community and later wished to return. "I confess, at times I was tempted to doubt Mr. Noyes's inspiration," one man wrote. "I now see that it was the temptation of the devil. . . . I believe Noyes to be a man chosen by God to lead his people, and teach them the way of life and salvation." And so while the Oneidans might profess their scorn for legality, in fact their lives were closely circumscribed by unwritten rules—rules laid down by Noyes, applied to individual cases by criticism committees, and enforced, when Noyes and the central members deemed it necessary, by the withholding of sexual privileges. This sanction was invoked against, among others, William Hinds, who was soon afterward to become a leading figure in the Community. "Wm. has been gradually coming under restrictions in his social experience because the leaders here found his fellowship turned the girls away from God and to himself," Noyes's son, Theodore, wrote to Tirzah Miller at Wallingford. "Mr. Hamilton says he must be converted from a hard heart."

The unwritten rules laid down by Noyes differed in some important ways from those by which ordinary—that is, sinful—Christians were called upon to live. To begin with, Noyes insisted that a true Christian was obligated to please not only God but his fellow Christians—a duty made easier, he liked to say, by the fact that pleasing others was the best way of pleasing oneself. "We miss happiness when we pursue it too directly," he warned. "When we would pour it into another's cup it overflows into our own." Thus the Oneidans were constantly instructed by Noyes and by their criticism committees in techniques of giving pleasure. In a home talk on "Provoking to Love," for example, Noyes advised his followers to be cheerful, to praise others freely, to cultivate a pleasing "suppleness of manners," and to acquire the art "of entering into another's plans with all our heart—of showing zeal and becoming enthusiastic in carrying out his schemes." On another occasion Oneidans were urged to be flexible in small matters. "Pliancy of will seems to be specially pleasing to Christ," the *Circular* reported; "it gives the social atmosphere a more than downy softness." One man was censured because "his utterance is labored, tedious, and awkward," another because he bored people, lecturing them on religion "with little reference to the proprieties of time and place." (His critics quickly added that "we would not have him less earnest or wise, but more winning.") A woman was praised for her industry, but cautioned that the power "of making society lively, or of refreshing others by a sweet gentle spirit, is often worth more than a great deal of industry with the hands." Stiffness and reserve were frowned on as barriers to friendship and love. Noyes said the people he (and presumably God) liked best were "quick to take fire . . . to manifest emotions, quick to laugh when there is occasion for it, and quick to weep."

Another important rule at Oneida was that egotism in any form must be ruthlessly suppressed. A young man named John Sears was so concerned about not seeming egotistical that he stopped using the pronoun *I* in his letters. "John *does* get a little homesick once in a while," he wrote from Wallingford to his current sweetheart at Oneida. "But John *is* thankful for his circumstances & for all of God's goodness to him." One manifestation of egotism that Noyes was particularly at pains to stamp out was the spiritual disease he called diotrephiasis—the unhealthy preoccupation with doing things better than other people. The diary of an Oneidan named Frank Wayland-Smith reveals how powerfully Noyes disapproved of the private—and therefore, in his view, selfish—cultivation of artistic talent. Wayland-Smith was an accomplished violinist, but in the fall of 1878 he yielded to Noyes's insistence that his passion for the violin was interfering with his obligations to the Community. He handed over his violin, his music books, and his sheet music—they were, of course, Community property—and Noyes put them away in his closet. In his diary, Wayland-Smith recorded Noyes's assertion that in a community like Oneida "there is no use in any performer trying to attain anything like a professional degree of excellence." In Noyes's view, Wayland-Smith continued, "we must all be satisfied to be only mediocre. Music, he says, must always be subordinate to spirituality on the one hand, and to industry on the other." Wayland-Smith, who by this time had begun to feel faint stirrings of doubt about Noyes's infallibility, went on to speculate that the real reason Noyes didn't want accomplished musicians at Oneida was that his writ of authority was without force in the realm of art—"He is evidently quite jealous of the influence of music."*

The putting away of Frank Wayland-Smith's violin illustrates a third fundamental (though unwritten) rule at Oneida. When the wishes of an individual conflicted with the good of the Community, as interpreted by its leader, it was the individual who had to give way. Young people might prefer to dance and have sex exclusively with other young people, but if the harmony of the Community demanded it, they must dance and go to bed, at least some of the time, with their elders and spiritual betters. An independent mind was acceptable only when "combined with a true taste for social harmony, and a reverence of the superior judgment of others." As this formula suggests, while every Oneidan might have an equal vote in settling certain practical matters, Oneida was far from being a democratic society. Each person was assigned to a place in the spiritual hierarchy of the Community, and it was mainly by willing deference to one's superiors that Oneidans gained promotion to a higher spiritual station. At Oneida, Noyes wrote, there was no place for "independence, reckless spirits. Every member shall stand below a wiser in his or her place, and love to submit to those who are above." Most Oneidans found

---

* Actually, striving for distinction in any field was regarded by Noyes as a diotrephian aberration requiring heavy applications of mutual criticism. This view was emphasized in his response to the observations of a prominent Canadian educator who complained, after a visit to the Community, that it offered no opportunity "for genius or special talent to develop itself or to outshine its fellows." Noyes took the position that this was, in fact, a compliment. "We never expected or desired to produce a Byron, a Napoleon or a Michelangelo," he said complacently. "A system that would foster [such] abnormal or excessive development in the individual," he added, would inevitably "do so at the expense of the mass," whose interests must be paramount.

over the years that submission to the will of God and his viceroy, Noyes, was a reasonable price to pay for the advantages of life in the Community, including the heady excitement of taking part in a great spiritual adventure. But there were some who were galled by the lack of freedom and left Oneida. They included Noyes's own nephew, Joseph Skinner, who complained that "he and every other person were boys to [Noyes], whose judgments they must accept." He quit the Community, he told his uncle, "with the purpose of the Pilgrim Fathers, to find 'liberty of conscience.' " Others who did not leave shared some of Joseph Skinner's feelings. A woman named Helen Barron told a friend after the Community broke up that she would not like to go to heaven and find it was like Oneida: "She said the tyranny was so great, it was such a relief to be free." The friend agreed, saying that "in the end you would not choose it because you were never free." Another woman, who had been one of Noyes's most devoted followers, discovered in herself, years after the breakup of the Community, a smoldering resentment of his despotic rule. Noyes, she wrote to a close friend from Community days, "said . . . once in one of my criticisms, because my hair was quite long, that it was really a question of salvation, whether I did as he wished in regard to my hair, or did as I wished. . . . *Now* it seems like man-worship to me, to do things and think a certain way because Mr. N thinks it the only way to do and think. . . . In the Community I never felt that I could have an opinion about anything and have it respected."

The Oneidans often assured themselves, and the readers of their publications, that the discipline of Community life, and specifically the discipline of mutual criticism, could cure all spiritual ills. The Community's first annual report, in 1849, included more than two dozen testimonials to its remarkable potency. One member said he had become "mild and gentle" and had "learned to respect the judgment of others, and to cultivate love and a community spirit." Many said they had overcome what one man described as "a rigid, overbearing will." Harriet Noyes said she had been cured of the hypo, the Onei-dans' name for depression. For years, she wrote, she had had "an evil eye, that looked down on the dark side of everything, and transformed good into evil." Now, she said, "my spirit has grown strong and courageous." A young man said he had become more active and practical after he had learned to curb "a dreamy imagination, which made me prone to build air castles." A young woman named Tryphena Seymour wrote, "The spirit of Christ which reigns in this association . . . has been like a refining fire to my whole character. Hidden selfishness has been brought to light and destroyed." Jonathan Burt, on whose land the Community had been established, said criticism had made him meek and humble.

There were similar testimonials in later years. In 1874 the *Circular* noted that criticism was working "to thoroughly purify persons of long-standing faults, and bring about almost instantaneous changes of character." Some of these changes were said to be nothing short of miraculous. "Criticism and suffering have made [S.] an earnest, God-fearing woman," a criticism committee reported. "She has found Christ in her heart. . . . She is very receptive to good influences, and she delights in the society of her superiors."

But there is ample evidence that Noyes was not as successful in making crooked sticks straight—or, rather, in bending them into the shape that he desired—as he and his followers wished to believe. A woman named Keziah Worden, who was among those testifying in 1849 to the beneficial effects of Community life, was not long afterward described as "an active unbeliever, a hiding-place and refuge for every disobedient spirit we have had to deal with." Tryphena Seymour, whose hidden selfishness had supposedly been consumed in the fire of Christ's spirit, was later said to be "laboring under the spirit of diseased egotism, pride, and love of attention." After criticism, people often wrote letters of thanks to their critics, in which they confessed to evil deeds and thoughts that should, in theory, long since have been washed away by the regular baths of criticisms they had been immersed in over the years. Joseph Skinner, who had spent all of his life at Putney and Oneida except for the three years when he had been a student at Yale, confessed that "throughout my life selfishness and egotism have been my chief motives." Chester Underwood, who had presumably been criticized time and again during the eight years he had belonged to the Community, was even harder on himself. "I hate and loathe my own life," he wrote. "There is nothing in it worth saving, and it is my prayer that it may *go to hell*, where it belongs."

Later, in Canada, Noyes made no bones about having failed in the enterprise of making over his followers' lives. Yet the astonishing fact about the Oneida experiment is not that it ultimately failed, but that it succeeded for a third of a century. And without some method, such as mutual criticism, for impelling members to subordinate their individual impulses and desires to the good of the Community, Oneida would likely have been split apart much sooner than it was by the explosive forces of envy, greed, and sexual rivalry. Moreover, while mutual criticism could not produce the miraculous improvements in character that the Oneidans claimed for it, it served another purpose. It forced each Oneidan to be an attentive spectator at the drama of his own existence, and to think long and hard about what he saw. At Oneida it was very hard to lead an unexamined life.

onfessing Christ as one's savior from sin, Noyes wrote not long after his conversion to Perfectionism, can dramatically improve the health of the confessor. In the Oneida Community's first annual report this assertion was supported by testimonials from members claiming that faith in Christ had cured them of asthma, sick headaches, weak lungs, kidney disease, and inflammation of the liver. Noyes wrote that he himself had been saved from consumption by the "enthusiasm and love" that coursed through the Community. He hoped, he added, that "these mighty influences will ere long bring forth the life-cholera"—that is, a transcendent cure-all—"before whose march disease shall vanish and death shall die." And while Noyes had to acknowledge as the years went by that disease was unlikely to vanish in his lifetime, or death to die, he insisted to the end on the primacy of faith and righteousness as remedies for bodily distress.

The Oneidans conceded that the low death rate of which they liked to boast, and the Community's relative freedom from disease, were due in part to the healthy lives they led. They ate lots of fruit and vegetables, got plenty of fresh air and exercise, drank little tea or coffee—they favored such substitutes as strawberry-leaf tea and a hot drink made from parched peas that they called "pea coffee"—and, after the first few years, got along without tobacco. The only alcohol they drank was the wine, made from cherries and gooseberries as well as from grapes, that was served on birthdays and other festive occasions.*

But while granting that there was some value to this regimen, Noyes argued that disease was essentially a spiritual phenomenon, and body-tenders who fussed about diet and exercise were missing the point. To be sick meant literally that one's body had been invaded by an evil spirit acting in concert with the devil, and Noyes reminded the Oneidans that they owed their good health not primarily to healthy living, but to their success in building a spiritual citadel into which the devil could not easily insinuate his agents. When disease did strike, the Oneidans were quick to look for a traitor inside the walls. During an epidemic of diphtheria in the 1860s, for example, suspicion fastened on a troublemaker named Mills, who had been ordered to leave Oneida after he had been found guilty of making unauthorized and unwholesome sexual advances to young girls in the Community. "Mills's case is one of the best proved cases of malignant sorcery we have ever seen," Noyes declared, adding that Mills "was guilty of active, conscious cooperation with those wicked spirits" responsible for the maiming and death of several Community members.

The best way to strengthen one's defenses against the devil and his servants, Noyes pointed out, was to lead a holy life and trust in Christ—a proposition whose obvious corollary was that anyone coming down with diphtheria or a sick headache must be spiritually deficient. If this were true, however, how was one to explain the illness and death, at the age of forty, of Noyes's brother-in-law, John Miller,

---

* Although the Oneidans had extensive vineyards, they did not market their wine, perhaps because they recognized their limitations as vintners. "I tasted three or four kinds of [their] homemade wine," an English journalist reported, "and agree with Brother Noyes that his people will be better without such drinks."

whose heroic work as the Community's financial manager, and whose hard-won faith in God and Noyes, should have armored him against the devil's keenest thrusts? And how explain why Noyes himself suffered periodically from headaches, backaches, and insomnia, not to mention the painful throat disorder that for years on end forced him, when he had something he wanted to say at an evening meeting, either to whisper it to an associate or write it on a slate? It is not clear how this latter question was answered by the Oneidans; most likely they assumed that Noyes, precisely because of the important task to which God had assigned him, would be attacked by the devil with greater persistence and ferocity than lesser mortals who did not pose so great a threat to the devil's designs on the world.

Evidence that righteousness and faith were no guarantee of freedom (or recovery) from disease did not at first soften Noyes's opposition to doctors and drugs—an opposition which, considering how little doctors of the time could do to cure the sick or even alleviate their distress, did no great harm to his followers. For many years the Oneidans called on physicians only for such offices as setting broken bones and sewing up cuts. The approved treatment for all illness was to concentrate on Christ's healing power. Explaining how he had rid himself of a chronic cough, one man said, "I was led to look to Christ for help, and confessed him in my throat and lungs, and said deep down in my heart that I was not going to cough, and by holding something tight over my mouth, and looking steadily to Christ for strength, I gained the victory over it."

But as time went on, more and more Oneidans questioned whether faith alone was the answer to disease. When diphtheria struck in 1863, taking the lives of five Community members, some of the first sufferers called in doctors and dosed themselves with borax, alum, and other supposed remedies. Noyes, who had been away when the epidemic began, soon put a stop to this. Speaking out loud in a meeting for the first time in years, and thereby demonstrating his own ability to exorcise by faith the evil spirit that had literally had him by the throat, he chided his followers for their faintheartedness. "He took a thorough stand against the employment of doctors, old women's nursing, and drugs," the official reporter noted. "He said he himself had been faithful to our original election of Christ in place of physicians, and should stick to him if half the Community died. He denounced these fiery washes for the sore throat, and recommended *ice* on the natural principle that we use water to put out fire."

But despite the uncompromising tenor of his remarks, Noyes had concluded, as his suggestion about ice indicated, that faith could use some allies in the war against disease. One thing sick people needed, Noyes said, was a generous application of criticism. This remedy had at one time been tried on children, with good results reported. In 1855 readers of the *Circular* were told of a girl with a bad earache who had submitted herself to criticism, whereupon a "good natured, loving spirit immediately took possession of her and she has been bright-eyed and happy ever since." Now, eight years later, Oneidans of all ages who came down with diphtheria were urged to call in a criticism committee, and many who did so reported remarkable cures. One woman said she had been thrown into "a profound sweat, till I felt as though I had been in a bath; and before the committee left the room, my headache, backache, and fever were all gone." She added that the criticism she received "had an edge to it, and literally separated me from the spirit of disease that was upon me." As proof of the efficacy of such criticism, the *Circular* noted that, of the fifty-nine diphtheria victims who had been worked on by criticism committees, every one had recovered.

Criticism was also recommended for other ailments and disorders. "We have seen it take effect at an advanced stage of chronic disease, and raise a person up apparently from death's door," the *Circular* reported. The paper added that while it might seem cruel to "apply a castigation to the character" of a sick person, this was "precisely the thing needed to cleanse and purify the system," and any pain or mortification was "only a sign that the remedy is applied at the right place and is taking effect." One of the chief benefits of forcing patients to focus on their spiritual failings, the Oneidans believed, was that this kept them from thinking about their aches and pains. As a Community handbook explained, criticism "stops the flow of thought toward the seat of the difficulty, and so tends directly to reduce inflammation."

During the diphtheria epidemic of 1863–1864 Noyes made another, and more significant, concession to the feeling at Oneida that there must be something beside trusting in Christ that a sick person could do to throw off his illness. For the first time Noyes allowed that what he called "natural means"—drugs, for example—could help cure the sick. In the same talk in which he insisted on the spiritual nature of disease, and ridiculed the idea of treating diphtheria with borax or alum, he urged on his followers a diphtheria remedy suggested by a newspaper report from France. Oneidans coming down with the disease were instructed to keep ice in their mouths, day and night, until the diphtheritic "canker," or membrane, disappeared. There could be no harm in this, Noyes said, as long as the sufferer realized that without faith in Christ no amount of ice would do any good. "Let this be our motto henceforth: *Inspired use of natural means*," he said. He went on to explain the relation between inspiration, or faith, and natural means. "Inspiration is the fire, and natural means are the fuel," he said. "We must not pile on so much wood as to choke the fire. Inspiration is growing to be a pretty fierce flame among us, and after a while, when the furnace is going with a roar, we can throw in bushels and cartloads of fuel, and it will take all without being smothered."

This formulation, stating that as long as one believed disease was not primarily a physical phenomenon it was all right to treat it with physical means, was in part a reflection of Noyes's growing interest in science. He had been greatly impressed by Darwin's *On the Origin of Species*, and the "inspired use of natural means" was Noyes's idea of how to bring science into a proper—that is, subordinate—relationship to religion, an enterprise to which he was now giving a lot of thought. He may also have concluded that, since God seemed in no hurry to complete the work of kingdom building that had been started at Putney, it would be cruel—and impolitic—for Noyes to deny his followers such means as medicine offered for easing pain, removing disabilities, and extending life. In any case, Noyes now proposed that Oneida should have a doctor "of our own folks": someone with unshakable faith in Christ plus a knowledge of "all that is good and valuable in the profession of medicine." He soon decided that two doctors would be better than one, and in the fall of 1864 Theodore Noyes and the Cragins' son, George, were named "conscripts to science" and sent off to Yale to study medicine.

But even with doctors of their own in residence, the Oneidans made sparing use of natural means—partly, it may be, because of a well-founded suspicion that most of the means known to physicians of the time had few, if any, curative or prophylactic powers. One exception that they recognized was the Turkish bath. At Theodore Noyes's suggestion, baths were installed at Oneida and Wallingford and were enthusiastically recommended, along with massage, not only for the prevention and cure of colds, headaches, fevers, nervousness, and fatigue, but for the pleasure, as a Community writer put it, of being "kneaded, rubbed, pressed, patted, spanked, squeezed, and tousled generally; after which you are sprinkled, rinsed, and deliciously soothed." Smallpox vaccine, too, was eventually put on the approved list, and so was quinine, for which members of the Wallingford Community were deeply grateful when, in 1871, more than half of them came down with malaria, or the ague, as it was known. But, as one of the victims, a young woman named Jessie Kinsley, recalled, the quinine was taken "with *criticism* as an *antidote to evil*," and no one was allowed to forget the true nature of the enemy. She could still hear, she wrote, the voice of her best friend "shouting with me at the ague devil as it gave me a final shake, to 'get out, get out, let Jessie get warm.'"

At Putney Noyes had encouraged his followers to hope that in a few years, or at most a few decades, they would be united with Christ and the members of the Primitive Church who had been raised into heaven some eighteen hundred years before. There was reason to suppose, Noyes's brother-in-law John Skinner wrote not long before the move from Putney to Oneida, that "there may be persons now living who will not taste of death." In the meantime there might be preliminary contacts with the Primitive Church; as Noyes hopefully predicted in 1846, "God may yet permit some traveler from our sphere to visit . . . and to study [it] from observation." In the early years the Oneidans felt so close to heaven that Mary Cragin issued a written invitation to the Primitive Church to send representatives "to call on us *in any way* or at *any time*," and promised "to do all that lies in our power to make such visit agreeable." Twenty years later, in 1871, when Noyes was nearing sixty, he wrote to one of his lieutenants, William Hinds, that "we are so near a second coming, or something like it, that I see no death before me."

It was, of course, politically expedient for Noyes to discourage talk about his death. And at times he saw fit to assure his followers that God would never deprive them of his leadership. Yet Noyes had long since conceded that he had been overoptimistic in thinking that the merging of heaven and earth was an imminent event; Oneidans, like other good Christians throughout the ages, would have to die before they could attain the immortality of heaven. He had been impelled to this conclusion, he said, by evidence, convincingly marshaled by the English geologist Charles Lyell, that the earth had not been created all at once a few thousand years ago, as the Bible had it, but had evolved slowly over millions of years. From this revelation, Noyes remarked at a Community banquet in 1860, "I took in an element of patience, and since then I have not been in so much of a *hurry* for the millennium, and for the manifestation of victory over death." He went on to elaborate this thought in one of the more felicitous of the sustained metaphors that were so distinctive a mark of his style as a speaker and writer. Geology, he said, had disclosed to him "the *time* in which the music of the universe is written. I hear in it the movement of the grand anthem of creation; and it enables me to correct my step so as to keep time with it. . . . I learned not to be desirous of dancing a jig, when everything around is moving to the time of a grand march."

If the Oneidans were, after all, destined to taste of death, Noyes was able to assure them that the taste would not be bitter. He conceded that Hades, which he distinguished from hell and where they would go when they died, was not so lively a place as the world they would be leaving. It was, in his words, rather "dark and sleepy," though lit by "a kind of moonlight, in which persons may go about and enjoy a partial degree of activity." But Noyes promised his followers that they would find their stay there agreeable, and that God, in his good time, would bring them back to earth, along with other Christians in Hades deemed worthy of immortality. On earth, clothed once again in their own bodies, they would be united with Christ and the members of the Primitive Church to enjoy forever the pleasures of a world over which God would now reign supreme.

To demonstrate their faith in the solidity of this arrangement, Oneidans were expected to show a casual and even cheerful attitude toward death. Funerals and gravestones were very simple, picnics and dances were never canceled because someone had died, and mourning was frowned on. Oneidans may have wept for their dead, but they were careful to do so in private, and funerals were customarily written up in Community publications as happy occasions. Thus, at the regular evening meeting after the death of a young woman named Florilla Nash, William Woolworth, the designated "father" of the Oneida family—Noyes at the time was living at Wallingford—praised the joyous spirit in which the Community had said its good-byes. "Mr. Woolworth remarked that they had a pleasant time burying Florilla this morning," the official reporter wrote. "Everyone appeared cheerful and light-hearted; and the whole thing seemed to him more like a picnic than a burial."

Chapter 13

*O*ne aim of Bible Communism was to emancipate women from the slavery to which, as Noyes saw it, they were customarily condemned in midnineteenth-century America. Looked at from the perspective of late-twentieth-century feminism, that emancipation was far from complete, and the record of how women fared at Oneida is filled with contradictions. But it is clear that they were granted rights, and offered a range of choices as to how they would dispose of their lives, that only the most radical feminists were beginning to claim—and then mainly in private—at the time Oneida was founded.

For one thing, women at Oneida were much freer than they would have been in the outside world to decide for themselves when, how often, and with whom they would have sex. That freedom was not unlimited. The rules of complex marriage did not permit monogamy. Nor did they sanction celibacy, sex being regarded by Noyes as a religious ordinance—an obligatory celebration of the goodness of God. (Christ, he once said, was determined that men and women should "love one another burningly . . . flow into each other's hearts.") Moreover, a woman who violated the rule of ascending fellowship—that is, who persisted in turning down proposals for sex from members of Noyes's inner circle of associates—was inviting public censure. Why, she would be asked, was she stubbornly passing up the opportunity to improve her character by intimate association with her spiritual superiors? But these restrictions were hardly as onerous as those imposed by conventional marriage, in which the wife had virtually no sexual rights at all, her husband being legally and even morally at liberty to use her body for his pleasure at will and on his own terms. At Oneida, by contrast, it was incumbent on men to make sex pleasurable for their partners—the Oneidans emphatically rejected the curious notion, advanced by most medical authorities, that normal women were incapable of enjoying sex—and a man who was sexually awkward or inconsiderate was not only plied with criticism and advice, but might have a hard time persuading anyone to go to bed with him until he had mended his ways.

Another and perhaps more important privilege that Bible Communism conferred on women was the freedom, thanks to male continence, to lead an active sex life without committing themselves to one pregnancy after another. This freedom was also enjoyed by women in the outside world whose husbands practiced coitus interruptus, which, at the time Oneida was founded, was the only reasonably reliable alternative to complete abstinence as a technique for limiting family size. But a husband might refuse to honor his wife's desire to avoid pregnancy. And when this happened she had no recourse other than to leave her husband (which was usually out of the question unless she had relatives willing to take her in) or to take the drastic step of forcing abstinence on him—and herself—by falling, consciously or unconsciously, into invalidism. At Oneida such measures were unnecessary. A man who was unable or unwilling to control his ejaculations could expect to be punished by sexual ostracism or, at least, to be limited in his choice of partners to women past menopause. Under the threat of such sanctions, Oneida men became reasonably skillful at avoiding what Noyes called the "propagative crisis"; in a community of well over two hundred adults, accidental pregnancies occurred at a rate of fewer than one a year.

Women at Oneida were free to have babies, as well as not to have them, provided the Community approved. For more than twenty years pregnancies were discouraged, on the ground that the Community was too poor to support a lot of children. But even then, a woman who had never had a baby, and who was getting up into her thirties, was usually given permission to become pregnant if she wished. And after the general ban on babies was lifted in 1869, when the Community began its ambitious attempt at scientific human breeding, a childless woman who was eager to have a baby was usually told to go ahead even if she did not strike the managers of the experiment as an ideal candidate for motherhood. The theory was that her spiritual or other deficiencies could be offset by choosing an especially well qualified man to be the father of her child.

When a woman at Oneida did have a child, she was relieved of many of the usual burdens of motherhood. For a year or so she was spared from most housekeeping chores so that she could concentrate on caring for her baby. At the end of this period she turned it over to the foster mothers in the Children's House. Mothers were not invariably happy about giving up their children to the care of the Community. But this was thought to be good not only for the children—there was much talk about the harmful effects of "sickly maternal tenderness"—but for the mothers as well. As a Community writer pointed out, "We do not believe that motherhood is the chief end of woman's life; that she was made for the children she can bear. She was made for God and herself." Women at Oneida were also spared much of the domestic drudgery that was the lot of most women in the outside world even when they had domestic help. In part this was because they were under no pressure, as most middle-class Victorian housewives felt they were, to justify their sheltered position in the home by fussing excessively over its furnishings and appointments. By Victorian standards the Mansion House was rather simply and barely furnished, and relatively easy to maintain. Moreover, cooking, housekeeping, and baby tending were far more efficient than in ordinary households. For these reasons—and because men helped out in the kitchen and with heavy cleaning—Community women, even before there were hired girls to do the laundry and certain other domestic chores, had much more time than the great majority of American women to read, study, and invite their souls.

They also had the opportunity, seldom found in the outside world, of living in close association with other women. Many found in long-lasting friendships with other women the emotional security and deep intimacy they were barred from seeking—except for brief periods—in relationships with men. Thus when two friends, Beulah Hendee and Annie Hatch, found themselves falling in love with the same man, Hatch, thanking Hendee for her assurance of "deep sincere love," wrote, "*That* certainly is more gratifying to me than to know that any man loves me, and be assured that Jacques or any other man *shall not* separate our hearts. I prize your friendship and love more than I do Jacques' and you shall have my confidence and the *first love* of my heart—next to God and my superiors."

◆   ◆   ◆

But while Oneidans agreed with such militant feminists as Victoria Woodhull and Tennessee Claflin that women in America were cruelly exploited by men, they differed with these and other leaders of the women's rights movement on a fundamental point. Again and again, in the *Circular* and other Community publications, they ridiculed the feminist claim that women were, or should be, the equals of men. "I am a woman, and am in favor of female suffrage, and more than that, of the abolition of marriage-slavery," a Community member observed; "and yet from my very soul I believe in the inherent superiority of man. His essential nature is the noblest. It is not only stronger than woman's, but finer-grained; not only more powerful intellectually, but richest in the affections." Like St. Paul—and like the orthodox Christian theologians of his own day—Noyes held that, in the spiritual hierarchy of the universe, God stood above Christ, Christ stood above man, and man stood above woman. It followed that a man who wholeheartedly accepted Christ as his master was entitled, in turn, "to command respect, subordination, and loving receptivity on the part of woman." Women would find happiness and the fulfillment of their destinies in serving such a man as his loving helpmeet. "The grand right I ask for women is to love the men and be loved by them," an Oneida woman asserted in the course of an attack on the doctrine of equality. "I want the right of the most intimate partnership with man. . . . I would rather be tyrannized over by him, than to be *independent* of him."

Noyes taught his followers that women owed their male masters more than just respect and loving receptivity. They had a further obligation to make men love them—if possible, to love them wildly. Thus, in summing up his criticism of Fanny Leonard, on the occasion when he compared her to a beautiful and fragrant plant, Noyes said enthusiastically, "If a woman has a pure heart, and it will do a man good to love her, I say to her, Come on, I don't care how bewitching you are—the more I am bewitched by real goodness the better." He went on to say that there was even "a sort of sly tact and art" that women could legitimately employ to make themselves bewitching. By contrast, women who were brisk and businesslike in their dealings with men, or who displayed the "self-asserting masculinity" that the Oneidans professed to see in the leaders of the women's rights movement, were likely to be treated harshly by their criticism committees. The ideal woman was, like Mary Cragin, one whose "only ambition was to be the servant of love."

In his insistence that women had a sacred duty to make men happy, Noyes was not far out of line with the views held by most contemporary editors of women's magazines and most authors of books on marriage and homemaking. But he differed radically from these authorities in his notions of what kind of helpmeet a woman should try to be. The same eulogist who praised Mary Cragin as a servant of love also praised her for her ability as an organizer and leader, and for her "active, powerful intellect." Noyes had no use for the widely held theory that women—middle-class women, that is, not those who worked as kitchen maids or in cotton mills—were by nature too fragile to think hard or work hard, and were therefore unqualified to meddle in the practical affairs of men, or to express strong opinions about anything other than matters of morality and household economy.* He assumed that God shared his own preference for women who were lively, frank, firm in their opinions, well informed and well organized, and physically as well as intellectually robust. "The standard of feminine character to which we aspire," Harriet Skinner wrote, "is the acquisition of healthy, vigorous bodies, active, fruitful minds, large hearts, and perfect sincerity of manners." In an age when it was fashionable for women to emphasize how different they were from men by proclaiming their helplessness and dependency, women at Oneida, though they were praised for being bewitching and lovable, were exhorted to "get rid of effeminacy," to cultivate "manliness and robustness of character," and not to shrink from "outdoor manly industry." In the hay fields and the printing shop and the editorial offices of the Community's publications, as well as in the trap shop, Oneida women worked side by side, and on equal terms, with men— a relationship in which a stance of clinging femininity was clearly inappropriate. Women at Oneida were free, too, from the restrictions of Victorian prudery. Writing to Noyes not long after the breakup of the Community, a former member named Gaylord Reeve recalled nos-

---

* Such attitudes were not unknown at Oneida, which is not surprising given Noyes's unyielding stand on the Pauline doctrine of male superiority. Suspecting —correctly—that she was to be replaced by a man as editor of the Community's weekly newspaper, which was about to come out in a new and enlarged format, Harriet Worden, a leading figure among the women at Oneida, protested bitterly to Noyes about the prejudice against her sex. "If it were right to envy, I should envy the men," she wrote sarcastically. "They are so wise and strong; and so confident, withal, in their wisdom & strength. They form such great plans, and are able to talk about them in such a large, disinterested way . . . that their opinions *pass for what they are worth*, every time. But woman, *per contra*, is such a creature of feeling she can scarcely give her views entirely free from personalities, and hence her judgment is received doubtfully. . . . She may feel as deeply, know as intelligently, & understand as thoroughly the premises in a certain case as her 'lord & master' man! But being a woman is evidence against her—she meekly bows to fate, and retires from the field of argument to attend babies and make pancakes."

talgically that women who had "not been my especial friends in a sexual sense" at Oneida had nevertheless spoken with him about sexual matters "in a simple manner as they might have done upon any other subject." This struck him, he said, as "something sweeter and purer than I've found in the world in general."

Noyes's belief that God intended woman to be man's comrade and fellow worker, rather than his ornamental pet, was reflected in the way that women dressed at Oneida. The style was set in the very early days when Harriet Noyes, Harriet Skinner, and Mary Cragin got together, in the loft of the Indian log house where the Noyeses and Cragins were temporarily quartered, to devise for themselves a more practical—and more "honest"—costume than the voluminous, ground-dragging dresses, worn over layers of petticoats, that were then in fashion. Acting on a suggestion of Noyes, they cut two long dresses off at the knees and used the discarded material to fashion ankle-length trousers, or pantalets, that would preserve the wearer's modesty without restricting her freedom of movement. This costume, antedating by a year or so the similar outfit later popularized by Amelia Bloomer, was quickly copied by other women at Oneida. A few long dresses were kept on hand for the use of women who were going to travel from Oneida to, say, Wallingford, and who were anxious to avoid being jeered at while changing trains in New York. Long dresses were also regularly worn by a few women who had joined the Community when they were well on in years, and who were further distinguished from younger women by the title "Lady." (Noyes's mother, Polly, was "Lady Noyes.") But the standard wear for women at Oneida was a dress with a fitted waist, high neck, leg-of-mutton sleeves, and a full skirt that fell about two inches below the knee. It was worn without a corset, and over trousers of the same pattern and material: calico in summer, flannel or linsey-woolsey in winter.

Community women further defied convention by cutting their hair off to less than shoulder length. Their purpose was to save, for more worthwhile pursuits, the time needed to comb, brush, and put up long hair. For the sake of comfort and practicality they wore low shoes with low heels instead of the high-heeled, high-laced boots then fashionable for street wear. "The Gaiter style, with rubber in the sides, is the favorite, on account of the facility with which it is put on," an Oneida woman reported. "It is a matter of strife here, by the way, who shall dress the quickest, one minute being all that the most expert demand." Plainness was prized along with practicality; a woman who wore too-elaborate dresses, or any but the simplest jewelry, was sure to be criticized for surrendering to the "dress spirit," Noyes's name for feminine vanity. "We have no 'heavers,' nor 'plumpers,' nor 'false calves,' nor 'rouge'; and perhaps we don't look as well as your city belle who is puffed and padded and painted," a female contributor wrote defiantly in the *Circular*, "but we are *genuine* from head to toe."

✦　　✦　　✦

Noyes saw women as having great intellectual capacities—nearly as great as those of men. Women at Oneida were praised like precocious children for reading Malthus and Plato "with great relish," and when the Community launched its own short-lived college, more than half of the sixty-five students were women. But although eleven men were sent away to Yale and other colleges over the years, and although more and more colleges were opening their doors to women in the 1860s and 1870s, Oneida women had to get what education they could at home. This may have reflected a feeling that if a student was going to be put through college at Community expense he should be trained in useful skills—the men who went to college studied medicine, law, engineering, and architecture—while women, however great their potential as thinkers, were deficient in the practical intelligence required for arguing a lawsuit, designing a dam, or running a big or complicated enterprise. "Let [women] have the Press," the *Circular* proclaimed in 1853, reassuring its male readers that there would still be plenty of work for men to do "in subduing the earth . . . and directing the great movements of civilization."

As this condescending assessment suggests, while Oneida men had no doubts about their superiority to women—Noyes once declared that "by nature woman in her understanding and spirit is a *smaller pattern* of man"—they were nevertheless more willing than the world at large to let some women try their hands at certain jobs traditionally reserved for men. For years the Community's bag factory was run by a woman, and at two different times a woman held the important job of editing the *Circular*. Women also worked as bookkeepers and office managers, and a few were even taught to do simple work with machine tools.

Still, while the conventional line of demarcation between men's and women's work was blurred at Oneida, most women spent most of their working hours tending babies, filling lamps, waiting on table, making beds, ironing clothes, and doing other domestic chores. Unless a woman was among the minority holding full-time jobs in, say, the printing office or the silk mill, she was assigned as a "mother" to one or more men; this meant that it was her job to pick up his clothes from the laundry each week and do any necessary mending before returning them to his room. Women also made their own clothes, and the clothes the children wore, while men ordered theirs—unlike the women, they dressed conventionally—from a Community tailor. With the exception of the *Circular* and the bag shop, women rarely had any part in the management of the Community's business enterprises. The business board, which met once a week, was made up entirely of men, and men ran the silk mill, the trap factory, the farm, and the canning business. A man was in charge of the Children's House, where he was assisted by women who bathed, dressed, fed, and otherwise attended to the needs of its residents.

Noyes's belief in the inferiority of women in general did not, however, prevent him from seeking the advice of particular women whose sagacity and judgment he had come to respect. They included his wife and, most notably, his sister, Harriet Skinner, who wielded considerable power by virtue of her authority as "mother" of the Community to head off or break up sexual liaisons that she deemed inappropriate. But when Noyes was away from Oneida it was always a man who was named to stand in for him, and to interpret Noyes's wishes and commands as Noyes interpreted God's. Women were entitled to vote at the evening meetings, and in 1875, when for six nights running the Community debated the merits of Noyes's plan to have his son Theodore succeed him as leader, several women spoke at length. But men ran the meetings, and men did most of the talking, while the women listened and caught up on their sewing. This was the case even when it was women who were being talked about. On an evening, for instance, when the discussion turned to the baffling question of why so many women had recently sprained their ankles, women either had nothing to say about the matter, or were too shy to say it. (Noyes closed the discussion by attributing the sprains to "faintness of heart," and vaguely prescribing "a bath of healing spirit" as the best preventive.)

Women at Oneida seem to have welcomed the chance to associate with men, both as lovers and as friends, on a more equal footing than the rest of the world usually permitted. But they were not all so happy about Noyes's determination to liberate them from the bonds of feminine vanity. Even after Mary Cragin, in the early days at Oneida, had set an example by throwing into the fire a too-beautiful dress that a lover had given her for Christmas, women in the Community continued to spend far too much time, as Noyes saw it, worrying about how they looked.

The difficulty Noyes encountered in subduing the dress spirit may have stemmed in part from a seeming contradiction in the instructions he gave his female followers. On the one hand, they were urged to make men happy: to cultivate a manner and spirit, as Noyes once said in speaking of Mary Cragin, "that will make a man crazy." On the other hand, they were told that they must not try to make men crazy by making themselves beautiful, because to do so would be to encourage idolatry. In any case, it was not until 1865, after the Community had been in existence for seventeen years, that Noyes felt justified in announcing that, at long last, Oneida women had freed themselves "from bondage to the spirit of dress and ornament."

This proclamation of victory was premature, however. Three years later women began dyeing their hair, a practice that Noyes deplored, and that was halted—or so the *Circular* reported—after "the men protested with righteous indignation and the women became convicted [sic] that . . . by doing one such untruthful thing they made themselves guilty of all the vanities and hypocrisies of the world." Even women who stood high in Noyes's estimation were not proof against the seductions of the dress spirit. They included Noyes's favorite niece and confidante, Tirzah Miller, who, as editor of the *Circular* in 1868, probably wrote the words just quoted about the folly of dyeing one's hair, but who, a few years later, was scolded for having too many dresses. "I used to think last summer that you put on a different dress every day," her aunt, Harriet Skinner, wrote her disapprovingly. "I think your dresses now would last you five years according to my standards."

Some women were never reconciled to the way they looked in their short dresses and pantalets, which struck most visitors as—to quote the writer Charles Nordhoff—"fatally lacking in beauty and charm." Corinna Ackley Noyes, a granddaughter of Noyes who spent her early childhood in the Community, recalled in her charming memoir, *The Days of My Youth*, how much she detested "those awful, shapeless pantalettes. I can remember to this day how they always hurt me. I hated to look at our women below the knee and how lovely, how graceful were the long dresses and the long hair of the women 'outside.' " Elsewhere in her memoir she noted that often when she happened to pass Noyes's room in the Mansion House she would see him sitting in his armchair, thinking with his eyes closed. One day "he saw me and asked if I wouldn't like to come in, that he had something pretty to show me. Then he took me on his knee, opened up a desk drawer, and there, on a bed of cotton wool, were all the women's bracelets. I had never seen so much jewelry before. They were dazzling, beautiful, but I didn't dare ask why they were there. Later I learned they had been temporarily banned to crucify the women's vanity and were later returned when their owners had conquered the 'Dress Spirit.' " But vanity refused to stay crucified, and one of the harbingers of the Community's approaching end was the reappearance at Oneida, soon after Noyes's flight to Canada in the summer of 1879, of long hair and long dresses.

Chapter 14

*O*ne of the most troublesome questions designers of utopias have had to wrestle with is what to do about children. To Noyes, and to some other nineteenth-century planners and builders of communities, it seemed clear that the European monastic orders, and America's own Shaker communities, had endured partly because the fabric of their communal life was not strained by the fierce possessiveness of parental love. Emerson, a close though skeptical observer of American experiments in communal living, argued that for the most part they had been doomed because mothers would not allow the community to take over the raising of their children. Rudely comparing such mothers to barnyard hens, he wrote, "Eggs might be hatched in ovens, but the hen on her own account preferred the old way. A hen without her chickens was but half a hen." Robert Owen and Charles Fourier would have agreed with Emerson that close ties between parents and children were incompatible with true communal life. But unlike Emerson, who ranged himself on the side of maternal possessiveness, they argued that these ties must be broken or greatly attenuated in the interest of human happiness. This was not, of course, a new idea. Two thousand years before, Plato had proposed in *The Republic* that children be reared by the state and never told who their parents were.

The Oneidans did not go quite so far. Children knew who their mothers were, and their fathers, too—unless, as occasionally happened, a mother had become pregnant by accident and could not be sure whose child she had borne. Babies were ordinarily cared for by their mothers until they were weaned and had learned to walk, and thereafter they regularly visited, or were visited by, their mothers and sometimes their fathers as well. But as Noyes repeatedly emphasized, children at Oneida belonged to God and the Community, not to their parents. From the time they were fifteen months old they all lived together and were bathed, fed, dressed, comforted, entertained, punished, and instructed in the principles of Christian conduct and Bible Communism by the foster fathers and mothers assigned to duty at the Children's House.

In the Community's first annual report Noyes noted with satisfaction that objections to this arrangement had been easily overcome. While there had been "some melodramatic scenes" when the children had first been moved into quarters of their own, the "wounds of philoprogenitiveness" had soon been healed as mothers came to value "their own freedom and opportunity of education, and the improved condition of their children, more than the luxury of a sickly maternal tenderness."

But women proved not to be so eager to free themselves from the restraints of motherhood as Noyes had optimistically claimed. Repeatedly he and other Community leaders found it necessary to admonish mothers of small children not to interfere with the children's appointed guardians and preceptors. "We have proved it over and over again," an editorialist asserted testily in the *Circular* in 1871, "that the mother's care is like hot-bed warmth, while the Children's House care is like the open air and sunshine." Even women who had grown up in the Community and who ranked high in its spiritual hierarchy were at times unable to control their philoprogenitiveness. They included Alice Ackley, a beautiful young woman and one of the Community's most talented musicians, whose daughter, Corinna Ackley Noyes, recalled in *The Days of My Youth* how hard it had been for both mother and daughter to accept their separation. Shortly after being parted from Corinna, Alice Ackley, on request, had dutifully composed, for the encouragement of other young mothers, a testimonial to the virtues of communal child care. "I now realize, as I had not before," she had written, "that the old way of each mother caring exclusively for her own child begets selfishness and idolatry." Yet in the months that followed she gave in again and again to the "mother spirit," in punishment for which she was forbidden to speak to Corinna for days or weeks at a time. "What she felt during these periods I can only guess," her daughter wrote, "but I can remember my own feelings well when, during one two-week period of separation, I caught a glimpse of her passing through a hallway near the Children's House and rushed after her, screaming. She knew—what I was too young to know—that if she stopped to talk with me another week might be added to our sentence. There was no time to explain. Hoping, I suppose, to escape, she stepped quickly into a nearby room. But I was as quick as she. I rushed after her, flung myself upon her, clutching her around the knees, crying and begging her not to leave me, until some Children's House mother, hearing the commotion, came and carried me away."

Behavior like Corinna's was not uncommon. Like philoprogenitiveness, it was seen as a sign of a bad spirit and was subject to punishment. Victims of this bad spirit included Pierrepont Noyes, a cousin of Corinna, whom he was later to marry. In his own memoir, *My Father's House*—he was a son of John Humphrey Noyes—he recalled an occasion when he had been disciplined by "Papa" Kelly, who ran the Children's House. He had had a tantrum because his weekly visit to his mother had been canceled, and Kelly "seized me and shook me and commanded me in a voice charged with indignation and authority—just such a voice as I imagined Jesus Christ used when casting out devils—'Be still, Pip, be still!' Then, firmly, 'You have evidently got sticky to your mother. You may stay away from her another week.' " A contemporary of Corinna and Pierrepont Noyes later remembered a little girl—almost surely it was Corinna—who would stand outside her mother's window "and call to her, even though the mother wasn't supposed to answer."

But with that one exception, this former resident of the Children's House recalled, "all the children seemed happy enough." They included Pierrepont Noyes, who persuasively suggests that it was the mothers, not the children, who had the harder time adapting to the Community system. His own mother was Harriet Worden, and though she was a protégé and confidante of John Humphrey Noyes, she had to struggle not to give way to idolatrous love for her children. Concluding his account of how he was punished for stickiness, Pierrepont Noyes writes, "The turbulence was mine, but the greater tragedy was my mother's." He goes on to relate how, when he was allowed to visit his mother's room, he would be playing on the floor and she would bend over him and ask, "Darling, do you love me?" In response, "I always melted. My marbles and blocks were forgotten. I would reach up and put my arms about her neck. I remember how tightly she held me and how long, as though she would never let me go."

In John Humphrey Noyes's view, clinging to one's children was a lesser fault than other forms of selfish love. "I feel a certain respect for this tenacious philoprogenitiveness," he said. "It is mighty, and I respect anything that is mighty." But like many another reformer before and after him, Noyes could see no virtue in leaving the moral and spiritual formation of a child to adults whose only qualification for the task was that they happened to be its parents. Also, and perhaps more important, letting parents raise their own children would divide the Community into little clusters of adults and children whose loyalty to one another must inevitably conflict with the greater loyalty they owed, if they wished to be true Christians, to God and to his appointed deputy at Oneida. There was room for only one family at Oneida, the one of which Noyes was the father and head.

✦   ✦   ✦

Although children spent little time with their parents at Oneida, they got lots of attention and affection from other adults, who were encouraged to play the part of aunts, uncles, and grandparents. Volunteers spelled the regular staff of the Children's House, helped with outings and picnics, and read to the children or told them stories at bedtime. Until 1869, when a big new children's wing was added to the Mansion House in anticipation of the Community's foray into scientific human breeding, many children slept on trundle beds in the rooms of adults who acted as nighttime foster parents. For a while every child spent an hour each evening visiting an adult who read to her, or helped her with a composition, or simply played with her. At the end of a week the assignments were shuffled, and each child got a new reader or entertainer.

In general the Community took enormous pride and delight in the children, and when, at Noyes's suggestion, a daily "children's hour" was inaugurated in 1868 it was a big attraction. At first it was held in the upper sitting room of the Mansion House, where, for half an hour before supper, children danced, sang, and stood on tables to recite poetry. One evening the entire group, twenty-three in all, climbed to the gallery that partly encircled the room and "leaned their bright faces over the balustrade and sang 'Beautiful River.'" On other occasions, the *Circular* noted with amusement, "a circle is formed and the little ones 'keel over,' all pitching in, till the carpet is covered with indistinguishable little heaps in every kind of shape and motion." Soon so many adults were crowding into the upper sitting room that the children's hour was moved to the big family hall, where the children sang, recited, and played games on the stage. The hall was also the scene of a regular Sunday evening ceremony, begun soon after the first of the stirpicults were born, at which babies were weighed and shown off to the Community. "Little Humphrey, just beginning to take steps," a reporter wrote after one weighing, "quits his mother's hand amidst the cheers of all beholding, and walks half the length of the stage."

Adults were encouraged to befriend and even make protégés of children—other people's children. It was thought that because such friendships would be untainted by parental possessiveness they would be healthy for both parties. Noting that crosses of the affections, as he called them, would "certainly add to the pleasure of our social music," Noyes said, "It is very pleasant for me to find that I can love another man's child as well as I can my own." Often a child would pick out a man to be his or her father—an affectionate and companionable father unlike the strict, disciplinarian "father" of the Children's House. Sometimes this happened because a child had been accidentally conceived and didn't know who his father was. More commonly a child would have discovered that his real father wasn't interested in him, or just didn't have time for a child. Pierrepont Noyes informally adopted, and was adopted by, a close friend of his mother's, Abram Burt, a gentle, simple man who "had me with him as much as the regulations permitted; mended my skates and sled; took me down in the mill where I played in the shavings and made little things with sticks while he worked." As for Pierrepont's real father, John Humphrey Noyes, "he seemed a great man, or better perhaps a great power. I was told that he was my father, but he seemed the father of all of us, just as God is the Father of all of us." Pierrepont goes on to speculate that his father could not afford to have favorites among the children of the Community, but had to cultivate "a feeling of general paternity." He adds, "I do remember that on one or two occasions when I was allowed to go to his room . . . he took me in his lap and caressed me affectionately; once he gave me a cookie." Noyes had a collection of tops of many colors and sizes. Once, when Pierrepont had gone to his room with two of his half-brothers, "he started [the tops] spinning all at once and let us throw handkerchiefs at them to see who could stop the most tops. . . . I think he was really fond of his children, but for everyday affection I turned to Uncle Abram."

✦   ✦   ✦

As soon as they could talk, children were taught to "confess Christ." At first, Corinna Ackley Noyes writes, "it was just 'fess Christ,' and to me remained so for some time before I knew the whole formula: 'I confess Christ a good spirit in me.' " Children were reminded of their duty to God, were criticized and punished when they failed to live up to his expectations, and were lectured on unselfishness, whose virtues the littlest children were taught to celebrate by reciting a poem that concluded:

> *I*-spirit
> With me never shall stay,
> *We*-spirit
> Makes us happy and gay.

The author of these lines was Mary Cragin, who was Oneida's first schoolmistress and who became the official "mother" of the children living at the Community's Brooklyn branch. In her zeal to make perfect Christians of her charges she even took steps to stop the girls from playing with dolls, a pastime that struck her as spiritually unsound. A committee was formed, consisting of Mary Cragin and two of the girls: Sarah Burt, age eleven, and Mary Prindle, ten. Offering striking proof of Mary Cragin's persuasive powers—in the words of one of her eulogists, "She could become a child to children, and not lose their respect; play with them, and lead them to God"—the committee's report quoted Sarah Burt:

> My doll seduces me into a heedless spirit. . . . I notice that as soon as I begin to play with my doll, I get frivolous and do not love to study. I have asked Christ to help me do the thing that will please him about it, and should rather put my doll in the fire and see her burn up than play with her any more; because I think that she gets my attention away from Christ.

Mary Prindle agreed. Playing with her doll, she said, made her "silly and frivolous, and then I have to be criticized." The committee concluded that treating dolls like living beings "is acting and speaking a lie"; that "we do not want our philoprogenitiveness to grow any faster than God sees is best for us"; and that the "doll-spirit" was the "same spirit that seduces women to . . . be so taken up with their children that they have no time to attend to Christ, and get an education for heaven."

Noyes agreed, observing solemnly that the doll-spirit "is a species of idolatry, and should be classed with the worship of graven images." With his approval the dolls at Brooklyn were stripped of their clothes and burned up in the fire while—so Mary Cragin reported—"all hands rejoiced in their condemnation." The same fate overtook the dolls at Oneida. At the appointed hour, Harriet Worden recalled, "we all formed a circle round the large stove, each girl carrying . . . her long-cherished favorite, and marching in time to a song; as we came opposite the stove-door, we threw our dolls into the angry-looking flames, and saw them perish before our eyes." The ban on dolls was never lifted.

Children were encouraged to testify how God had helped them in their daily lives. At one children's hour an eleven-year-old boy said "he was tempted to tell a wrong story, but God had made him feel so bad about it that he confessed his temptation and the lying spirit left him." Another boy said he had been stuck on his arithmetic lesson, but after asking God to help him, and confessing Christ, he had been able to work the problems. There were also daily meetings for religious instruction. In the 1870s these were held at five-thirty every afternoon in the big South Room of the Children's House. "The older children," Corinna Noyes writes, "sat in the front rows in the little oak armchairs designed and made in the Carpentry Shop. The larger children sat at the back of the room. Papa Kelly would then take over. First we were asked to sit very still for a few minutes to get a 'quiet spirit.' Then Mr. Kelly would read verses from the New Testament, after which we would say the Lord's Prayer or the 23rd Psalm and then we were told to confess Christ." Sometimes Corinna's mother led the children in singing hymns; sometimes, in Pierrepont Noyes's words, there were "serious talks about our souls and the way children might please God."

Long after the religious excitement of the 1830s had died down elsewhere in America, it flared up periodically at Oneida. At these times of religious revival children sometimes experienced conversions such as Noyes himself had described, when, after declaring his freedom from sin, he had lain on his bed in New Haven and felt streams of eternal love gushing through his heart. In *A Lasting Spring*, her fine and loving account of growing up at Oneida, Jessie Kinsley recalls her own conversion at the age of ten. At the time she had been getting religious instruction from her schoolteacher, a Mrs. Bushnell, "a natural Evangelist and filled with religious fervor." Listening to one of her teacher's talks, Kinsley became "convicted of unbelief and sin," and found to her dismay that simply saying "I confess Christ in me a good spirit" did not set things right. "I remember this great pain," her account continues, "and then one day suddenly saying aloud in school, 'I confess Christ in me my savior from sin,' and bursting into tears. . . . With those words had come the understanding of Faith. Christ *in me* seemed the surest thing in the world, there was no more doubt of keeping out the Devil. Christ would keep him out, all good was right at hand."

Even when it did not result in dramatic conversions, the religious and moral training that children got at Oneida powerfully reinforced their sense of being different from—and spiritually superior to—children in the world outside. Oneida children were not allowed to mix with outsiders, and Pierrepont Noyes recalls the shock of his first encounter, at the age of eight or nine, with ordinary children. He and one of his half-brothers were returning from a visit to the trap shop when they were chased by some boys from a nearby Irish settlement called Turkey Street. The pursuers jeered, called them bastards* and "Christ boys," and challenged them to fight. This was bad enough, since Oneida children were forbidden even to speak to outside children, let alone fight with them—or, for that matter, to fight with anyone at all. But Pierrepont was even more horrified by the challengers' language. " 'God damn' and 'Jesus Christ' hurled at us by

---

* Pierrepont's mother assured him that "we consider you children more legitimate than any children in the world," adding, "you need never feel badly about that."

boys of my own age froze my blood," he writes. "How dared they? Deliberately courting damnation! An older boy, called Tom, grabbed my arm and thrust his face in front of me. He sneered, 'God-damn goody Community boys.' . . . All other emotions I may have felt have faded from the picture save only surprise and horror at the unbeliev- able exhibition of human depravity we had encountered."

Besides learning to please God, children were also required, from the age of six or seven on, to work for an hour or two each day. They filled woodboxes, scoured knives in the kitchen, sewed, braided palm- leaf hats, made trap chains, and joined adults in hoeing weeds, husking corn, and gathering butternuts. School took up two or three hours more. Four- and five-year-olds attended a kindergarten, known as Aunt Susan's school, where they colored with crayons, played with blocks and an abacus, and learned how to mix watercolors. Older children went to school in a building known as the Seminary, where adult classes were also held, and where they studied reading, writing, arithmetic, geography, and drawing. They also learned to set type, since many compositors were needed in the printing office to get out the *Circular* and other publications. Some days, too, there were "walking schools." These were rambles in the course of which their schoolmaster, a keen naturalist who had been a college instructor be- fore joining the Community, taught his pupils about plants and insects and the habits of woodchucks. Children also attended a singing school and regularly performed, as a chorus, for the Community and outside visitors. Some children took piano lessons as well. On reaching the age of twelve or thirteen, when they graduated from the Children's House and became junior members of the adult Community, children no longer had to go to school. But many teenagers, like many of their elders, regularly took classes in mathematics, English, Latin, and the sciences, often gaining a sufficiently solid grounding in these subjects to qualify them for college.

By the middle of the nineteenth century more and more American fathers were spending long hours each day in offices and factories, seeing their families only at night and on Sundays, and raising children was coming to be seen as exclusively a woman's job. But in Noyes's view this was a poor arrangement. The proper molding of children's characters required "masculine power and execution" and the "exacting and truthful severity" that only men could provide. Accordingly, the staff of the Children's House was headed by a man, and discipline was strict. Looking back on his childhood in the Community's early years, an Oneidan wrote, "Sometimes the rod was applied in special cases, and I have known the entire room full of noisy children switched in turn on general principles to keep down the flesh and the devil."

✦   ✦   ✦

In his book *The Communistic Societies of the United States*, published in 1875, Charles Nordhoff reported that on a visit to Oneida he had found the children "a little subdued and desolate, as though they missed the exclusive love and care of a father and mother." But Nordhoff abhorred the notion of complex marriage and communal child-rearing, and he may simply have seen what he wanted to see. Certainly his impression does not square with the recollections of people who grew up in the Community. In 1961 a sociologist, William Kephart, interviewed several former Community children, by then in their eighties and nineties, who were still living in the Mansion House. Without exception, he reported, they "felt certain that childhood in the Old Community was a happy and exhilarating experience." Corinna Noyes, too, once she got over her longing to be with her mother, was a happy child. The childhood landscape she evokes in *The Days of My Youth* is flooded with sunlight and peopled by congenial cousins and siblings and by interesting and loving grown-ups.

Pierrepont Noyes had some mild reservations about life in the Children's House. He was bored by the daily children's meetings, and near the end of *My Father's House* he complains, half ironically, that as a young man forced to make his way in a strange and perilous world, into which he had been thrust by the breaking up of the Community, he had had to slough off "the reverences, the obediences, the timidities so carefully cultivated by Papa Kelly."

But his childhood, as he remembered it, was crowded with variety and excitement. With his playmates in the Children's House he fished, trapped, swam in Oneida Creek, walked in the woods, sledded, skated, visited the Community's workshops and factories, and marched out in the early morning to pick strawberries from plants still white with dew—this last an adventure so joyous as to make him think, "Outsiders never have such fun as our people." In summary, he writes, "We lived, in the south wing, like a great family of brothers and sisters. We felt surrounded by a larger family of grown folks who seemed also brothers and sisters. On them we relied as a bulwark for our protection." At times, he goes on to say, the grown folks seemed chiefly bent on "detecting our spiritual delinquencies and applying remedies." But, their purpose, he recognized, was "to insure our healthy development into men and women like themselves," and he could not fault them for that.

The only cloud that really darkened the bright skies of Pierrepont Noyes's childhood—at any rate, the only one he mentions—was the fear that something terrible might happen to the Community. He recalls a cold, overcast fall day when his mind was filled with foreboding because of a rumor he had heard. A group of clergymen had vowed to wipe out the Community, and the word had spread in the Children's House that a famous medium, or fortune-teller, had declared that the clergymen were destined to succeed. In a passage that movingly conveys his feeling as a child for Oneida and its creator, Pierrepont Noyes writes:

I remember crossing the South Terrace, walking slowly, listening to the wind in the trees, staring now at darker clouds coming over the west hill and again at the familiar outline of the Mansion House, the only home I had ever known, and wondering—wondering, with fear in my heart—whether such a thing were possible. I pictured our people, the men and women I knew so well, the only men and women I really did know, with their backs to the wall, fighting a losing fight against the ravening wolves of a wicked, anti-Christian Outside.

I asked myself why—why did they want to destroy us? . . . I answered the question in the only way my limited experience made possible: "They are envious."

So, the hosts of envy and wickedness were about to attack our Garden of Eden! I thought of my mother and Uncle Abram and the boys and myself. Self-pity seethed in my heart.

As I stood there, utterly forlorn, my father came out the south door and walked in an opposite direction. Instantly, the sight of his broad back and vigorous stride reassured me. It was impossible! Father Noyes had a firm hold on a stronger power than the hosts of wickedness. He would protect his people. My fear was gone.

oyes's arrest in 1847 on charges of fornication and adultery convinced him there was no longer any point in trying to maintain the secrecy in which the new sexual order at Putney had until then been shrouded. On the contrary, he concluded that the cause of Bible Communism might best be served by a frank and detailed exposition of his theories about love, sex, and marriage—theories whose application under proper supervision (meaning supervision by Noyes) he saw as indispensable to the establishment of God's kingdom on earth. So, soon after arriving at Oneida, at the beginning of 1848, he settled down to write. Working in the best room of the house where he was staying, in which a new parlor stove had been installed for his comfort, he composed a treatise to which he gave the title "Bible Argument; Defining the Relations of the Sexes in the Kingdom of Heaven."

Noyes could be wordy and tedious, but in writing the "Bible Argument" he was at the top of his literary form. Forceful, closely reasoned, and ornamented with a wealth of arresting metaphors, it is perhaps the best thing he ever wrote. One may doubt that there is sex in heaven, or that there is any heaven at all; and there is more to be said for monogamy than Noyes allows. But while much of what he has to say about sex and religion is likely to strike a modern reader as quirky and bizarre, the case that he makes against conventional marriage, and in favor of a system that might be described as principled free love, is nevertheless a powerful one.

Noyes admits at the outset of his "Bible Argument" that the Bible says nothing about sexual arrangements in heaven. The reason, he ingeniously explains, is that there was no point in God's revealing these arrangements prior to the time—the midnineteenth century—when he was ready to unite his true followers on earth with Christ and the members of the Primitive Church. But monogamy is clearly incompatible with the Bible's emphasis on universal love. It is absurd, Noyes writes, to suppose that men and women who have achieved the freedom of "grace without law" that Paul held out to all who truly believed in Christ "should be allowed and required to love in all directions, and yet be forbidden to express love in its most natural and beautiful form, except in one direction." As for the mistaken notion that there is no sex in heaven, Noyes notes that it was plainly God's design, in creating man and woman, "to give love more intense expression than is possible between persons of the same sex." How can one then imagine, he asks, that God would "abandon that design by unsexing his children, or impede it by legal restrictions on sexual intercourse in the heavenly state."

In building his case against monogamy, Noyes invokes nature and common sense as well as God and St. Paul. For most people, he argues, marriage is a prison that "gives to sexual appetite only a scanty and monotonous allowance." Even in a marriage based originally on love, he writes, the partners soon discover "that their susceptibility to love is not burnt out by one honeymoon, or satisfied by one lover. On the contrary, the secret history of the human heart [shows it] capable of loving any number of times and any number of persons." It is true that there may be "special pairings" in the kingdom of heaven; there, everyone will be at liberty to find "a mate whose nature best matches his own, and whom of course he will love most." But to love most does not mean to love exclusively. "The fact that a man loves peaches best," Noyes remarks, launching into a metaphor that critics pounced on with cries of prurient indignation, "is no reason why he should not, on suitable occasions, eat apples or cherries"—provided, of course, that the eater has earned the right to such a varied diet by freeing himself from sin.

Having disposed of monogamy, Noyes moves on to challenge the conventional Christian view that, when God endowed man with the capacity for sexual pleasure, he was simply acting to ensure the continuation of the human race. Noyes dismisses this as a total misreading of God's intention. Sex has two distinct functions, he writes—the amative and the propagative. And the amative function is by far the more important—a priority that God revealed, Noyes argues, when he made it possible (Noyes does not say how) for Adam and Eve, before the Fall, to enjoy sex without having to worry about unwanted pregnancies.

God, however, does not value sexual intercourse primarily because it gives his children pleasure, but because it is—or can be, for true Christians—a form of worship, bringing the worshipers face-to-face with the power and sweetness of divine love. Sexual shame is therefore a form of blasphemy. "To be ashamed of the sexual organs, is to be ashamed of the most perfect instruments of love and unity," he writes. "To be ashamed of sexual conjunction, is to be ashamed of the image of the glory of God—the physical symbol of life indwelling in life, which is the mystery of the gospel." Indeed, when a man and a woman unite their bodies in the right spirit, sexual intercourse becomes a sacrament, like the Lord's Supper, which should properly be surrounded by "all the hallowed associations which attach to the festivities and hospitalities of Christmas or Thanksgiving."

If sex is a celebration of God's goodness, Christians should not have to hold back from participating in its rites for fear of giving birth to unwanted children. The privileges enjoyed by Adam and Eve can readily be reclaimed, Noyes asserts, by eliminating ejaculation from the act of love. Anticipating objections that this is flying in the face of nature, Noyes argues that nothing could be further from the truth.

What is unnatural, as well as clearly contrary to God's intentions, is to expend semen for any purpose other than propagation—as in coitus interruptus, of which Noyes disapproved on both hygienic and esthetic grounds. "God," he writes, "cannot have designed that men should sow seed by the wayside, where they do not expect it to grow." Conceding that sex without ejaculation demands discipline, Noyes reassures his male readers that it is "natural and easy to spiritual men, however difficult it may be to the sensual." Always an able propagandist, he goes on to say that mastery of the technique of male continence is not only a mark of spiritual superiority, but permits lovers to "enjoy the highest bliss of sexual fellowship for any length of time, and from day to day, without satiety or exhaustion; and thus marriage [sic] life may become permanently sweeter than courtship, or even the honeymoon."

Nearing the end of his argument of the case for free love, Noyes asserts that monogamy and "exclusive" love are incompatible with the perfect communism, first experienced by the early Christians on the day of Pentecost, that will prevail in the kingdom of heaven. "Love, in the exclusive form, has jealousy for its complement," he writes; "and jealousy brings on strife and division." Denouncing ordinary conjugal life as "only a double kind of egotism [which] obstructs community life," he scoffs at the idea, advanced by some Perfectionists, that God has chosen one, and only one, proper mate for every man and woman on earth. "If the sexual organs were so constructed that they would match only in pairs," he writes, "we might believe that the affections which are connected with them attract only in pairs."

"Bible Argument" ends with some thoughts on the regulation of sex in God's kingdom. Noyes acknowledges that free love without proper supervision inevitably opens the way to the depredations of greedy and selfish sensualists. As a consequence, he and his disciples "neither license or encourage any one to attempt the practice of these incendiary theories, without clear directions from the government in the heavens." That government, Noyes warns, "will not employ self-seekers," and anyone who tries to do away with monogamy without God's express authorization "will plunge himself in consuming fire."

The task of guiding true Christians on the dangerous pathway to sexual freedom can be entrusted only to someone who, through spiritual self-crucifixion, has achieved true holiness—in other words, to someone very much like Noyes. At Oneida, the reassuring message ran, free love would be in safe hands.

✦   ✦   ✦

In setting forth at length the principles governing sex at Oneida, Noyes was aiming not so much at winning converts to Bible Communism as he was at disarming its enemies. His hope was to persuade the world that the Oneidans' sexual arrangements were commanded by God and the Bible and were therefore protected by the Constitution's guarantees of freedom of conscience and religion. Accordingly, as soon as "Bible Argument" was off the press, copies were sent to the governor of New York and other public officials. In a brief preface Noyes noted that the Community was publishing its sexual theories "only in self-defense" and not to proselytize. Application of those theories, he promised, would be confined to the Community's "own family circle, not invading society around it."

For a while Noyes's strategy seemed to be working. In 1851, however, the Community came under heavy attack from the Oneida County district attorney, Samuel Garvin. Garvin apparently had not been on the mailing list for "Bible Argument," and his attention was drawn to the sexual practices of the Oneidans by a quarrel between the Community and one of its neighbors—a quarrel that, at the outset, had nothing to do with sex. The neighbor was a man named Hubbard, whose daughter, Tryphena, had been converted to Perfectionism soon after Noyes's arrival at Oneida. In the summer of 1848 she joined the Community after marrying one of its members, Henry Seymour; the marriage had apparently been arranged by the Community's leaders to avoid raising questions about sexual practices at Oneida at a time when these were still a closely held secret. Three years later, while the couple were living at a Community outpost some miles removed from Oneida, she began acting strangely—"crying nights, wandering about, frightening the children, and talking incoherently," as one account had it. In the belief that physical punishment was the best way to quiet her down, her husband, to the later embarrassment and dismay of the Community's leaders, beat her with a rawhide whip until her back was black and blue.

When her father learned of this, he first threatened to horsewhip his son-in-law, and then complained to Garvin, on whose recommendation a grand jury indicted Henry Seymour for assault and battery. Before the case came to trial, however, Noyes's brother-in-law, John Miller, managed to patch things up. Tryphena had been taken to an insane asylum in the nearby city of Utica, and Miller and Seymour agreed that when she was released she would not return to the Community. Instead, she would be entrusted to the care of her father and brother, to whom the Community would pay an annual sum for her support: $125 if she came out a well woman, $200 if she was still "unsound in body or mind." Their indignation soothed by this generously applied financial balm, the Hubbards apparently asked Garvin to drop the charges against Seymour, and the case was thereupon dismissed.

But Garvin had made it clear that wife-beating was not the only offense he was determined to put a stop to at Oneida. In his presentation to the grand jury of the case against Seymour he had called as witnesses nine members of the Oneida Community, including several women, and had questioned them very closely about the Community's sexual practices. Hoping to forestall the indictments for adultery or fornication that Garvin obviously was aiming for, the Oneidans called on their neighbors for help. A petition was circulated praising members of the Community as "good neighbors, and quiet, peaceable citizens," "persons of good moral character," and "lovers of justice and good order." The petition concluded with the assertion that "we have no sympathy with the recent attempts"—that is, by Garvin—"to disturb their peace." Even though it was no longer a secret that the Oneidans went in for free love, the statement was signed by most of the local farmers, lawyers, and businessmen to whom it was presented, including a former Oneida County district attorney, Timothy Jenkins, a wealthy landowner who had recently served two terms as Oneida's representative in Congress.

This did not move Garvin, who obtained indictments against several Community members. (Noyes, having lived in Brooklyn for the past three years, was not among them.) While the Oneidans nervously waited to see if Garvin would actually bring them to trial, they were attacked from another quarter. A leading religious weekly, the New York *Observer*, ran a long editorial, which seemed certain to be widely quoted and reprinted, denouncing the Community as "this foul body," and asserting that its members lived "in a state of vile concubinage and even worse." Noyes's "Bible Argument," the editorialist indignantly protested, "sets forth a theory of promiscuous intercourse of the sexes as compatible with the highest state of holiness . . . [a theory] so loathsome in its details, so shocking to all the sensibilities even of the coarsest of decent people, that we cannot defile the columns of our paper with their recital."

Noyes's instinctive preference when confronted by powerful enemies was for appeasement or flight. In the face of this new attack, and of Garvin's stubborn hostility, he decided to order a retreat, which he announced to the public in the pages of the *Circular*. In reply to the *Observer*, he insisted that a "legal scrutiny of the household habits of the Oneida Community" would surely "disclose less careless familiarity of the sexes—less approach to anything like a 'bacchanalian' revelry . . . than is found in an equal circle of what is called good society." Nevertheless, because Oneida's sexual customs were "looked upon with jealousy and offense by surrounding society," the Community would resume "the marriage morality of the world" and henceforth abstain from all sexual behavior that might be held to be in violation of the law.

Noyes followed this statement of capitulation with an assertion that he could hardly, even for a moment, have believed to be true. The Community, he wrote, had taken up complex marriage only as an experiment, and was now content to bring it to a close. "We land from our long voyage of exploration improved and refreshed," he said blandly. "That voyage with its gales and icebergs and elemental perils is done—passed into history; and we emerge now under new circumstances, ready for new enterprises."

Soon after this announcement Garvin let it be known that he was not going to prosecute after all. The delighted Oneidans decided to celebrate, and at the same time show their gratitude for the support they had been given, by inviting their neighbors to a garden party. On the appointed day some three hundred guests showed up to inspect the Mansion House, to be entertained by the children's choir, and to eat strawberries and cream at rustic tables scattered about in shady spots, or in a sweet-smelling cedar bower erected for the occasion in the children's playground.

There was more trouble to come, however. John Miller, hoping to convert the Community's truce with Garvin into a permanent peace, went to Garvin's office in Utica, the county seat, and invited him to visit Oneida. Garvin, denouncing the Community as "worse than any whorehouse," refused. To Miller's consternation he went on to say, as Miller recalled their conversation, that he "was determined to break us up and if we were not off before the September court, he would give us 'such an overhauling as we never had yet.' "

When the news reached Noyes in Brooklyn, his first impulse once again was to surrender. Gloomily recording his impression that "the Lord wants to scatter us," he suggested that it might be best for most of the Community's members—presumably including those most likely to be prosecuted—to disperse to branch communities outside Garvin's jurisdiction. But Miller and the other leaders at Oneida were less inclined to run up the white flag. Garvin's decision to reopen hostilities, it appeared, had been prompted by a new complaint from the Hubbards. They were now insisting that every man in the Community who had had sexual intercourse with Tryphena, other than her legal husband, should be punished for the crime of seduction. As he had before, however, Miller bought the Hubbards off: for $350, they agreed to "ground arms" permanently in their fight against the Community. As evidence of their change of heart they joined other neighbors of the Community in signing a second petition urging Garvin to call off all proceedings against the Oneidans.

This Garvin agreed to do. The Community's leaders relaxed, and Noyes soon recovered his nerve. Only five months after he had solemnly proclaimed the end of complex marriage he authorized its reintroduction. In the late summer of 1852, in an article in the *Circular*, he even boldly included "Cultivation of Free Love" in a list of principles that the Community stood for. There was no reaction from Garvin, who was either unaware of this indiscretion or had concluded there was nothing to be gained by antagonizing the voters who had rallied in such numbers to the Community's defense. However that may be, he soon afterward formally vacated all pending indictments.

◆   ◆   ◆

Although nothing more was heard from Garvin, the Oneidans were threatened from time to time by other enemies. One was William Mills, a former member of the Community who was expelled in 1864 for introducing eleven- and twelve-year-old girls to "perverting and licentious excitements." (He was gently removed from the Mansion House and deposited in a snowdrift when he declined to leave under his own power.) In retaliation for his banishment, Mills declared his intention of exposing the shameful secrets of sex at Oneida. Among other things, he told people that the Oneidans drew lots for sexual partners. As it happened, this was an arrangement suggested by Mills himself at a time when he was having no luck in persuading Community women to sleep with him. But the plan had never been put into effect, Noyes having rejected it as totally at odds with the spirit of complex marriage. Luckily for the Oneidans, Mills was an inveterate and fairly transparent liar and was unlikely to impress many of his hearers as a reliable witness. But Noyes, whose customary mood of rosy optimism about God's plans for Oneida was easily disturbed, nervously raised the possibility that Mills would "bring upon us again the wrath of the magistrates and the mob, break us up and plunder the ruins." So the Community decided to buy Mills's silence by paying him $2,250.

Not long after this successful attempt at blackmail, the Community was denounced by another ex-member, Charles Guiteau, who was destined, fourteen years later, to assassinate President Garfield. Guiteau had been a misfit at Oneida—like Mills, he had a hard time finding sexual partners—and after leaving the Community in 1866 he printed up an "appeal" calling for its extirpation as a moral cancer. In this document, which he sent to the attorney general in Washington, as well as to a number of New York editors, ministers, and public officials, he asserted that the Community had been founded solely to satisfy Noyes's sexual appetites and that, night after night, innocent girls and young women were "sacrificed to an experience easier imagined than described." Girls who were born in the Community, he claimed, "were forced to cohabit at such an early period that it dwarfed them," and as a result most Oneida women were "small and thin and homely."

Nothing came of this effort to make trouble for the Community, and when a number of newspapers and magazines, three or four years later, ran articles praising the Oneidans as good businessmen but denouncing them as sexual monsters, the Community's leaders felt secure enough to react with amusement rather than alarm. "The word filth, with its derivatives filthy, filthiness, etc., occurs nine times," the *Circular* noted with good-natured resignation in a review of a series of articles on Oneida that had appeared in the popular *Frank Leslie's Illustrated Newspaper*: "abomination, abominable, etc. [occur] six times; depravity, depraved, etc., six times; lust, four times; blasphemy, three times; licentiousness, three times; bestial, foul, and terrible, each twice; with single specimens of such words as horrid, diabolical, scattered everywhere in wonderful profusion." The *Circular* went on to report that when the last article in the series had been read aloud at an evening meeting it "brought down the house again and again with the heartiest merriment." Three years later, when the Presbyterian Synod of Central New York tried to mount a crusade against the Community, its charges were the subject of articles and editorials in a number of newspapers. But the synod noted sadly that "with a single known exception [they] were more complimentary to the Community than to the Synod itself."

✦   ✦   ✦

Indeed, as the years went by, lurid reports like the series printed in *Frank Leslie's Illustrated Newspaper* were more than offset by accounts by visitors to Oneida who found much to praise in what they saw and heard. One of these was an English journalist, William Hepworth Dixon, who included a lengthy report on Oneida in a book called *New America*, published in 1867, that was widely read not only in England but in other European countries and in America as well. Dixon's account was marred by inaccuracies. As Noyes pointed out, this was not surprising, since he had spent only forty-three hours at Oneida and had used up a lot of this time sleeping, visiting a nearby Indian village, giving a lecture on the Holy Land to the assembled Oneidans, and recovering from a severe headache. In any case, Noyes wrote, trying hard to strike a note of good-natured tolerance, Dixon should not be judged as a historian, "but as an entertaining, off-hand book-wright, who tells the truth as near as he can remember it in the hurry and heat of artistic composition."

The truth as Dixon saw it was that Oneida was a significant and strikingly successful social experiment, and this perception was shared by a procession of writers, scholars, politicians, and editors who followed him to Oneida. Among them, to give just two examples, was the well-known Boston writer Thomas Wentworth Higginson and a Frenchman, Elie Reclus, who reported in a Brussels sociological journal that he had liked just about everything he had seen except the dreadful clothes—"*cet accoutrement hermaphrodite*"—the women wore. As Oneida's fame spread and word of its eminent respectability got around, its members were edified and entertained by lecturers, singers, and musicians—they included the great Norwegian violinist Ole Bull—who had been booked for appearances in the nearby cities of Syracuse or Utica and who made a point of visiting Oneida. And while some clergymen continued to denounce the depravity of Noyes and his followers, others came to Oneida, held serious theological discussions with their hosts, and, like Dixon, were invited to lecture in the family hall.

The Oneida Community was, in fact, one of the chief tourist attractions in its part of the world. Each Fourth of July, and on almost every pleasant summer Sunday, hundreds of visitors wandered about the grounds, consumed great quantities of strawberries and cream, lemonade, ice cream, and other refreshments, and were entertained by the Community's band and its children's choir. In the year 1866 alone, more than six thousand names were entered in the visitors' register. Three years later, service was begun on a new railroad line, the Midland, that bisected the Community's property. There was a station only a three-minute walk from the Mansion House and here, on summer weekends, trainloads of excursionists arrived to spend a day at the Community. (Visitors were understandably curious about the sexual customs of their hosts—they often asked to see the huge round bed in which they had heard that the entire Community slept —and for answers to their questions they were referred to a handbook they could buy for a few cents.) Some of the excursions were organized by churches. In August 1870, the *Circular* reported that the Universalist church of the nearby town of Fulton had held its yearly Sabbath-school picnic at Oneida, and that there had been so many picnickers, nearly a thousand in all, that the concert scheduled for their entertainment had to be given twice so that everyone who wanted could attend.

To the very end the Oneidans continued to get on well with their neighbors. The concerts they regularly gave for their workmen and for residents of nearby villages often included comic songs and skits, dramatic recitations, and tableaux that drew overflow audiences to the family hall. Occasionally the Community's hospitality was returned. "Just before the close of meeting this evening," a Community reporter noted in the summer of 1867, "someone announced that the fire company from [the village of] Oneida intended making us a call. Soon music was heard in the distance, and the dancing of torch lights seen approaching." The musicians belonged to the firemen's band, which marched around in front of the Mansion House for a while and was then invited inside for refreshments and "a pleasant interchange of music."

As the Community prospered, building mills and workshops and furnishing well-paid work for local residents, it commanded increasing respect. Outsiders might disapprove of free love, or "universal love," as the Oneidans preferred to call it. But it was hard to think badly of people who were so straitlaced, so generous, and so successful in business. (Most Americans, whatever their religious persuasion, inclined to the Calvinist belief that the ability to make money, except when there was clear evidence that it was made dishonestly, was a sign of God's grace.) "No finer example of quiet industry and inflexible honesty can be found," the Utica *Observer* asserted in an editorial defending the Community against its Presbyterian critics. "Its products are the best of their class, are just what they are represented to be, and command the best prices wherever they are offered. Its dealings are open, straightforward, and honorable. . . . Its cash business cannot fall far short of a million dollars yearly." Almost as an afterthought the *Observer* added, "Its members use neither tobacco nor strong drink, are models of good order, tenderly care for each other, and treat the world outside with uniform courtesy and respect."

hen Noyes asserted in 1852 that in their sexual adventuring the Oneidans had been beset by "gales and icebergs and elemental perils," he was making what was, for him, a highly unusual concession to the realities of complex marriage. His public comments on the course of universal love at Oneida were far more often along the lines of his boast, in the Community's second annual report, that "Amativeness, the lion of the tribe of human passions, is conquered and civilized among us." In fact, getting complex marriage established at Oneida was a long and turbulent process, requiring much tinkering with the machinery by its designer, and attended by much unhappiness.

One difficulty was that many Oneidans were distinctly uncomfortable with Noyes's notion of complex marriage as a dance in which there should be no wallflowers—or, more precisely, as a form of worship in which true Christians were not only privileged, but more or less obligated, to take part. At a time when the New York *Observer* was worrying about unbridled lust at Oneida, Noyes was worrying because there was too little sex. As he observed ruefully, "We have all been more Shakers than Bacchanalians" and in the early years he repeatedly called on his followers to shed their inhibitions and claim the freedom of sexual choice that complex marriage offered.

His exhortations could be playful and even roguish. On one occasion he had been given a cigar by four young men, all of whom had recently shared with him the privilege of sleeping with a young woman named Julia Dunn. Noyes was pleased with the gift, and in a letter addressed to "the South Garret Lodge of Free and Accepted Lovers" he promised to "smoke the segar in the society of . . . our common sweetheart." Thanking them for their diligence in the service of complex marriage—and for demonstrating that a group of men could make love to the same woman and still all love one another—he went on to suggest that they could do even more for the cause. "I propose," he wrote, "that we young men . . . study to be liberal and diffusive in our love and attention to the other sex" so as to hasten "the grand consummation" of the courtship going on at Oneida "between all the men as one man and all the women as one woman." Getting down to cases, he added, "To this end let us consider whether we may not do good, get good, and feel good by drawing nearer than we have to certain worthy young ladies whose charms have not yet been fully appreciated, such as L.B.H. and N." He concluded by urging the free and accepted lovers not to overlook the charms of older women.

In insisting that Oneidans should lead more active sex lives, and with a greater variety of partners, Noyes made it clear that he was expressing the will of God. The frontiers of the kingdom of heaven, he warned, were closed to monogamists. "You may say that you have no taste for anybody but your wife," he said. "But your taste may be diseased. God will not have in his kingdom those who cannot love all that he loves." On another occasion, addressing the spiritual leaders of the Community, he said that the most important thing they could do to speed the establishment of God's kingdom on earth was to pitch in and make complex marriage work. "I am bold to say in the name of Jesus Christ," he declared, "that . . . the use of amativeness is what is going to drive the Devil out of the world."

Nevertheless, for years the current of universal love flowed sluggishly. In 1852, John Skinner, Noyes's brother-in-law and one of the central members of the Community, made a survey of sexual activity at Oneida. The results, he noted, showed that the abandonment of complex marriage, which Noyes had just announced, was going to make a lot less difference than outsiders might suppose. "The actual amount of sexual intercourse . . ." he wrote, "has been scarcely one seventh (and many of the members judge it has been hardly one tenth) of the amount that occurs in ordinary married life."

One difficulty was the persistence of old habits and old loyalties. Many who joined the Community in its first year were not seekers after sexual freedom and had learned what would be expected of them sexually only after coming to Oneida. Married couples might agree in principle that monogamy had no place in the kingdom of heaven and yet find it impossible to avoid the feeling, when they came to the point of actually sleeping with new partners, that they were doing something terribly wrong. This may account in part for the impotence that many men complained of in the early days.

Another impediment to the free flow of sexual love was a fear of falling into, or being accused of, pleasure seeking. This was the offense of using sexual allure to humiliate or abase one's sexual partners, or of treating those partners purely as instruments for one's own physical gratification. To be acceptable to God, Noyes warned, sexual intercourse must be an expression of true love and respect for one's partner. It must also be elevating, and one of the worst varieties of pleasure seeking, or false love, as it was also called, was the kind of reckless infatuation that blinded lovers to one another's faults and excluded by its intensity all thoughts of God and spiritual improvement. Even someone as well schooled in holiness as Mary Cragin could not, at least on one occasion, resist pleasure seeking of this sort. Her downfall came when it was first decided, in 1849, that the best way to ease ardent young bachelors into the swing of complex marriage, and at the same time to teach them to regard sex as a spiritual exercise, might be to pair them up for a time with older and spiritually wiser women. When Mary Cragin was assigned to tutor a young man named George

Hamilton, she threw herself into her pedagogical task with such abandon that she apparently forgot all about her duty to lead him closer to God.

In this case it was clear that one of the lovers had, as Noyes gently put it, "lost her equilibrium." But the line between false love and the true Christian variety was a difficult one to draw, and many Oneidans in the early years were inhibited from making advances to new sexual partners for fear of being criticized for loving them in the wrong way. "Amativeness has been under so much judgment," Harriet Skinner wrote after living at Oneida for two years, "that the sexes are more divided, if anything, than in the world. As Charlotte [her sister, Charlotte Miller] says, all criticism and no love does not work well. . . . At present the men keep bachelors' hall, and the women are kind of forlorn."

◆   ◆   ◆

The most serious obstacle Noyes faced in trying to make complex marriage work was jealousy and its concomitants: the marriage spirit, the claiming spirit, exclusiveness, idolatry, and special love. As John Miller later recalled the first years at Oneida, "We had to have our watch constantly on duty to prevent our social building from being burned up in the fire of jealousy." Sewall Newhouse, the trap maker, became so angry when he found his wife strolling in the garden with another man that he jumped on his rival and had to be dragged away. When one man told his wife that he wanted to sleep with a certain young woman, she dutifully consented, even volunteering to serve as his ambassador in proposing the desired "interview." But as she later told John Miller, she had had no idea how much it would hurt. "She [had] thought it would be relief to her to have him free," Miller reported to Noyes, "but she found that she didn't know what it was *to die.* She didn't sleep any for nearly a week, and cried a good deal of the time." Young people often found the thought of sharing their sweethearts unbearable. A sixteen-year-old named John Norton threatened suicide when a beautiful young woman with whom he had been having an affair left Oneida for Brooklyn, where she would presumably soon have other lovers. "You say you cannot forget Helen," Noyes wrote the unhappy teenager. "I do not wish you to forget her, nor to love her less. But cannot you love her without *claiming* her, and quarreling with us and with God about her, and almost shooting yourself on her account?"

Often in the Community's early years Noyes even had to lecture his wife, Harriet, on the evils of jealousy and the claiming spirit. In 1849, before leaving with Mary Cragin for their week's visit to Niagara Falls, he suggested to Harriet that he had planned the trip partly for *her* benefit. It would help, he explained, to expand her heart "into the free love of the family of God," and thus "perfect the union" (he did not say exactly how) between Harriet and himself. But the claiming spirit had too strong a grip on Harriet to be exorcised even by such heroic measures, and nine months later she admitted at a meeting of the Brooklyn family that she still bitterly resented Noyes's partiality to Mary Cragin. Noyes, conceding that he loved Mary better, said that Harriet—with God's help—must reconcile herself to this, and to the fact that Mary was not only brighter than she was, but her superior in other ways as well. "It is essential," he said unctuously, "that someone should learn to rejoice in the superiority of another. We cannot all be first." Not surprisingly, Harriet seems to have derived little comfort from this self-serving pronouncement. She remained irritable and unhappy. Noyes, complaining that she was "a great burden" to him, continued his efforts to free her from bondage to the claiming spirit. "Friday evening . . ." the official reporter noted after a family meeting in Brooklyn, "Mr. Noyes talked about jealousy being proof of shallow love. If a woman loved a man enough to enter into the depths of his heart, she would sympathize in his love for other women, and would love those whom he loved." Noyes did not mention Harriet's name, but there was no question whom he was talking about.

As it turned out, neither Mary Cragin nor Noyes himself had completely mastered the lesson that Noyes was so bent on teaching Harriet. A year or so after moving to Brooklyn, Noyes revealed that he hoped to be reunited with his old sweetheart, Abigail Merwin. She was now a widow, living outside New Haven, and Noyes sent ambassadors to urge her to join the Community. He admitted that the prospect of Abigail's coming to Brooklyn had "stirred up the principality of the marriage spirit" in his breast—that is, he had had visions of having Abigail entirely to himself—and that he knew he would have to struggle hard with its temptations if she should come. But he promised Harriet and Mary that "Abigail Merwin cannot take your place" and assured them they could count on God to "make an end to the claiming spirit in the association." This did not suffice to quell the fierce pains of jealousy to which Mary Cragin now found, to her great embarrassment, she was not, after all, immune. She was "tormented," she wrote a friend, by the fear of having to yield to Abigail her place in Noyes's affections. "I do not know how much egotism remains," she added, "but I want to have all there is tempted out and destroyed."

Fortunately for Mary Cragin, she was not put to the test. A few months later, after Abigail had refused to see two emissaries from Brooklyn, Noyes announced that he was no longer in love with her. His only aim in trying to get her to join the Community, he asserted, was to save her from the devil—"I can now do without her, and have no hankerings for her." This seems to have been wishful thinking. Soon afterward, Abigail agreed to see Mary Cragin, who informed her—with what feelings we can only guess—that Noyes still loved her and was eager for her to visit him and the Brooklyn family. Abigail refused, saying she did not believe the kingdom of God had come and did not hold with the abolition of marriage. "She said Mr. Noyes was a married man," Mary reported to Harriet Noyes, "and that if he had any such love for her as was represented, it was a sin in his heart." Two months later Noyes was still talking, albeit somewhat vaguely, of a reunion with Abigail. "Mr. Noyes said he should pursue her forever," Mary Cragin told Harriet. "If she died, if she made up her bed in hell, it would make no difference to him."

✦ ✦ ✦

In July 1851 Mary Cragin was drowned when a sloop in which she was sailing on the Hudson River capsized and sank in a squall. She was lovingly eulogized, at evening meetings and in the columns of the *Circular*, as a saint, or something near it—a woman who, after terrible struggles with sin and the devil, had come to exemplify the beauty of sexual love and its astonishing power to link man and God. Years later, Noyes admitted that he had loved her more intensely, and more *particularly*, than the canons of universal love allowed. But her death, he said, had freed him once and for all from the toils of "sexual specialty." Nothing more was heard of his passion for Abigail, and his active sex life—Noyes felt it his duty, as the Community's spiritual director, to show by example how to love in the true Christian spirit —was apparently from then on untainted by favoritism or possessiveness.

After Mary Cragin's death, too, Noyes no longer found occasion to scold Harriet for jealousy. "I feel myself in better relations with Harriet than ever," he told the Brooklyn family. "She has gained a power over her feelings that makes her cheerful and happy." The change Noyes perceived seems to have been real and lasting. Four years later a Community reporter, summarizing what had been said of Harriet at a criticism session, wrote, "She was a real spiritual mother . . . a beautiful lover [who] combined love with simplicity and sincerity; did not trifle, but treated love with sacredness. She was free from the marriage spirit." Harriet Noyes, then forty, did not take Mary Cragin's place—Noyes never pretended to find her "intoxicating," as he had found Mary—but she was deeply devoted to Noyes and for the rest of his life she was his closest confidante and friend among the women of the Community. With the possible exception of Harriet Skinner, she was also the woman whose judgment he most respected. A much younger woman, who knew her well when she was in her sixties, recalled Harriet Noyes as quick-moving, with thick, close-cropped, curly gray hair, and eyes "deep-set in a somewhat rugged face, full of intellectual thought and spiritual beauty"—a woman who lived "in a world filled with faith and hope [in which she] saw a providence in everything that happened."

✦   ✦   ✦

Not everyone at Oneida was as successful as John and Harriet Noyes in triumphing over jealousy, the marriage spirit, and the devil's other allies in his campaign to destroy the kingdom of universal love over which Noyes ruled. But by the mid-1850s Noyes had devised a set of rules and conventions that transformed complex marriage from a theory about love and sex in heaven into a workable human institution. The machinery creaked, jammed, almost broke down at times, and had to be constantly modified and repaired by its inventor. But for twenty-five years it ran smoothly enough to demonstrate that men and women could love one another, respect one another, and get emotional and spiritual joy from sex, without conforming either to the laws of marriage or to the conventions of romantic love, which state that true love must be, or must be felt to be, exclusive and undying.

merican newspaper readers in the 1850s were offered a rich journalistic diet of free love, a term that Noyes had invented but that had been appropriated by other sexual reformers of whose doctrines and practices he sternly disapproved. Some of these reformers, like some of the early Perfectionists, wanted no restraints at all on sex. Prominent among these was the "Free Lovist" Stephen Pearl Andrews, who grandly proclaimed that "Man and Woman who do love can live together in Purity without any mummery"—that is, marriage vows—"at all." Together with Josiah Warren, author of the doctrine of individual sovereignty—everyone entitled to do exactly what he or she likes—Andrews founded, on Long Island, a short-lived anarchist community called Modern Times. At Modern Times, according to one account, "conjugality took on an air of spontaneity. Colonists tied a red thread on their finger to announce themselves wed and untied it when they regarded themselves unwed." Other advocates of perfect sexual freedom included Thomas and Mary Nichols, who were later converted to Catholicism but who, in the 1850s, circulated printed lists of people who had signified their eagerness to taste the delights of free love.

Although censorious clergymen and editorial writers often lumped Noyes with free lovers like Andrews and the Nicholses, the differences were great. Love and sex at Oneida were free only in a very qualified sense. Noyes's followers might be at liberty to have sexual relations with a variety of partners. But under the reign of universal love, a term that Noyes came to favor over free love as a description of Oneida's sexual regimen, men and women could love and sleep with one another only on terms laid down by Noyes and enforced by a range of stiff penalties.

✦   ✦   ✦

One major restriction on sexual freedom at Oneida was, of course, the rule that unless a couple wanted a baby and had been specifically authorized to have one, the man must refrain from ejaculating during intercourse. Mastery of the technique of sex without orgasm had to be demonstrated before a man was admitted to the full privileges of complex marriage. A boy reaching puberty, and considered to be ready for sex, was customarily paired with women who were past menopause until he had acquired the necessary self-control. A gynecologist who visited Oneida was told by women whom he questioned that most men had little difficulty in restraining themselves. Those whose control faltered were, like novices, restricted in their choice of sexual partners to women who were past child-bearing age until their performance was brought up to standard.

As a contraceptive technique, male continence was clearly a success. By the late 1850s some two hundred adults were living at Oneida and its branches, and many of them, having learned what was expected of them as lovers, had overcome their earlier inhibitions and were enjoying very active sex lives. (Noyes's niece, Tirzah Miller, estimated that a reasonably popular woman might have intercourse two or three times a week, and it was not unusual for a woman to sleep with several different men in the course of a month.) Until 1869, when the Oneidans began their experiment in scientific human breeding, pregnancies were seldom authorized. This meant that when men and women got together for sex they were, with rare exceptions, bound by the rule of male continence. Nevertheless, during the Community's first twenty-one years there was, as noted earlier, an average of only about one accidental pregnancy a year.

When stirpiculture got under way, accidents became a bit more frequent. One reason may have been that men got so used to having orgasms while sleeping with women whom they were authorized to impregnate that they could not easily go back, when having nonpropagative sex, to "making sexual intercourse a quiet affair, like conversation," as Noyes once recommended. In these years there may also have been pregnancies that were unauthorized but not accidental. Couples who had been denied permission to have a baby, on the ground that they were not good breeding stock, may in some instances have decided to go ahead and have one anyway. (The offspring of such unions were treated exactly the same as authorized stirpicults.) Some women may have become pregnant—or tried to—without their partners' willing collaboration. "She tried to make me lose control," one man complained in a postcoital diary entry.

While there was no question about the effectiveness of male continence in preventing unwanted pregnancies, in the opinion of many contemporary medical authorities it was bound to damage the health of its practitioners. Suppressing ejaculation, they believed, not only put an intolerable strain on a man's nerves, but would also in time make him sterile as well. Many physicians believed that male continence was bad for women, too. They pointed out that, like coitus interruptus or the use of a condom, it robbed a woman of the benefits of the "sedative and relaxing seminal fluid," an infusion of which was considered an indispensable aid to natural and healthy release from sexual tension. The Oneidans were understandably eager to scotch such theories. In 1870 Noyes's son Theodore, in an article in the New York *Medical Gazette*, argued that male continence, properly practiced, could not in any instance be linked to such nervous disorders as were to be found at Oneida. He also noted that microscopic examination revealed "abundant and active zoosperms" in the semen of Oneida men. As long as men were careful to keep well back from the brink of orgasm, the younger Noyes concluded, male continence was "not injurious to either male or female, while it gives rise to all those emotions which are refining and ennobling to both men and women."

Although Theodore Noyes had recently taken his medical degree at Yale, and although the editors of the *Medical Gazette* praised his report as "a model of careful observation and discriminative appreciation," doctors remained skeptical. Seeking independent confirmation of Theodore's findings, the Community invited a Syracuse, New York, physician named Ely Van de Warker to examine a group of Oneida women with a view to determining if their health had in any way been impaired by their peculiar sex lives. His findings were published in the *American Journal of Obstetrics* under the title "A Gynecological Study of the Oneida Community." Although Van de Warker made no effort to hide his distaste for what he described as "one of the most artificial sexual mal-relations known to history," he reported that he had found no evidence that male continence, or any other feature of Oneida's sexual customs, had damaged the health of the women he had seen. Taking particular note of Charles Guiteau's charge that Oneida women had been stunted by the early age—typically, thirteen or fourteen—at which they had been introduced to sex, Van de Warker wrote, "However repugnant it may be . . . we cannot resist the conclusion that sexual intercourse at this tender age does not arrest the steady tendency to a fine and robust womanhood."

Male continence was well liked by the women at Oneida. It not only freed them from the fear of undesired pregnancies, but pleasantly lengthened the act of coition. Coitus might continue for an hour or more, during which time it was customary for the man, who ordinarily entered his partner from the rear—she would be lying on her side, with one leg drawn up—to engage in prolonged manual play. According to Hilda Herrick Noyes, a grandniece of Noyes who became a physician, and who made it her business after the breakup of the Community to find out what she could about its sexual practices, "the men prided themselves on giving the women their orgasm."

PLATE I. *Community members pose on the South Lawn of their communal home, the Mansion House (c. 1870).*

PLATE II. *John Humphrey Noyes, founder and leader of the Oneida Community, was in his early sixties when he sat for this photograph.*

PLATE III. *Although one might not guess it from this portrait (above), Mary Cragin, with whom John Humphrey Noyes fell passionately in love, was a woman of enormous sexual drive and magnetism. "Her only ambition was to be the servant of love," a Community eulogist wrote after her death by drowning in 1851, "and she was beautifully and wonderfully made for this office."*

PLATE IV. *Group portrait, c. 1870. John Humphrey Noyes, hands clasped in front of him, stands directly behind the little boy in the checked shirt sitting on the grass.*

PLATE V. *John Humphrey Noyes publicly scolded his wife, Harriet (left), for her jealousy of Mary Cragin (Plate III). But she learned to suppress the "claiming spirit" and became—along with Noyes's sister Harriet Skinner—one of his two closest and most influential advisors.*

PLATE VI. *Noyes's sister Harriet Skinner (right) played a large role in the regulation of Community affairs—particularly in deciding the tricky question of who should sleep with whom.*

PLATE VII. *Harriet Worden, a fierce advocate for the rights of women within the Community, was for years editor of the* Circular, *the newspaper that went out each week to sympathizers around the country.*

PLATE VIII. *Croquet was so much the rage at Oneida that people even played it in winter, wearing overcoats and gloves.*

PLATE IX. *At this "bag bee" on the lawn of the Mansion House, Oneidans are stitching up the traveling bags that for a while they manufactured and sold.*

PLATE X. *The Oneidans at one time marketed this ingeniously fitted-out traveling lunch bag, invented by John Humphrey Noyes himself.*

PLATE XI. *Tirzah Miller, who, like Harriet Worden (Plate VII), put in a stretch as editor of the* Circular, *led—and recorded in her diary—a highly active and turbulent sex life. A niece of John Humphrey Noyes, she was his close confidante and for many years perhaps his favorite sexual partner.*

PLATE XII. *In this picture of the Oneida Community orchestra, John Humphrey Noyes is eighth from the right. Noyes considered music a form of worship second only to sexual love; he was, by all accounts, a terrible violinist.*

PLATE XIII. *This women's singing group (above) was one manifestation of the Oneidans' rich musical life. An 1864 census listed two orchestras, a brass band, a choir of twenty-five singers, two male quartets, and a "club of eight male voices."*

PLATE XIV. *Community children in front of a rustic summer house on the North Lawn of the Mansion House. Most were products of the Oneidans' efforts to produce a spiritually superior race of men and women by "stirpiculture," or scientific human breeding.*

PLATE XV. *Ann Bailey, who for a while was the official "mother" of the women at Oneida, was driven out of the Community by John Humphrey Noyes. He charged that in the course of a long "amative and spiritual connection" she had exerted an evil influence over his son Theodore.*

PLATE XVI. *Theodore Noyes, eldest son of John Humphrey Noyes, studied medicine at Yale and lost his faith in Christ. Despite this apostasy, the elder Noyes tried repeatedly (and unsuccessfully) to install Theodore as his successor—efforts that helped bring about the breakup of the Community.*

PLATE XVII. *In the 1870s a group of clergymen vowed to stamp out what one called "this Utopia of obscenity" at Oneida. This 1879 cartoon from* Puck *is representative of the derision with which their efforts were generally greeted in the press.*

PLATE XVIII. *Pierrepont Noyes was the son of John Humphrey Noyes and Harriet Worden (Plate VII). While still in his twenties, he was named general manager of Oneida Community, Ltd., the company organized to take over the Community's business assets after the breakup. He built it into one of the world's leading manufacturers of silverware.*

PLATE XIX. *The "Stone Cottage," overlooking Niagara Falls from the Canadian side, was John Humphrey Noyes's home during the years between his secret flight from Oneida in 1879 and his death, at seventy-four, in 1886.*

But for men, male continence not surprisingly could have an unpleasant side effect. Coitus interruptus was forbidden at Oneida, Noyes holding that it led a man to concentrate too much on his own physical pleasure and not enough on God and his partner. (He also argued that it wasted a precious fluid that men were better off retaining except when its expenditure was required for procreation.) And while one Oneida man told Hilda Noyes that he himself "never remembered any local congestion following an interview," he conceded that other men were not invariably immune to the severe pain that can result when prolonged sexual arousal is not relieved by ejaculation. He somewhat improbably insisted, however, that he had never heard of anyone seeking relief from such pain by masturbation—a practice of which Noyes took as dim a view as any conventional moralist or medical authority of his day. At Oneida the only approved remedy for postcoital discomfort was cold water.

In a testimonial written for the Community's first annual report, one man asserted that sex as practiced at Oneida "expands and elevates the heart, roots out and destroys selfishness in its various forms—destroys isolation—unlocks a fountain in the soul unknown before, and leads us to the boundless ocean of God's love." One need not be a cynic to speculate that, under the stern rule of male continence, men may have thought hard about God during sex as a good way to avoid thinking about the exquisite sexual pleasure they were obliged to forgo. But it is likely that the restraint and quietness imposed by male continence may, in some instances, have transformed sexual intercourse into a quasi-religious experience—an affirmation of the superiority of spiritual to physical love. But this is only guesswork. Such diaries and letters of Oneidans as have survived and are accessible to historians offer few clues as to how men at Oneida really felt about—and coped with—sex without orgasm. All that can be said with confidence is that few of them found it so frustrating that they left the Community. Of the men and boys who were on the Community's rolls in 1853, at the end of its first five years, just under 60 percent were still members a quarter century later when Noyes went off to Canada.

✦   ✦   ✦

Although Noyes held that true Christians would, in general, be instructed by God in how to conduct themselves, and so would have no need for laws and regulations, he came to the conclusion in 1852 that, in the matter of sex, it might be well to put God's intentions in writing. Accordingly he issued a set of "Rules for Sexual Intercourse." They specified, among other things, that men and women must sleep apart. "Their coming together should not be to sleep but to edify and enjoy," Noyes explained. "Over-familiarity dulls the edge of sexual passion." Ordinarily a man would go to his partner's room for sex, but in the early years, when many Oneidans did not have rooms of their own, a few rooms were set aside for sexual trysts. These trysts, Noyes instructed his followers, should be limited to an hour or two, after which the man should return to his bed. The stated aim of this regulation was to prevent satiety. As Noyes observed, once again equating sexual intercourse with eating, "It is an excellent rule to leave the table while the appetite is still good." But there may have been another reason why he did not want lovers to spend whole nights together. He may have feared that such prolonged intimacy, and privacy, would undermine their defenses against the fever of idolatrous love.

Another rule on Noyes's list was that invitations for "love interviews" should be extended through a third person. These invitations were expected to come from the man, though there was nothing to keep a woman from hinting that an invitation would be welcome. One reason for requiring a go-between was to spare a woman the embarrassment of having to tell a man to his face that she didn't want to go to bed with him. The rule also served the far more important purpose of enabling Noyes to control the sex lives of his followers. The intermediaries designated to receive and transmit proposals for sex were always central members, like Harriet Noyes or one of Noyes's sisters. They not only kept Noyes and his chief male deputies posted as to who was sleeping with whom, but they could refuse, either on their own authority or after checking with Noyes, to approve a proposed liaison. Given the lack of privacy at Oneida, it was all but impossible to carry on an unsanctioned love affair in secret; to carry one on in public would be to court severe criticism, the banishment of one party or the other to a branch community, or even expulsion.

Although it was all right for Oneidans to have love affairs that went on for weeks or months, the leaders were quick to terminate an affair that showed signs of being contaminated by jealousy or idolatry. (One such sign might be the reluctance of the partners to sleep with anyone else.) Another common ground for vetoing a liaison was that it violated the rule of ascending fellowship, specifying that young people should, more often than not, choose—or accept—sexual partners who were their spiritual superiors.

Thus, teenage boys, even after they had become proficient in the technique of male continence, were required to have sex mainly with much older women, standing high in the Community's spiritual hierarchy, from whom they might learn to subordinate the love of pleasure to the love of God. Young girls, as has been noted, were introduced to sex—usually soon after they had begun to menstruate —by Noyes himself or, in the last years of the Community, by one of his most trusted associates. When a woman had reached her late teens, she might now and then be permitted to go to bed with a contemporary if the couple could convince the elders of the Community that, as a young Oneidan explained, "they will not get into bondage to one another so as to make their love exclusive and idolatrous." But, as a rule, it was only when a woman was in her twenties that she became free routinely to accept as lovers men her own age or younger. From Noyes's standpoint, the virtual ban on what the *Circular* referred to as "mere boy-and-girl love affairs" had other advantages beside that of instilling in the young the proper attitude toward sex. It also tended to keep young people from forming an exclusive clique that would fortify what Noyes regarded as the natural but deplorable disposition of the young to resist the teachings of their elders. And it gave many older people a wider choice of attractive sexual partners than they might otherwise have enjoyed.

The power to regulate the sexual diet on which Oneidans fed gave the Community's leaders a powerful disciplinary tool. A man charged with pleasure seeking in sex was likely to discover that he was welcome only in the beds of certain older women charged with helping him to mend his ways. A member who was hardhearted toward God and Noyes and who proved impervious to criticism might find himself cut off even from such uplifting encounters. William Mills, whose expulsion from the Community was preceded by a complete sexual boycott, appealed in vain to Harriet Skinner to have pity on him. He assured her that the interview he was seeking was "not for secual [sic] purpose, but for spiritual interchange," but Harriet, apparently unconvinced by this disclaimer, turned him down, explaining with schoolmistressy condescension that such an encounter "would be no way to promote our fellowship. The way would be by your becoming a good man, which I know you can be if you will." In 1867 the Oneidans' little Community newspaper, the *Daily Journal*, reported that a man named Otis Miller "in his present state of hardness, has been requested not to obtrude his presence upon the family in their sitting rooms or library. Accordingly he has been furnished with a room in the . . . garret with a stove in it, that he may not be under the necessity of going to other rooms to warm." Unlike Mills, Miller eventually confessed his faults—he was, he agreed sadly, "egotistical, shiftless, lazy, and wicked"—and was restored to good standing after demonstrating his determination "to lay down his individuality, and organize into the Community spirit."

Sex was used to reward as well as to punish. The privilege of acting as a mentor to the young under the rule of ascending fellowship was a powerful incentive to please God and Noyes. And arguably it was Noyes's control of access to the embraces of the young—particularly of the young and attractive women, who by and large were ready to abide by his wishes in accepting or rejecting lovers—that, more than anything else, enabled him to govern at Oneida so long and so effectively.

✦   ✦   ✦

By the mid-1850s many of the rough edges of complex marriage had been smoothed away. If jealousy had not been abolished, it had at least been contained. Yet at Oneida, as in the outside world, love and sex could still be a source of great anguish. In 1861, when members were asked if their sexual experience during the past year had been "encouraging or otherwise," two out of five said it had been otherwise.

Dissatisfaction with complex marriage took many forms. Young people wanted to be freer to have lovers their own age. Older women who were not especially attractive often felt sexually deprived. At an evening meeting in 1861 a communication was read from a woman who complained that, without God's guidance, "the young and handsome and attractive will be likely to monopolize a large share of the rewards [of complex marriage] when perhaps in some cases . . . they do not merit so much as some who are outwardly less attractive." She added wistfully, "I wish it were more popular than it is for the young to love the old, the handsome to love the less so, the educated the less educated, in short, that love might be truly free, permeating and pervading all hearts." In a society as suffused with sexual feeling as Oneida by this time had come to be, it was particularly galling to be a wallflower.

Another cause of unhappiness was the failure of lovers to measure up to the standards set for them by Noyes. Men were criticized for treating their partners like mistresses, and women for using their sexual power to enslave lovers rather than to elevate them spiritually. One man accused a former lover, a young woman who was a leader in Community affairs, of having made him feel that it was much more important to please her than to please God and Noyes. "All I wanted to know was what she wanted of me and that [is what] I was going to do, let come what would," he told her criticism committee, adding that, toward the end of their affair, he had come to feel "that I was in a great machine that was going slowly around and was grinding me to powder."

But the main source of anguish and frustration in the sexual lives of the Oneidans was Noyes's refusal to tolerate love affairs that threatened, by their intensity or exclusivity, to deafen the lovers to the voices of God and the Community. "One might as well think of loving some particular tune and no other," Noyes asserted, "as to think of loving some particular woman to the exclusion of all others. What we love in the particular tune, is *music,* and what we love in the particular woman, is *love*—and love is God." Yet however hard they tried to resist, many Oneidans were bowled over by romantic love. They included Charles Cragin, a son of Mary and George Cragin and a man greatly looked up to by young people in the Community. After his death from malaria it turned out that he had been consumed by selfish love for a young woman named Edith Waters, who soon afterward died of tuberculosis. His secret was revealed in his diary, passages from which were read to the Community as a lesson in how not to love. Years later a young woman who had been one of his admirers recalled these passages as being full of "passionate and pathetic love for my precious [Edith] who was too ill to know much of them, or of their criticism . . . they seemed to me then wild and wrong, almost wicked."

Beulah Hendee, at a time when she was painfully recovering from a love affair which she (but apparently not her lover) would gladly have prolonged, wrote to a friend at Wallingford, "Father Noyes says the great thing for us to learn, is not to give our hearts to *any* man. He said they would surely abuse us so long as we did it." She added bravely, "All my experience nowadays is teaching me that lesson— teaching me to be truly independent and free." Yet within a few months she was again passionately in love, this time with the man whom she was to marry after the abandonment of complex marriage at Oneida. Many love letters written by Oneidans betray a passionate intensity, and a longing for the love of one person—and one person alone—that was not in keeping with the limited emotional commitment that Noyes prescribed for lovers. A young man named John Sears, who had been sent to Wallingford to take charge of a new factory there, was inconsolable at being separated from his sweetheart at Oneida. "You do not know," he wrote, "how I long to see you sometimes, & tell you lots of things that I cannot write on paper. I had a time last week of being dreadful homesick . . . & I would have given all I possessed to have been at [Oneida] where I could have gone up in your room & told you just how I felt."

✦　　✦　　✦

It would be a mistake, however, to put too much emphasis on what one Community elder referred to at an evening meeting as "all the difficulties, embarrassments and torments" that people experienced in their sexual lives. All parties to the bitter factional disputes that led to the Community's breakup were committed to complex marriage; they differed only in their views on how it should be regulated. Theodore Noyes, an intelligent and thoughtful man who maintained in his later years a sympathetic but detached attitude toward the experiment in which he had been so deeply involved, was convinced that complex marriage had given Oneidans "a higher average of happiness than in the same class in monogamic marriage." One reason, he wrote in 1892, was that when sexual discords arose, "there was more chance of resolution into a chord of happiness than in monogamic discords" and, therefore, "a higher average of happiness, sexually."

This is, of course, an unprovable proposition. But it would seem, judging from the results of the 1861 questionnaire, that more Oneidans than not were tolerably content with their sex lives. Some managed to immunize themselves against the dread infection of romantic love by which Noyes himself had been so seriously imperiled. Affectionate and tender in their sexual encounters, respectful of their partners and solicitous for their pleasure, they had schooled themselves to follow Noyes's advice and not give away their hearts.

Others, taking advantage of that loophole in the law of universal love that made it permissible to love one person best of all, were able to enjoy the deep emotional commitment and trust that is nurtured, in principle at least, by conventional matrimony. As long as a man and a woman were ready to have sex with others and to accord the same privilege to their special partners, and as long as they would accept criticism of their partners without becoming defensive, they were unlikely to be found guilty of selfish and idolatrous love. At a criticism session in 1849, for instance, Noyes held up as a shining example "the special companionship" of Stephen and Fanny Leonard. Everyone would agree, he said, that "there is not a couple more fond of each other, more sweetly united and affectionate than they are, and at the same time there is no couple more independent of each other, more perfectly free from jealousy and exclusiveness. No man would feel himself in any danger of being regarded as an intruder, or as liable to excite any evil thoughts, in loving Mrs. Leonard. Everybody would expect Mr. Leonard would be glad of it; it would excite in him a feeling of complacency instead of jealousy."

Since Fanny Leonard was one of Noyes's favorite sexual partners at this time, he had a powerful motive for flattering her husband on his generosity. But whatever Stephen Leonard's true feelings may have been on this occasion, there is evidence that Oneidans were often able to accept with reasonable grace, if not with wild enthusiasm, the knowledge that someone with whom they were deeply in love was having, and enjoying, sexual intercourse with others. Tolerance in these circumstances was easier, however, when the injured party, as the world would view the matter, was assured of remaining first in his or her lover's or spouse's affections. "Seymour I hope you will not make too much of what has been said about Mr. T and myself," a woman in her mid-fifties wrote from Wallingford to her husband at Oneida. "I did not know but what you would think we were very deeply involved—but not so; we have had quite a pleasant time in loving but now his heart seems turned in another direction."

✦   ✦   ✦

Complex marriage forced each Oneidan to think of his or her capacity to love, and be loved, with a sustained concentration rarely to be found in the world outside. One of the chief tasks Noyes set for his followers was to learn to love their sexual partners in ways that would deepen their love for the Community and for God. "The fulfillment of complex marriage was an 'ordinance,' " an Oneidan explained to her daughter long after the breakup of the Community. It was, she went on, "a loving 'ordinance of fellowship,' more earnest than the kiss or the everyday handclasp, no doubt, but simple, sacred, without guile, not unrestrained passion, but a 'communion of spirit and body.' " Oneidans even had a special song to remind themselves that sexual love was a form of Godly fellowship, justified only when it served as a pathway to God. A man would look directly at a woman and sing:

> I love you, O my sister,
> But the Love of God is better,
> Yes the Love of God is better—
> O the Love of God is best.

The woman would reply in the same words, substituting "brother" for "sister," and then the entire company would join in singing:

> Yes, the Love of God is better,
> O the Love of God is better,
> Hallelujah, Hallelujah—
> Yes, the Love of God is best.

Not everyone at Oneida succeeded in regarding sex as a particularly earnest handclasp. But even in the alternation of ecstasy and despair that many Oneidans experienced in complex marriage, they were likely to feel that they were perfecting their union with God. A letter written by a thirty-four-year-old woman describes how a newly begun love affair had awakened "my heart anew to communistic love." She had been recovering, she wrote from Wallingford to a friend at Oneida, from an affair that had been broken off by her lover at a time when she was still deeply in love with him. As a result, she had thought she would never again have anything to do with men. And so when another man wanted her to sleep with him she was at first determined to say no. But just being with him, she said, "seemed to let me feel that I *had a heart*, and gave me new courage to let it be warmed and melted—that perhaps God would give me a new experience." Like the devoted disciple of Noyes that she was, however, she had prayed that God would restore her capacity to love not just her lover, but the big family to which she belonged. Her prayers were answered: "I found myself really loving [her new lover]—but the best thing was, that I found my heart warming and enlarging toward all the brothers here—and my heart has been filled with a desire to seek *unselfishly* to please those around me, even at the sacrifice of my own tastes & inclinations."

If love was an ordinance at Oneida it was not meant to be a solemn one. Noyes's view of love had much in common with that of the Elizabethan poets, in that he was determined to eliminate from love and sex the monotony, the boredom, and the absence of all surprise and spontaneity that he saw as the curse of monogamy. He urged his followers to pattern their love affairs on courtship, not on marriage. In the presence of visitors, it is true, Oneidans were at pains to maintain an almost Shaker-like decorum. Men and women did not kiss in public, or even put their arms around one another. Yet the social atmosphere was charged with sexual excitement. At any moment a man and a woman could move swiftly from acquaintance or friendship to the mutual discoveries and heady intimacy of sexual love, and, with God's approval, this experience could be repeated again and again with other partners. In her memoir, *A Lasting Spring*, Jessie Kinsley recalls "the changing and the steadfast lovers. Some heartache, much happiness. . . . One formed no habits to dull the edge of love except, perhaps, as one was obliged to maintain too rigidly the principle of Ascending Fellowship." Along with the bookish rusticity that one reporter found at Oneida, and the Oneidans' stern pursuit of spiritual and moral perfection, there was a sense of high and never-ending sexual adventure. Pierrepont Noyes, who was nine when complex marriage ended, remembered "our grown folks" as having displayed a loving sensitivity in their relations with one another in which (he later theorized) the remembrance and anticipation of sexual gratification could have played only a part. "I believe," he wrote, "that the opportunity for romantic friendship also played a part in rendering life more colorful than elsewhere. Even elderly people, whose physical passions had burned low, preserved the fine essence of earlier associations; child as I was, I sensed a spirit of high romance surrounding them, a vital, youthful interest in life that looked from their eyes and spoke in their voices and manners."

Chapter 18

n a conversation with one of his lieutenants in 1871, Noyes confidently asserted that "I see no death before me." He added, "I do not know what changes are coming, but whatever they may be I have not the least idea that I shall cease to be the central life and manager of the Community." In an excellent unpublished documentary history of the Oneida Community, Noyes's nephew, George Wallingford Noyes, wrote that this declaration "seems to have been taken as a challenge by the powers of evil." Noyes was "assailed by pains in the back, a burning throat, disordered heart, pressure on the brain and terrible nights." He was then living at Wallingford, where ground was being cleared for a new dam on the Quinnipiac River, and despite his illness he "pitched into the work with all his might, splitting rocks and felling trees." After a sleepless night he would often get up at four o'clock and go to work. By the end of that summer, during which he turned sixty, Noyes had largely recovered his health. But his recent ordeal, together with the death of his brother George, who had been his literary collaborator as well as the editor of the *Circular*, was a discouraging reminder that God was in no rush to hand Noyes and his followers that victory over disease and death that for a time had seemed so close at hand.

Noyes once confided to his son Theodore that he put "a pretty free construction" on the Bible. "I take the ground," he explained, "that the account of the creation may be, if you please, an invention, a fable, a poem, and yet be inspired and convey substantial truth." Theodore suspected that his father at times had secret doubts as to the literal truth of the New Testament as well—or, rather, that he doubted the validity of his own highly idiosyncratic interpretation of the Gospel, from which Bible Communism got its legitimacy. In any case, Noyes never retreated from his claim that God had picked him to clear the way for Christ and the heavenly hosts to take possession of the earth. But when it came to tactics he was flexible enough, and as the millennium receded into the future, from time to time he issued new instructions to his followers concerning the role that God had given them in the great drama on which the curtain had been raised at Putney.

At the outset Noyes saw the community he had established at Oneida as having two distinct though related purposes. One purpose was to enable Perfectionists to foil the devil by leading, under Noyes's inspired guidance, a truly holy life. At the same time Oneida would serve as a bridgehead in Christ's campaign to conquer the world. Here the faithful would gather and, through the medium of a free daily newspaper, summon people everywhere to cast aside sin and thereby prepare themselves for the fast-approaching time when heaven and earth would be united and death would die. Oneida obviously would be unable to accommodate all who wished to live in perfect holiness. But other, similar communities would spring up by the hundreds and thousands, and Oneida's responsibility would be to furnish them with leaders. "The opening and promise before our young people is to be the heads of Communities," Noyes declared in 1866. He added optimistically, "The demand for Communism is going to be enormous. I should not think it strange if within two years we should be scattered to the four winds, except for a skeleton organization and that changing all the time."

As it turned out, no such community was ever founded (Wallingford was never anything but an Oneida branch). One reason was that the demand for communism was not, in fact, enormous. The great religious storms that had howled across the land in the 1830s had blown themselves out and showed no signs of returning. As time went by, fewer and fewer people seemed ready to give up their homes and their privacy, the comforts of matrimony, and the care of their children in order to save themselves and the world.

But this does not explain why it was that when converts to Perfectionism did appeal to Oneida for help in founding new communities, no help was forthcoming. The reason usually given was that the petitioners were not divinely inspired. An editorial in the *Circular* warned against would-be community builders who "rig themselves out with a complete set-up of the doctrines and social regulations we have developed," but whose aims were purely secular. It would "delight our hearts to see ten thousand Communities started," the editorial continued, but it would be "suicidal for us to encourage people to start Communities until the true work of inspiration comes."

There was, of course, nothing to stop Noyes from doing what he had so grandly promised in 1866. He could have commissioned some of his followers at Oneida, whose devotion to Christ and Bible Communism was all he could desire, to go out and start new communities. The most plausible explanation of why he did not do this is that he could not bear the idea of having rival dukedoms in the kingdom of heaven. The role in which he felt most comfortable, and in which he was most effective as a leader, was as the head of a family whose members were bound to him by a conviction, continually refreshed by personal contact, that their salvation lay in complete submission to his authority. As events were to show, Noyes had little aptitude or stomach for coping with dissenters from his rule, and his reluctance to see other communities spring up may have reflected a realistic apprehension that they would inevitably have their own ideas about communism. This in turn could well lead to disaffection and schism at

Oneida, and destroy the gratifying authority he had enjoyed as the father, under God, of the family he had gathered there.

However that may be, after 1866 there was little further talk of Oneida as the mother from whose womb new communities would spring. Oneida's success, it was said, was due to very special circumstances, notably including its good fortune in having Noyes as its leader. The Oneidans' duty to God was to furnish mankind with a shining example of true Christian life even though it was an example that could not, at least for the time being, be generally copied. "Let us see and show how much God can do for man and society on a single spot," Theodore Noyes wrote. "This will be a better service to the cause than any amount of crude unfinished experimenting and premature expansion." By 1870 John Noyes was suggesting that if socialism was to come it would not be through the founding of communities like Oneida—"exceptional associations [which] may be formed here and there by careful selection and special good fortune"—but through those very churches whose leaders Noyes had once declared to be non-Christians because they sinned. "We believe," he explained somewhat vaguely (and surprisingly) in his *History of American Socialisms*, "that a church that is capable of genuine revival could modulate into daily meetings, criticism, and all the self-denials of Communism, far more easily than any gathering [called together] for the sole purpose of founding a Community."

Noyes's growing conviction that very few people were ready for Bible Communism was reflected in Oneida's own admission policies. Many who joined the Community in its early years were not equipped for the psychological and moral rigors of communal life and soon departed, either of their own volition or by request. (Seceders, as they were called, were automatically given back any capital they had contributed to the Community; youthful seceders were customarily given a small sum of money to help them get a start in the outside world.) As a result, it was decided in the 1850s that it was not enough for a prospective member to confess Christ his savior from sin and declare his loyalty to Noyes. An applicant would also have to demonstrate, both through correspondence and on a visit to Oneida, during which he would be encouraged to submit himself to the Community for criticism, that he was ready and able to lay down the selfishness of his past life on the altar of communal harmony.

In the late 1860s and early 1870s, after the publication of William Hepworth Dixon's friendly, if breezily condescending, account of life at Oneida, applications poured in. Most of them were rejected out of hand. For every "earnest, God-fearing" applicant, the *Circular* complained in 1870, there were perhaps a hundred who were totally unfit for communism. "Owenites, infidels, spiritualists, irresponsible free lovers, and the riffraff of defunct Communities stand ready to take possession of every social experiment," the *Circular* continued. "It has required constant vigilance and hard fighting to keep such useless material out of the Oneida Community." Most people wanting to join the Community, the newspaper observed a couple of years later, "have no adequate conception of what they seek." Some, it was said, were simply bored and eager for a change. Others were "weak and sickly," or were looking for a "social paradise"—that is, for freedom from all sexual restraints—or had "failed in business and didn't know what to do with themselves."

There were also applicants who did meet the Community's standards, and from time to time a few of these were accepted. They included a group of families, survivors of a one-time free-love colony in Berlin Heights, Ohio, who had satisfied the Community, after years of correspondence and many visits to Oneida, that they were ready to accept the discipline of Bible Communism, and who were taken in in 1874. But apart from this group, only about a dozen new members were accepted during the last ten years of the Community's existence, even though this meant turning down applicants with excellent credentials. The reason for their rejection was that Noyes, perhaps fearing that his control of the Community would be weakened if it got too big, seems to have decided in the late 1860s that membership—at any rate, adult membership—was about as large as it ought to be. At the time, some two hundred and fifty people were living at Oneida and its branches. Over the next ten years membership grew to just over three hundred, but this increase was accounted for by the fifty-seven children born after stirpiculture was begun in 1869.

The decision not to start new communities, and to limit Oneida's membership to a carefully vetted spiritual elite, reflected a significant change in Noyes's view of the role that God had assigned to Oneida. The notion that Oneida existed to serve its members gave way to the notion that the members should serve Oneida. The perfection of individual character came to seem less important than the perfection of the Community.

This was a task, moreover, from which the Oneidans must not allow themselves to be distracted. Many Americans who, like Noyes, had been caught up in the religious excitement of the 1830s later shifted their energy and attention to causes other than the salvation of souls. Most notably they became abolitionists. But even though Noyes had been a founder of one of the first antislavery societies in America, he insisted that the abolitionists were putting the cart before the horse. If people could just be persuaded to accept Christ as their savior from sin, he pointed out, slavery and other forms of oppression and inhumanity would fade away.

Thus, while the Oneidans sympathized with the Union cause when war at last broke out, they felt no obligation to change their ways in order to hasten a Union victory. As the *Circular* smugly observed in 1863, "We consider ourselves fellow-conscripts with the new-made soldiers but drawn to serve in a different field. Indeed . . . we have been in camp for the last sixteen years, pioneering in a grand struggle against worse foes to the common welfare"—the reference was presumably to the devil and his minions—"than the southern 'secesh.' " The Oneidans' detached attitude toward the war was made easier by a bureaucratic mix-up as a result of which Oneida's young men were not required to register for the draft. The war's main effect on Oneida was to increase the demand for its products, which put a lot of money in the Community treasury.

To some subscribers to the *Circular* who counted themselves good Christians, Oneida's refusal to join in movements aimed at making the world a better place looked very much like selfishness. One such reader characterized the Oneidans as "selfish aristocrats who, from the secure heights of [their] Communistic walls, look down and enjoy the fratricidal struggle in the arena beneath." But Noyes insisted that the task God had set for the Oneidans was to show future generations that under the right circumstances—meaning under the right leadership—a carefully chosen band of Christians could live together in holy harmony. As one member wrote after the Community's demise, Oneida had given the world an object lesson, "a true outline of Heavenly Institutions . . . furnishing invaluable help to future builders whenever the world is advanced enough to tolerate their work." Oneida, he said, had been "an anticipative and imperfect miniature of the Kingdom of Heaven on earth."

✦   ✦   ✦

As it became clear to Noyes and his followers that rescuing the world from the devil would be the work of many centuries, and as American's fervor for salvation was undermined by the materialistic worldview of science, or gave way to a preoccupation with money and making it, the tone of voice in which the Oneidans addressed the world changed radically. At Putney, and in the early years of the Oneida Community, the *Free Church Circular* and its successors dealt almost entirely with the kingdom of heaven and the means of attaining it. "We propose to offer the world freely the news of salvation," an editorial declared in 1850, adding that the Oneidans were impelled to do this "because the facts are in us, and we must 'bear witness of the truth.' " To be sure, the diet that Noyes offered his readers included some non-theological hors d'oeuvres. Among the items in the *Circular* of June 26, 1856, for example, were a poem by Tennyson, a report on "Extension of the Telegraph to Australia," and an article headed "Silk-Peddler's Report—Observations, etc." But most of the issue was taken up with articles and editorials carrying such headings as "The Bible View of Prayer," "Prepare for Inspiration," "The Spirit of Immortality," "The Eternal Kingdom" (a reprint of a talk by Noyes), "True Education" (offered only by Bible Communism), and

"What is Religion?" (Answer: "Having the life of Christ pervade our hearts and minds, our nervous and spiritual systems—thus making us throughout new creatures, resurrection beings.")

By 1864, however, Noyes had concluded that if the Oneidans were to be successful in spreading God's truth they must allow for America's growing preoccupation with this world rather than the next. The *Circular*, announcing that its chief aim henceforward was to be "entertaining and useful," took on a new and more secular character. Addressing himself to readers who might be bothered by this change, Noyes argued that if the Community and its newspaper were to divorce themselves from the intellectual and material concerns of the age, they would be doing Christ a poor service. The power of science to illuminate the mysteries of the natural world and to transform the conditions of men's lives were manifestations of Christ's power and were to be seen as advancing heaven's cause. "The religion of heaven is not a drowsy affair of sitting on benches and psalm-singing," he wrote. "It is mighty and masculine and magnetic; it knows everything and can do everything, from teaching a child to pray to building an ironclad."

The new *Circular*, edited by Noyes's brother George, continued to print, and reprint, religious talks by Noyes, along with pieces on such subjects as the errors of the Swedenborgians and how to fight disease with faith. But these were far outnumbered by items of quite a different sort. An April 1876 number of the *Circular* included an article on how to grow strawberries; a lively review of Thoreau's *A Week on the Concord and Merrimac*, accompanied by some extracts from the book; a gracefully written column called "Foot Notes," consisting of miniature essays on trees, plagiarism, and the Hartford Turnpike; a piece about the water supply of ancient Jerusalem, reprinted from *Scientific American*; an article on "The Barbaric Element in Music"; and another on plans for a railroad that would be propelled through a tube by compressed air. The paper also reported, in an agreeably chatty style and often at considerable length, on daily life at Oneida and Wallingford.

But while Americans seemed eager to read titillating accounts of

life at Oneida in their magazines and newspapers, and to come to
Oneida to eat strawberries and marvel at the women with their short
hair and short dresses, fewer and fewer people were interested in
Noyes's views on salvation—even when those views were buffered by
articles on trees and compressed-air railroads, and even when the paper
that carried them could be had absolutely free of charge. Whereas the
Circular had once claimed ten thousand readers, by the end of 1875
there were perhaps only a quarter as many. Of the eight hundred
copies mailed out each week, nearly seven hundred went to nonpaying
subscribers. In 1876 the Oneidans settled on two measures they hoped
would win new readers and put the paper on a paying basis. Free
subscriptions were discontinued, and the paper's character was
changed again, this time much more drastically. Renamed the *American Socialist*, its mission was defined as making "a public record of
facts relating to the progress of Socialism everywhere." Seeming to
abandon—for itself, if not for the Oneida Community—any claim to
exclusive possession of God's truth, the new paper promised to treat
the Oneida Community "only as one of many examples of successful
communism." The *American Socialist* was more serious in tone than
its predecessor, and narrower in focus. Its contents ran heavily to accounts of communistic experiments, past and present, and to articles
with titles like "A Model Factory Village." Bible Communism all but
disappeared from its pages. There were occasional religious editorials
—an early one put forth the notion that Christ was the first socialist
—but they were written in a modest, tentative spirit quite different
from the oracular certitude with which the *Circular* in earlier days had
invariably spoken on religious topics.

Some nineteenth-century Christians saw science as a deadly foe with
which there could be no compromise. This was not to be wondered
at, considering that science's ingenious and persuasive theories of how
the world and man had evolved seemed calculated to destroy the very
foundations of Christianity. Noyes, however, instead of denouncing

science as the work of the devil, chose to clasp it to his bosom in a warm—actually, suffocating—Christian embrace. He hungrily devoured the works of the British geologist Charles Lyell and, later, of Charles Darwin. At the urging of David Croly, the editor of the New York *World*, who visited Oneida in 1868, he immersed himself in the writings of the French philosopher Auguste Comte, the father of positivism and one of revealed religion's most formidable enemies. In a letter published in the *World*, Noyes argued that Christianity really had nothing to fear from Comte's insistence that the only true knowledge was grounded in the positive certainties of science—a position with which Noyes said he was in complete agreement. After all, he wrote, his old theology professor at Yale, Nathaniel Taylor, had taught his students "to follow the truth, lead where it will and cost what it will." Describing this as "the first precept of science," he observed complacently, "Under that precept I have traveled far enough into the regions of free-thinking to shake hands with the scouts of Positivism, and yet I have no thought of abandoning Bible religion. . . . I have followed Lyell into the geological ages . . . and even Darwin into his endless genealogies, and yet I am as sure [as ever] that Christ is king of the world." The sovereignty of Christ, Noyes suggested, was to be regarded either as a scientific truth or as a truth beyond the reach of science.

The Oneidans, following Noyes's example, had already taken up science as enthusiastically as they had gone in for band music and croquet. They read *Nature* and the *Journal of Applied Chemistry*; attended evening lectures on geology, the ideas of Comte, and the chemistry of cooking; took courses in astronomy and physics; and learned the techniques of analytical chemistry in a former ice house that had been fitted out as a laboratory by Theodore Noyes. Science and its applications were principal topics of discussion at regular late-morning meetings in the upper sitting room. "Positivism, Calvinism & Spiritualism are viewed and reviewed," a participant noted, "with not infrequent digressions to water-powers, silk-manufacture, and stirpiculture."

In 1870 Noyes announced that "God designs to bring science and religion together and solder them into one," and that the soldering was destined to be accomplished at Oneida. The first step had already been taken with the inauguration of stirpiculture, an enterprise in which Darwin's science, together with the empirical knowledge of live-stock breeders, was to be employed in the production of a spiritually superior race of men. As the *Circular* pointed out, God himself had used the technique of inbreeding to produce in the Jews, whom Noyes greatly admired, a "better receptivity to inspiration and obedience." What God had done for the Jews, Noyes and his followers—with Darwin's help and God's inspiration—would try to do for the entire world.

he notion of resorting to scientific human breeding for the spiritual perfection of mankind was first addressed by Noyes in 1846. Noting that some physiologists favored such a scheme, he argued in the pages of the *Spiritual Magazine* that there was a better (and quicker) way. By choosing the path of Bible Communism, men and women could free themselves from sin and attain perfection within their own lifetimes. In arguing for this alternative, Noyes was no doubt influenced by the faith cures and other signs he saw at Putney pointing to the swift approach of the Resurrection— signs that would, a year later, persuade him and his followers to declare formally (and, as it turned out, prematurely) that the kingdom of heaven had arrived.

But the possibilities of stirpiculture continued to intrigue Noyes. And by 1856, having reconciled himself to God's apparent determination to take his time about extending his sway on earth, Noyes suggested a change of strategy in the war that he and his followers were waging against the devil. "God has not prospered us in proselytism," he observed. "We should give up insisting that God should convert the world immediately, and have instead a far-reaching purpose to save the world by combining regeneration with generation." In other words, the Oneidans whose regeneration—that is, spiritual perfection—was most advanced should pair up to produce children who would inherit their parents' superior spiritual traits.

In 1856, however, the Oneidans were not yet ready for such an undertaking. They were still struggling to get on their feet financially, and, perhaps more important, the memory of their bruising encounters with Utica's District Attorney Garvin were still fresh. To set about producing a big crop of babies as long as there was any danger that the Community would be broken up would be highly imprudent.

But Oneida was soon to enter a golden age. By the mid-1860s its businesses were highly profitable and the outside world, while plainly in no hurry to embrace Bible Communism, seemed as much inclined to admire as to deplore the Oneidans' radical experiment in communal living. Hoping to extend its influence abroad, in the summer of 1867 the Community sent two of its members—Noyes's brother George, then the editor of the *Circular*, and Charles Joslyn, who not only was Oneida's most accomplished musician but had recently been admitted to the New York bar—on what amounted to a European sales trip. They placed samples of Oneida products in the Paris Exposition of 1867, were guests of honor at a dinner given by followers of Fourier, dined in London with the Bishop of Gloucester, explained the Community's birth-control method to the noted English biologist Thomas Henry Huxley—Huxley was said to have been "a good deal impressed"—and set up agencies for the sale of Community publications in London and Paris.

Oneida was flourishing spiritually as well as financially. Earlier discords in the harmony of Community life had died away, and a whole year passed without the departure of a single "seceder." There was rejoicing when, in 1865, Noyes's son Theodore, a student at the Yale Medical School and a leader among the younger members of the Community, announced that he had overcome earlier doubts about the divinity of Christ and the divine authority claimed by his father. Two years later, on a vacation from Yale, he inaugurated a religious revival among the young people at Oneida. Religious meetings, in which many older members soon joined, were held each day at noon. It was a time, John Noyes exulted, when "hard spirits retreated, good spirits prevailed and rejoiced." In his history of the Oneida Community, George Wallingford Noyes wrote that "the year August 1866 to August 1867 may not inaptly be called the culminating year of the experiment."

Over the years Noyes's enthusiasm for stirpiculture had been heightened by his reading of Darwin, whose insistence on the plasticity of living forms, Noyes observed, provided a solid scientific basis for the selective breeding of humans that Plato had advocated.* Buoyed by the mounting evidence that God was smiling on Oneida, Noyes concluded that the time had come to undertake the world's first experiment in scientific human propagation. "Without immodesty," he wrote, "we may ask all who love God and mankind to pray that we may succeed, for our success will surely be the dawn of a better day to the world."

✦   ✦   ✦

Stirpiculture would obviously entail a significant extension of the control that the Community's elders already exercised over the sex lives of its members. From a spiritual point of view, not all Oneidans were equally good breeding stock, and someone—ultimately, Noyes himself—would have to decide who could have babies, and with whom. Expressing their readiness to accept such control, fifty-three young women—those from whom the mothers of the first generation of so-called stirpiculults would be selected—signed a statement placing

---

* Noyes saw science as an exciting game that anybody, himself included, could play. Speaking at an evening meeting with the easy confidence of a man who had taught his followers to regard his pronouncements on religious subjects as divinely inspired, Noyes suggested that Darwin and Genesis could be reconciled by assuming that man was descended from snakes. "The Bible itself," he explained, "gives an account of a race that dwelt on the earth before man was created. It walked upright, had speech, was highly ingenious, and was called 'the serpent.' "

themselves completely at Noyes's disposal. Declaring that "we do not belong to ourselves in any respect, but . . . belong first to *God*, and second to Mr. Noyes as God's true representative," they promised to "put aside all envy, childishness, and self-seeking, and . . . if necessary, become martyrs to science, and cheerfully renounce all desire to become mothers, if for any reason Mr. Noyes deem us unfit." A similar statement was signed by thirty-eight young men.

At first the decision as to who could have babies was made by Noyes himself, in consultation with his informal cabinet of central members. Later, in 1875, the job was assigned to a Stirpicultural Committee, consisting of six women and six men, two of whom were graduates of the Yale Medical School. But after fifteen months, perhaps because the selection of parents was too important in the politics of the Community to be delegated to a committee, Noyes and his senior advisers again took over.

The standard procedure was for a man and a woman to apply to the authorities for permission to have a baby—although in perhaps one out of four cases where permission was granted the pairing had been suggested by the central members or by the Stirpicultural Committee. When a couple's application had been approved, the woman would have sexual relations only with her designated partner until she either became pregnant or had given up trying; men were at liberty to sleep with other women, and occasionally did so. When couples applying to have babies were turned down—in the fifteen months that the Stirpicultural Committee was running the experiment, nine out of fifty-one applications were rejected—an effort was made to find another and more suitable partner for the woman. Very few women who wanted to have children were considered such poor stirpicultural material that their deficiencies could not be compensated for by a mate of sufficiently high spiritual attainments. Couples who had babies by accident—or had them on purpose but without authorization—were not disciplined for their offenses; the offspring of such unions were treated exactly like the approved stirpicults and were often included with them in statistical analyses of the experiment.

When a couple had been given permission to try for a baby, this was ordinarily announced at an evening meeting, on the theory that the baby would be the child of the *Community*, not of its biological parents. For a time such unions were formally celebrated like weddings. A woman named Charlotte Leonard, writing to her mother at Wallingford in the spring of 1873, described one such ceremony, held in the big hall of the Mansion House. "The stage was cleared, & Edward Inslee & Tirzah [Miller] walked to the front of the stage & kneeled together, their heads bowed, & having hold of hands." The audience then rose and sang, to the tune of "Old Hundred," a song titled "Blessing on Begetting," written by Tirzah's brother George:

> Great Giver of the righteous seed,
> Before Thy throne Thy children plead
> That they are nevermore their own
> But live to worship Thee alone. . . .
>
> And on these two, Oh Lord, who kneel,
> Our blessing with Thy blessing seal;
> And grant in coming joyous days
> A noble child to lisp Thy praise.

After the singing, Charlotte Leonard reported, a dozen or more couples went up onto the stage and kissed the prospective parents, who then entertained the company with a duet for horn and piano.

The disappointment of would-be parents who were turned down by the Stirpicultural Committee sometimes ran deep. One "martyr to science" named Mary Jones, who wanted to have a baby by a man named Victor Hawley, was told that this was out of the question; no reason seems to have been given. At the committee's prompting, she moved from Oneida to Wallingford, became pregnant (with official permission) by Theodore Noyes, and soon returned to Oneida. There, she was tenderly cared for throughout an extremely difficult pregnancy by her unhappy lover Victor. "My God, My God," he wrote in his diary upon learning of her pregnancy, "what has she been through as well as I? Will they tear the hearts out of both of us? When shall we ever be happy together again?" In the face of criticism that he had fallen into the trap of special love, Victor spent hours each day with Mary. He brought her oranges, eggnog, wild strawberries, and oysters; read the New Testament to her; recorded the growing size of her stomach and felt the baby move; cuddled her to help her sleep, gave her massages, and—when she felt up to it—had sex with her. (On one occasion, after massaging Mary's hips and legs, he wrote, "They did not stop aching so I went to bed with her and had connection and the pain all left her.") Despite Victor's ministrations, the baby was stillborn, and within a few months the two lovers left the Community to get married.

✦   ✦   ✦

In 1869, as stirpiculture was getting under way at Oneida, the British anthropologist Sir Francis Galton published his classic *Hereditary Genius*. It was Galton's work that provided the scientific underpinning for the eugenics movement, whose goal was to improve the human race through selective breeding, and which was to enjoy a considerable vogue in both Europe and America over the next half century. In an essay called "Scientific Propagation," published in 1870 in the magazine *Modern Thinker*, Noyes wrote enthusiastically of Galton's demonstration that not only physical traits, but moral characteristics and "spiritual proclivities" are "as transmissible [by inheritance] as the speed of horses." Unlike the speed of a racehorse, of course, the spiritual attainments of humans cannot be measured with a stopwatch. But as George Bernard Shaw, a firm believer in eugenics, later pointed out, the task of choosing the right parents was simplified for the Oneidans, "the question of what sort of men they should strive to breed being settled at once by the obvious desirability of breeding another Noyes." That this is pretty much what Noyes had in mind is suggested by the fact that, as noted, nine of the fifty-eight babies at Oneida whose parents were scientifically selected for parenthood were fathered by Noyes himself.

To get the maximum benefit from the Noyes bloodline, Noyes

encouraged unions in which both parties had good Noyes blood. While he saw no good reason why healthy siblings should not unite for stirpicultural purposes, he did not follow through on this conviction, apparently believing that the time was not right for an assault on what he described as "the last citadel of social falsehood, which forbids the union of brothers and sisters." He did, however, promote uncle-niece combinations. His own niece Tirzah, with whom he had for many years a close and passionate relationship that might—in others —have been denounced as special love, had her first child by Noyes's brother George, and Noyes told her that he, too, would like to have a child by her. As she recalled the conversation, "I told him I should like that. . . . He said to combine with me would be intensifying the Noyes blood more than anything else he could do." At the time, Tirzah was pregnant by Edward Inslee, and nothing came of Noyes's plan, but he did later have a child by another niece, Helen Miller.

In principle, parents were chosen primarily for their spiritual qualities, with some importance being assigned to intellectual, moral, and physical characteristics. But other considerations often weighed heavily. Having Noyes blood, for example, qualified some Community members for parenthood who would otherwise almost surely have been turned down. A principal case in point was that of Theodore Noyes. He was well educated and highly intelligent, but his health was poor—a contemporary described him as "corpulent and somewhat inclined to apoplexy"—and not long after the experiment in stirpiculture got under way he had what was diagnosed as a nervous breakdown and spent four months recovering at a nearby sanitarium. More important, for a long time in the early 1870s he was, in the view of a close friend, "an infidel, if not an atheist"—a state of disbelief from which he never totally recovered. He was nevertheless allowed to father four children. The privilege of fatherhood was also granted to Theodore's half-brother Victor, the child of John Noyes and Mary Cragin, even though, at the age of twenty-four, he would be one of the very youngest of the designated fathers, most of whom were selected from among the older (and presumably spiritually more advanced) men of the Community. More significantly, like Theodore, some years earlier he had rebelled against his father's religious views, and Noyes, who seems to have regarded this as a symptom of insanity, had had him committed to an insane asylum in Utica.*

The selection of Theodore Noyes and Victor Cragin as breeding stock was quite in keeping with Noyes's belief in the importance of bloodlines. In his *Modern Thinker* article he contended that men with good blood in their veins could pass the virtues of that blood to future generations even if they themselves were not particularly good. (Noyes did not explain how someone with good blood could be bad.) "Providence," he wrote, "frequently allows very superior men to be also very attractive to women, and very licentious." He went on to argue that evil as such men may be, their licentiousness may actually benefit later generations. As an example he cited Pierpont Edwards, the roué son of the great New England preacher and theologian Jonathan Edwards. "Who can say," he asked in all seriousness, "how much the present race of men in Connecticut owe to the numberless adulteries and fornications of Pierrepont [sic] Edwards? Corrupt as he was, he must have distributed a good deal of the blood of his noble father . . . and so we may hope the human race got a secret profit out of him."

In deciding who was to have babies, Noyes was often motivated by considerations other than the spiritual standing of the prospective parents and whether they had Noyes blood. Thus, Charlotte Leonard, in her report on the betrothal, as it were, of Edward Inslee and Tirzah Miller, commented that the union had been blessed by Noyes mainly

---

* In a moving letter to his father, written from the Utica asylum when he was nineteen, Victor said he had never felt better in mind or body, and pleaded with Noyes not to let him "rust out my life at . . . this Hell upon Earth." As for their religious differences, he wrote: "Can't you give me a trial? God knows I have had (and have now) no personal feeling toward you or the Community. It has been (and is) with me a question of principle; of right and wrong, and if I find hereafter that I have been in error, I will gladly humble myself at your feet." Noyes adamantly rejected this plea, warning that Victor could not hope to be discharged until he had acknowledged that he had, in fact, been insane, and until he had shown his readiness to "wipe out all the notions that you have adopted during your insanity, and begin again, as a little child." Whether Victor yielded to this harsh ultimatum is not clear, but a week later he was back at Oneida.

because he thought it would be good for Edward—and for the Community—if he were to become a father. "Edward has lately been going through a good deal of temptation about going away," she wrote, "& has at last come out of it all with Mr. Noyes's help, & now Mr. Noyes thinks it will help to fasten him I suppose to have a child." As it turned out, Inslee was a cruel disappointment to Noyes, who years later denounced him as an agent of evil spirits, a man "absolutely impenetrable to conviction of wrong."

In another case a young woman named Leonora Hatch asked Noyes for advice on how best to cure herself of her "exclusive idolatry" of a man named Edwin Burnham. Noyes told her he had been praying about her, and suggested that she have a baby. She agreed, saying she thought a baby would bind her to the Community, and adding that she wanted Noyes to be the father. Noyes consulted his wife and his sister, Harriet Skinner, who both agreed that this would be a good idea, and in due course a son, Guy, was born. Like Edward Inslee, Leonora turned against Noyes, going so far as to let it be known, after Noyes had gone into exile in Canada, that if he should ever be brought to trial for sexual offenses she was ready to testify that he had forced her to have a child by him. To reassure Noyes that the accusation was groundless, and would never stand up in court, Tirzah Miller wrote to him in Niagara setting forth in detail her knowledge of the affair. In her letter, which offers a revealing glimpse of the inner workings of stirpiculture, she wrote that Leonora herself had told her that it was *she* who had proposed to Noyes that he be the father of her child. As further evidence of her eagerness to have a child by him, Tirzah recalled a conversation she had had with Leonora after she had slept with Noyes for the first time—the first time, at any rate, when the rule of coitus reservatus did not apply: "She came to me in great anxiety one day, & said she was afraid it was your intention to only 'try' *once* during the month (as had been your usual practice) & she wished you would try a number of times so as to make a sure thing of it." The letter continues: "I advised her to tell you her desire herself. She did so & came back to me all aglow with the success of her interview with you. She gave me distinctly to understand that she had pretty much taken the business into her own hands & was going to 'make him do it'—her own expression."

✦   ✦   ✦

In 1891, the *American Anthropologist* published an appraisal of the experiment in human breeding at Oneida that had ended abruptly with the abandonment of complex marriage in 1879 and the subsequent breakup of the Community. Its author, a Dr. Anita Newcomb McGee of the Johns Hopkins Medical School, had interviewed, or obtained detailed information about, twenty-two stirpicults, aged eighteen to twenty-two, then living in Oneida. She found them an impressive group: "The boys are tall—several over six feet—broadshouldered, and finely proportioned; the girls are robust and well built." Two of the young men were in college, one was a college graduate, one was in medical school, and ten were in business, all but one of them working in supervisory or white-collar jobs. Of the six women, one was in and another about to enter college; a third was "a student of the kindergarten system." McGee's report continues, "As an index of the calibre of the offspring of stirpiculture, it may be mentioned that favorite amusement is found in a debating society of three girls and four of the boys, which meets during the summer when all are at home." The chief aim of stirpiculture at Oneida was to produce humans who were *spiritually* superior, and in this regard the author noted that the early results were not encouraging. "It is a surprise . . ." she wrote, "that in spite of their early doctrinal training only a very few are church members and but one is a Perfectionist."*

That the stirpicults McGee saw and talked to were healthy, robust, and well adjusted is, as she conceded, at least as much a tribute to the way they were reared at Oneida as to the way their parents were selected. And that they were doing well in the world could be credited

---

* This was disputed by a former member of the Community who wrote the author after publication of her paper that he knew of *three* stirpicults who were Perfectionists.

to the fact that many of the young people she interviewed had fathers who were managers of one of the thriving enterprises spun off when the Community was dissolved, and that most of them had grown up in moderately prosperous circumstances. The real significance of the Oneida experiment in child production and child rearing was not that it proved or disproved the proposition that scientific breeding was the way to improve humankind. Rather, it demonstrated that growing up in the Children's House not only made for a happy childhood, but gave its graduates an excellent start in life. For Noyes, however, even though he conceded that not much in the way of human improvement could be accomplished in one generation, there had to be something more to stirpiculture than this. Writing to Tirzah Miller a year after the breakup of the Community, he noted that since the children born under the stirpicultural regime had the whole Community as their parents, they were likely to be "better, so far as natural inheritance is concerned, than their immediate parents." How could it be possible, he went on to ask, "that a child [could be] born in that seething mass of miraculous life without partaking of its genius?" But this was less a scientific hypothesis than an effort to assuage the all but unbearable grief that at times overwhelmed Noyes in his last years as he mourned his lost kingdom.

oyes often said that it was his—and God's—intention that he should never cease to be the ultimate authority in the affairs of the Oneida Community even if, as he once declared, "I should pass into the spiritual world." But by the mid-1870s he was in uncertain health and so deaf that he could no longer hear what was said at meetings. At times the recurrence of his old throat ailment made it difficult for him to speak. And while he left no doubt that he would remain God's viceroy at Oneida, there was nothing in his commission from God to keep him from delegating some of his authority. Accordingly, he said, it was now his intention "to provide a personal leader" who would relieve him of responsibility for the direct management of Community affairs.

The person best fitted for this task, Noyes asserted, was his son Theodore. This came as no great surprise. As early as 1867 Noyes had made clear his conviction that Theodore was qualified for a leading part in the government of the Community. At that time, as a result of a nationwide credit squeeze, in a period when Oneida's business enterprises were expanding rapidly, the Community had found itself stripped of working capital and heavily in debt—a condition requiring, as Noyes put it, that "we solemnly submit our business and organization to God for pruning." To help God wield the shears, the Community accepted Noyes's suggestion that Theodore be placed in charge of all business operations. He was then twenty-six and had just finished his medical education at Yale. A handsome man, somewhat plump, with a full, dark beard, he was highly popular with the young women of the Community. He had a clear, analytical mind, and even though completely lacking in business experience, he proved so skillful a pruner that within a year the Community was out of debt and had built up a cash reserve. Under his management, expansion was resumed—construction was begun at Wallingford of a new dam on the Quinnipiac River to provide more power for the Community's job-printing and silk-spinning businesses—and earnings soared.

But while Noyes's confidence in Theodore's talents as a businessman was amply vindicated, as the years went by he became increasingly unhappy about Theodore's high-handed methods. Noyes, to be sure, was himself an autocrat. In important matters, especially matters of religion, he knew—and let it be known—that God did not intend him to be overridden by his followers. In most circumstances, though, he believed in government by consensus and was ready to modify or even abandon schemes to which cogent objections were raised. "In many things the Community was a pure Democracy," Theodore Noyes recalled after his father's death. The elder Noyes "had the unusual art of governing firmly, while he allowed the largest possible liberty," Theodore explained, adding that "Father's final control was so unquestioned that he could leave things to run themselves for months at a time—sure that he could bring everything right at a touch."

Theodore, however, notably lacked his father's tolerance for the messy processes of democracy. In the course of straightening out Oneida's business affairs he had effectively deprived the Community of any opportunity to review business decisions, as they had been reviewed in the past at open meetings of the Community's Business Board. This not only flew in the face of Noyes's belief in a modified town-meeting form of government, but had the bad effect, in his view, of distancing the business managers from the moral and spiritual life of the Community, making it easy for them to forget that their first obligation was to be good Christians, not good businessmen.

In 1872 Noyes stepped in. The Business Board, he said, must be revived and business arrangements once again brought under the moral sway of the Community. "If Theodore feels able to guide the whole thing himself," he observed tartly, "he is a greater man than I am. . . . Let us throw all these things open to the daylight. Let all the departments offer themselves for criticism, and have no irritability about it." Soon afterward, Theodore had his nervous breakdown and went off to recuperate at a "water cure" in western New York. When he returned to Oneida four months later, he took no further part for the time being in the Community's business affairs, serving instead, with Mary Cragin's son George, as community physician.

Theodore's breakdown had been precipitated by an intense emotional crisis brought on by a recurrence of the doubts that had plagued him, while he was a student at Yale, about the divinity of Christ and the legitimacy of his father's commission from God. At that earlier time he had quickly returned to the fold, declaring that "I don't want and won't have any independence of [the] movement of which Father is the center." But positivism and the German rationalists—those writers, like Goethe, who took an "infernal" delight, as Noyes saw it, in undermining the supernatural foundations of Christianity—were making their malign influence felt at Oneida. To Noyes's dismay, their converts included his sister Harriet's son Joseph, who had taken a degree in civil engineering at the Sheffield Scientific School at Yale. In 1873, finding himself at odds with the religious beliefs of the Community, he left Oneida for good, telling his father that he could no longer endure being ostracized by his own mother and treated as a naughty child by Noyes.

This was a great blow to Noyes, but a greater one was soon to fall. A few weeks after Joseph's departure, Theodore confessed that he shared Joseph's views. He said he had come to doubt not only the divinity of Christ but the very existence of God. Like Joseph, he soon left Oneida, with a $50 stake provided by the Community and no clear idea of what he wanted to do with his life.

But Oneida's hold on him was powerful. He concluded almost at once that what he most wanted was to return to the Community, provided he would not be required to renounce his agnosticism. The elder Noyes consented, stipulating only that the prodigal return "with an honest wish and purpose, to conquer his doubts." To Noyes's profound relief, Theodore, who had been staying in New York, took the next train back to Oneida, where the question of his readmission to the Community was taken up at an evening meeting. The Community could afford to lose Joseph Skinner, but the thought of losing Theodore was intolerable—not only because of the grief his loss would cause his father, but because of the high regard in which he himself was held. The undemocratic management of the Community's businesses under his administration had not diminished his personal popularity, and so, despite Theodore's admission that in his present state of mind he could give no more than tentative and formal adherence to his father's religious views, his request for readmission was greeted with cheers. According to George W. Noyes's account, "The belief was general that Theodore was on the right track. . . . The question of reinstating [him] in his membership was put to a vote and unanimously approved, after which the hearts of all beat more freely."

Noyes still clung to the hope that Theodore would someday succeed him—or, at any rate, serve as his chief deputy, or prime minister. But it would be helpful if he could first be freed from the curse of positivism, and to aid in this rescue mission Noyes turned to the spirits of the dead.

For many years he had regularly looked for guidance and inspiration to a small group of such spirits, consisting of Christ, his apostles, and the one hundred forty-four thousand members of the Primitive Church who had been taken up into heaven by Christ at the time of the destruction of the Temple of Jerusalem. Noyes had no doubt about his ability to receive messages from them—or about the uniqueness of that ability. As the Community's most perspicacious chronicler, Frank Wayland-Smith, noted in his diary, "I do not know of a single person in the Community whom he would consider fit to get at the mind of the spirits—except himself; and he has no hesitation in saying that he gets at it exactly, every time." In Noyes's communication with the elite of the spirit world, Theodore Noyes recalled, his father did not resort to "the mummery of ordinary spiritualism." Instead, when he had an idea he would "hold still and consult the spiritual world" by letting the idea fill his mind until he could determine if it was good enough to qualify as divinely inspired. Noyes had previously discouraged his followers from joining in the craze for Ouija boards, table rappings, and mediumistic trances that swept the country in the mid-nineteenth century. It was not that he doubted the ability of mediums to transmit messages from the dead; his complaint was rather that most such messages came not from members of the Primitive Church, but from inhabitants of Hades. And Hades, in his view, was populated almost exclusively by beings less advanced spiritually than the true Christians at Oneida—beings from whom the Oneidans could therefore learn nothing useful or improving. Nevertheless, Noyes now suggested that Theodore undertake a thoroughgoing investigation of spiritualism. His hope was that regular attendance at séances might wean the doubting Theodore away from scientific materialism by convincing him of the existence of a spirit world—and that this conviction would in time lead him to a renewed belief in the divinity of Christ.

Theodore accepted the assignment with enthusiasm. Taking advantage of his father's newly relaxed attitude toward spiritualism, he developed half a dozen home-grown mediums at Oneida, and every day, an Oneidan remembered years later, the voices of the dead were heard at séances "in the 'dark room' in the north garret where we sat around a table and people *shook*." He also traveled about New England and New York, attending sessions with well-known mediums. He was sometimes accompanied by his close friend Frank Wayland-Smith, who had recently dropped out of the Yale Law School for health reasons, and the two men became adept at detecting fakery. But they also encountered phenomena that, as Wayland-Smith wrote, could be explained only by assuming the existence of "an invisible, intelligent force which can affect matter . . . but which we do not yet fully understand."

The medicine that his father had prescribed appeared to be working, and in 1875 Frank Wayland-Smith suggested to the elder Noyes that Theodore's spiritual recovery had progressed to a point where he could once again be considered for an important leadership job. Noyes was then living at Wallingford, and Wayland-Smith said the job he had in mind was "father" of the Oneida family, a post whose occupant had day-to-day responsibility, under Noyes's supervision, for the conduct of affairs at Oneida when Noyes was not in residence. The present father, William Woolworth, had said he would be happy to turn the job over to someone else, and Noyes leaped at the idea of Theodore's taking Woolworth's place. He decided, however, that this was a matter for the Community to decide, and in March 1875 Theodore's fitness for the position was debated at six successive evening meetings at Oneida. The elder Noyes, who remained in Wallingford, did not take part.

There was strong support for Theodore's candidacy. Harriet Skinner asserted that her nephew's apostasy was only theoretical. Theodore not only instructed his own little son to pray and "confess Christ," she said, but "is in the constant habit of prayer himself, not to God by name but to the highest spirit in the universe." James Herrick, the former Episcopalian minister, took a different line—one that struck many of his hearers as dangerous heresy. Making no attempt to prove that Theodore was really a good Christian, Herrick argued that under a leader like Theodore, a man with "a strong intellectual and scientific bias," the Community "will be broader, healthier, and will have a better chance of perpetuity than if built on a simply spiritual basis." In a similar vein, Frank Wayland-Smith praised his friend's habitual skepticism, saying that he "has given me a contempt for cant and hypocrisy which is very wholesome to one's moral nature."

But there were also widespread doubts about the elder Noyes's hopes for Theodore—doubts that were in time to play a big part in

the breakup of the Community. The departure from Perfectionist orthodoxy that the elder Noyes now seemed prepared to tolerate—in
his son, if in no one else—dismayed many Oneidans, who felt the
spiritual ground giving way beneath them. "What is the object of this
community?" a speaker asked. *"It is to make us good men and women.*
Well, is thinking God out of the universe going to make us better
men and women?" William Hinds, who had mastered his tendency to
unspiritual lovemaking and was now a leading member of the generation that had grown up at Oneida—he was soon to take over the
important job of editing the Community's weekly newspaper—gave
voice to a feeling shared by many when he argued that few would
have considered making Theodore the father of the Oneida family if
he had not been Noyes's son. Theodore's cautious assertions of belief
in an unspecified higher power were not enough to satisfy a critic like
Hinds. The Community, he insisted, could survive "only by keeping
alive and active the old spirit of faith in a living personal God, in a
living personal Devil, in a living personal Savior." On the sixth night
Theodore asked to be heard. He said he was convinced that "a fa-
natical tendency in some of the members needs the antidote of my
[skeptical] tendencies of mind." But he went on to say that he could
not be a good leader without the "kindness and charity" of those with
clearer views than his of the nature of God. And since, at the time,
such charity obviously struck many Oneidans as "a concession to the
Devil," he would be "well content to wait until I am wanted by all
hands." The meeting then decided to regard Theodore's nomination
as having been withdrawn, and voted unanimously to ask Woolworth
to continue as father of the Oneida family, which he agreed to do.

✦   ✦   ✦

This setback to Theodore's—and his father's—ambitions proved only
temporary. Soon after the six-day debate, Theodore joined his father
at Wallingford, and over the next few months they struggled to find
a common spiritual ground on which to stand. On one important
matter, at least, they were now in complete accord, Theodore having

come around to his father's view that the true object of business was character-building, not money-making. Accordingly, toward the end of 1875, when the leadership at Oneida asked for advice on the management of the Community's business operations, Noyes sent Theodore to Oneida with a proposal that, if accepted, would once again put him at the center of Community affairs. Two years before, when Theodore had been dismissed as chief business manager partly because of his failure to curb an excessive zeal for money-making, Noyes had called for a periodic "throwing aside of business, and a sitting, or lying down, a kneeling and shutting the eyes and going to God." Three months later, the *Circular* reported with satisfaction that many had indeed taken up this practice, which had come to be known as "going home to God." But by 1875 the Community's businessmen once more seemed too busy for God. Voicing again his concern about this state of affairs, Noyes told the Oneidans that he hoped they would invite him "to take a more general control of our business." At the same time he made it clear that if they did so, he intended to have Theodore act as his deputy. Theodore, for his part, assured the Community that his spiritual recovery had advanced to a point where he was now prepared to storm "the heights of belief which may lie between this earth and heaven."

When Noyes's proposal was taken up at an evening meeting toward the end of 1875, many who spoke said that if Noyes wanted Theodore to act as his deputy in straightening out the Community's business affairs, that was good enough for them. Some speakers, having hoped and prayed for Theodore's complete spiritual reconciliation with his father, were warmer in their support. "I think Theodore has changed, and am very glad he has," one man said. "I believe he will change, and grow better and better." The meeting ended with a unanimous vote "to put our entire business into Mr. Noyes's hands, and accept heartily any agent he may select."

"We have had a good time with Theodore," William Woolworth wrote reassuringly to Noyes, "and I think the whole Community hail the dawn of a better day."

But the spirit of secularism was now widespread and deeply rooted, as evidenced by a letter Theodore wrote to a superintendent of one of the Community's enterprises. This young manager had balked at taking orders from Erastus Hamilton, one of Noyes's oldest and most trusted associates, who had succeeded Woolworth as father of the Oneida family. Hamilton, Theodore wrote, "possesses moral qualities which you decidedly lack, and I agree with Father that what is wanted . . . at present is less disorganized liberty which drifts toward secularism in business [and] more . . . sturdy moral sense." He added, "When those of the young men who have bright faculties drift away from spirituality, shirking the struggle we must undergo to purify our souls, and take refuge in the excitements of business, I think we are lucky to have some left of the sterner sort." In the face of this reproof, the young superintendent resigned his job and "came to Wallingford to separate himself from the temptations of the world and seek a new spiritual experience."

Victory in this one skirmish did not mean that the battle against secularism had been won. But Theodore's performance so impressed his father that after he had been on the job for only four months, Noyes made a dramatic appeal to his followers to greatly broaden the rather narrow authority Theodore had been granted. In a letter to the Oneida family, he said the time had come for him to hand over to Theodore the reins of Community government. While acknowledging the troubling disagreement on the "great question" of Theodore's fitness for the job, Noyes asked that he be allowed to settle the matter. "Can you not trust me in this, as you have trusted me before?" he pleaded. "Am I not more likely than any of you to understand the merits of the question at issue, and the awful responsibility I am under to find and do the will of God?"

A few years earlier, if Noyes had invoked the will of God in calling for a vote of confidence, there would not have been a dissenting voice. But now Hamilton and the other leaders at Oneida, worried about the Community's reaction, waited several weeks before having his letter read at an evening meeting. Their concern proved well-founded. While most of the Oneida family voted to go along with Noyes's proposal, there were many who were prepared to accept Theodore as manager of the Community's business affairs, but not as inheritor of his father's throne. In the absence of a consensus, the matter of Theodore's succession was put aside.

The serious erosion of Noyes's authority that this action demonstrated had many causes. They included, most obviously, the doubts about Noyes's judgment that had been raised by his stubborn and repeated insistence on having his son as his successor. Another cause, Theodore later wrote, was related to Theodore's own investigations of the spirit world. These had resulted in some of Noyes's oldest and most loyal disciples becoming addicted to spiritualism, finding in the voices of the dead, despite Noyes's disdain for the inhabitants of Hades, a new source of spiritual strength. Theodore went on to suggest that the "new habits of independent thought" to which this led had opened the way for another innovation: the holding of Community revival meetings. Toward the end of 1876, with Noyes's approval, two Oneidans who had had experience in organizing such meetings before joining the Community launched a revival at Oneida that went on for months. At Wallingford, there was no such activity, and some Oneidans criticized the Wallingford family for infidelity and worldliness. In reply, a nephew of Noyes, George Miller, assailed the revivalists at Oneida for "narrowness and legality"—that is, for making verbal professions of faith, rather than deeds, the measure of spiritual attainment. Noyes himself grew increasingly unhappy about the revival—he was concerned that, among other things, its leaders were setting themselves up as rival wielders of spiritual authority—and in the spring of 1877, at his request, the meetings were called off.

This did not sit well with the revivalists, and at Wallingford, where he was once again living, Theodore suggested to his father that drastic measures were called for if the "narrow"—that is, hypocritically pious—spirit now evidenced at Oneida were to be conquered. His plan was to move the members of the Wallingford branch to Oneida, where the reunited family would be subject to the personal leadership of himself and his father.

Noyes approved the plan, which he said was calculated to achieve the very objectives aimed at by the revivalists. "If we can get all hearts interested in gathering together here," he told the Oneida family, "it will be a conversion to the whole Community." The Oneidans agreed, and some forty Community members who had been living at Wallingford moved to Oneida, leaving behind a crew of twenty to run the only business now to be carried on there, the manufacture of spoons. In the euphoria that accompanied his return to Oneida and the uniting of the two families, Noyes seized the opportunity to declare, without calling for any discussion or for a vote, that he was designating Theodore as his successor. Theodore, he said, was determined "to lead the Community back . . . into the subordination of money-making to spiritual interests." He urged his followers to give their new leader their wholehearted support. As for himself, he said that he would devote himself to editing the *American Socialist,* as the Community's newspaper was now called. "I shall in a certain sense cease to be a member of this Community," he declared, "and pass into the position of an outside friend and counselor." In a brief message Theodore said he anticipated that the Community would now be unified in "pursuit of truth in the great circle which embraces Spiritualism, Christianity, Communism, stirpiculture, and science of every kind."

But that hope was not to be realized. In his short and troubled reign, Theodore proved incapable of coping with the deep divisions that were opening up at Oneida. And even though Noyes resumed in 1878 the throne he had so recently—and optimistically—vacated, those divisions continued to widen, and in less than two years the Community had voted itself out of existence.

Chapter 21

Soon after Theodore assumed his new office in May 1877 a disquieting rumor made the rounds at Oneida. Its burden was that he and his principal female helper, a young woman named Ann Hobart whom he had appointed as general women's superintendent—ordinarily referred to as the "mother" of the Community—intended to set themselves up in a villa overlooking the Hudson River. From there, or from a palatial yacht they were said to be planning to buy, they would govern the Community by a system of written orders and administrative reports.

While there was no truth to the rumor, its nature and currency reflected the widespread antagonism that Theodore had provoked in his first months as leader. His critics were disturbed by, among other things, his attachment to "legalism," a term with a distinctly pejorative connotation in his father's lexicon. The elder Noyes repeatedly emphasized that, under Bible Communism, conduct was to be governed not by laws, but by divine guidance. In practice, this meant submitting to the judgment of God's deputy—Noyes. In talks at evening meetings, and in remarks at mutual-criticism sessions and in private meetings with those who sought his advice, Noyes let his followers know exactly what God expected of them.

Such personal and charismatic leadership was not to Theodore's taste—or within his capabilities. Unlike his father, he could not speak with divine authority. And while he was highly intelligent and had shown himself to be a brilliant teacher, he notably lacked his father's mastery of the arts of leadership. As a member of the Community remembered Theodore, he "had no stomach for meting out criticism and shrank from the personal administration of discipline." In his new position he seemed bent on subjecting the Community to rules and regulations of the kind his father had with rare exceptions scorned. To combat laziness and shirking, he announced that members would be required to turn in written reports showing what—and how much—work they had done each day. The new rule applied even to children. A graduate of the Children's House recalled being given "little pads, printed and lined, so that we could record each hour of the day. I can remember our enthusiasm over being able to do the same thing we saw grown folks doing."

A similar plan was put into effect to tighten the leadership's control of members' sex lives. In recent years, the old rule that all proposals for sexual interviews were to be submitted to Harriet Skinner, or to some other person high up in the Community's spiritual hierarchy, had been allowed to lapse. A degree of secrecy, or privacy, had crept into the business of sexual pairing, and couples had been forming liaisons that in earlier days would have been headed off—or, if entered into in the face of official disapproval, would have subjected the lovers to a powerful jolt of mutual criticism. At an evening meeting soon after he took office, Theodore spoke of the pressing need for a stricter "organization" of sexual life at Oneida. A few days later, at a women's meeting, Ann Hobart explained what he had in mind. She said he was particularly worried about the young women, some of whom, in his view, were damaging their health—presumably by too much sex—while others were being unfairly neglected as sexual partners. Still others, she quoted Theodore as saying, were spiritually retarded because they were being allowed to flout the rule of ascending fellowship. To get sex back on its old footing, Ann continued, all invitations for sexual "visits" were from then on to be extended only through "responsible women" acting as intermediaries. If an intermediary had any doubt as to the propriety of a visit, she was to consult one of three designated leaders. Even invitations that were deemed proper were to be reported regularly, in writing, to Theodore. Although this plan seemed to meet with general approval at the women's meeting, it was, in fact, resented by some young people as a restriction on the freedom they had gained from the shackles of ascending fellowship. More important, from the standpoint of Theodore's ability to command the loyalty and respect of the Community, some older members also were offended by the new regulatory scheme. While generally approving of its object, they regarded the formal logging in of sexual liaisons as an unacceptable deviation from John Noyes's insistence on government by grace and inspiration, rather than by law.

To the disappointment of many members it was also clear that the elder Noyes had been oversanguine in his spiritual prognosis for Theodore. In talks with Frank Wayland-Smith at this time, Theodore acknowledged that he did not consider Christ the son of God and asserted that, since he believed implicitly in Darwin's theory of natural selection, he saw no need to seek for a creator of the universe. Wayland-Smith noted in his journal that while Theodore did not try to convert others to his way of thinking, he was setting what many members considered a thoroughly bad example for the young by pointedly taking "little or no part in the religious exercises of the family, such as the Confession of Christ, expressions of faith, etc."

✦   ✦   ✦

What doomed Theodore's administration, however, was neither his fussy legalism nor, in Wayland-Smith's words, his "perversion from the faith of his father." Rather, it was his relationship with Ann Hobart. An attractive woman with curly hair, a beautiful complexion, and striking blue eyes, she had impressed Theodore, at the time of his investigation of spiritualism, with her gifts as a clairvoyant and "writing medium." She was also gifted with great intelligence and possessed a strong will, traits that impressed not only Theodore, but his father as well. When Noyes's younger sister, Charlotte Miller, died in 1874, Ann, then twenty-seven, had been appointed to succeed her in the important job of chief adviser to the girls and young women of the Community. Subsequently she and Theodore had begun a love affair so intense and protracted as quite possibly to have laid them open, had they held less exalted positions in the Community, to the serious charge of having fallen prey to the marriage spirit.

Theodore's appointment of Ann as women's superintendent, a job in which she was so closely associated with him in the management of affairs that the Community was in effect being ruled by a duumvirate, was not universally popular. Many women looked on Ann as a ruthless intriguer. She was said to have abused her position as counselor to the young women by separating them from lovers whom she wanted as sexual partners for herself. Noyes's niece Tirzah Miller complained that one of her former lovers, by whom she had had a child, had been driven out of the Community by Ann's plotting, and Noyes had to use all his formidable powers of persuasion to talk her out of leaving the Community herself rather than submit to Ann's rule. Ann also antagonized some older people, including the elder Noyes, by the disrespectful way in which she brushed aside her predecessor as Community mother, Noyes's sister Harriet. For the time being, however, having asserted that Theodore should have a free hand in picking his cabinet, Noyes kept his misgivings to himself.

But in the fall of 1877 he decided that Ann would have to go. She had come to him with disturbing accusations against Theodore, including the charge that he wanted to destroy complex marriage by doing away with male continence. Without confronting Theodore, Noyes made up his mind that the accusations were false or greatly exaggerated. In his view, Ann was simply trying to discredit Theodore as a means of tightening her hold over him. Noyes never made clear just how this scheme was supposed to work. But he was firmly persuaded that Ann exercised an evil influence on Theodore, that she was largely responsible for the legalistic tone of his administration, and that she must resign. He further concluded that, for Theodore's sake, the couple must be separated.

On the last day of 1877, Noyes wrote to Theodore, who had gone to Wallingford to be with Ann while she recuperated from an operation. He said there was widespread dissatisfaction with Ann and tactfully suggested that she was not in good enough health to fill the demanding job that had been given her. Her best course, he wrote, was to resign of her own free will and "subside into a quiet position as a good, humble woman in ordinary membership."

When there was no immediate reply from Theodore, Noyes took his case against Ann to the family at Oneida. He said that he had become seriously alarmed by the talk he had had with her six weeks before, when she had tried to convince him that Theodore "was acting directly contrary to my ways and wishes." Among other things, Noyes said, she had accused Theodore of becoming so infatuated with a certain young woman that he had tried to "appropriate" her exclusively for himself, in defiance of one of the bedrock principles of complex marriage. Forced to decide whether to "give up my confidence in Theodore or my confidence in Ann," Noyes said he had concluded that his duty was to support Theodore, and to "relieve him from his connection with her"—a connection which, according to Ann herself, Theodore had once described as "the greatest misfortune of his life." To show why Theodore might have felt this way, Noyes produced a statement from a former intimate of Ann's who said she had been shocked by the violence of Ann's quarrels with Theodore, and by the way she had belittled and bullied him. "She made a good deal of fun of his doctoring," the statement said, "and really talked very disrespectfully of him . . . I can scarcely remember an instance of his beating her in their discussions."

Noyes's decision that Ann must be separated both from her job and from her lover drew an anguished appeal from Theodore. In a letter to his father he admitted that Ann had made mistakes, but argued that often they were not really *her* mistakes. The same personality traits that had made her so effective as a spirit medium, he explained, led her at times, without realizing what she was doing, to act as a medium for the thoughts and feelings of living persons with whom she had been in close contact. Thus when she criticized or attacked him, she was doing so under hostile influences. If he deferred to her at such times it was only because he had learned that was the best way to cope with her moods, and "I have always gained my point by waiting until she had got into my spirit." In denouncing him to his father, Theodore went on, Ann had been under the "mesmeric influence" of two Community members—"legal moralists," as he described them—who could not tolerate his free-thinking agnosticism. Asserting that Ann "is now strongly bound to me," Theodore said he could see nothing to be gained "by separating me from such a friend as she has been." He concluded with the somewhat unconvincing suggestion of a new role for Ann—acting as a bridge between father and son across which "we can send messages of peace and concord."

Noyes, unimpressed, returned to the attack with new and harsher accusations. He and Theodore, he told the Oneida family, had exactly opposite theories about Theodore and Ann's relationship. Using a term that he had taught his followers to employ as a synonym for manipulation, Noyes said that while Theodore might insist that he had all along been "psychologizing" Ann, the shoe was on the other foot: "I hold that she has psychologized him from first to last and is the cause not only of the late unprincipled conduct which she complains of in him but of his whole departure from the faith of the Community." Ann's psychologizing of Theodore, he said, dated back ten years, to a time when Ann had undergone a religious conversion for which Theodore had felt chiefly responsible. "Nothing is so flattering to a spiritual man as to have an attractive woman become his convert," Noyes said, adding that Theodore's enthrallment by Ann reminded him of Abigail Merwin. "She was my special convert and bright particular star," he recalled, "and her fascination cost me years of delusions and sufferings."

As to Ann's susceptibility to mesmeric influences, Noyes said she had all along been under the sway of her father, a hardened nonbeliever named Seba Bailey, and of her brother Daniel, who had left the Community some years before after drinking too deeply of German rationalism. Noyes conceded that Ann had tried to escape their influence, going so far as to take her mother's name, Hobart. But she had been unable to throw off the Bailey character, one of whose chief traits, Noyes said, was diotrephiasis, the "who-shall-be-greatest mania," as he once defined the term. Noyes, a believer in phrenology, observed that even the shape of Ann's head was "of the Bailey type, strong in the love of power and weak in conscience and veneration." As a result of Theodore's "amative and spiritualistic connection" with Ann, he had been captured by the atheism of the Bailey family. Back in 1867, when Theodore thought he had brought Ann into unity with Christ, Noyes declared, he had in fact "plunged into the Bailey spirit, and that was the last we have seen of him in his own proper nature."

In the face of this barrage, Ann's normally formidable defenses crumbled. She confessed that for years she had taken pleasure in torturing her lovers, and that Theodore had been her principal victim. "I can think of a hundred times when I have by my ugliness made him suffer horribly," she said. She added that when they quarreled, she would hold out until Theodore came to her to make up. Then, "instead of being softened by his better spirit and example, it only hardened me and made me tyrannize over him the more." She said she had tried to prevent a complete reconciliation between Theodore and his father because "my mean and jealous heart was afraid of losing his love."

Some Oneidans were hopeful that, with Ann removed from office and no longer working to pit father against son, and with Theodore blessedly free from the Bailey influence, he would now come into his own as leader. But Theodore had had enough. Still attached to Ann, and angered by his father's treatment of her, he resigned his post, and at the beginning of 1878 the elder Noyes took back into his own hands the active management of Community affairs.

Moving quickly to relax some of the tensions generated by Theodore's administration, Noyes abolished the hated system of sexual bookkeeping and resumed his traditional role as chief enforcer of the unwritten rules of complex marriage. At the same time he took steps to bring Oneida's business affairs more directly under his—and the

Community's—control, specifying that all principal business managers must henceforth regularly submit themselves, as in earlier years, to the discipline of mutual criticism. Despite the frustration of his ambitions for Theodore, he seemed buoyant and cheerful as he made plans for the profitable entertainment of visitors to Oneida in the coming summer. Two prominent clergymen had just called down the wrath of God on the Community's depraved and shocking sexual practices, and Noyes observed delightedly that, if the past was any guide, this would bring even bigger crowds than usual to Oneida. "Mr. Noyes's mind," a diarist noted, "is full of projects for making money during the coming summer. . . . He intends to give daily concerts and have the children on the stage, and besides this he is going to have the outdoor brass band play twice every day and the military band for marching and an organization to play for dances." For his own entertainment, Noyes, whose direct dependence on divine guidance once again seemed to free him from the restraints of consistency, enthusiastically embraced the rituals of table-rapping and mediumistic trances that he had once scorned. Daily séances were held in his room, and he announced happily—if cryptically—that he now considered himself first and foremost a medium, rather than a preacher or writer.

Meanwhile, Theodore, at his father's request, had come back to Oneida from Wallingford. Without a job, he kept to himself, stayed away from the evening meetings, and had theological arguments with his father in writing and through intermediaries. Ann had hoped to follow him to Oneida, but the elder Noyes would not allow this. Giving up on Theodore and the Community, she got in touch with the apostate Joseph Skinner. While he was still at Oneida, Ann had had a child by him. She now invited him to visit her at Wallingford (a flagrant violation of an unwritten Community rule), and soon afterward she left to marry him and live in New Haven.

Theodore, blaming his father for driving Ann out of the Community, decided once again to leave Oneida for good. In the spring of 1878, withdrawing $3,500 from the Community treasury that had been left him by a relative, he went to New York. He had become an enthusiast for the therapeutic virtues of Turkish baths—everybody was taking them at Oneida—and in New York he entered into a partnership with a former Oneidan, Abel Easton, who had been running a Turkish bath there.

But history repeated itself. He quickly grew homesick and asked to be allowed to return to Oneida. Despite all that had happened, he and his father still clung to the hope that he might someday be reinstated as Community leader. They could not ignore, however, what Frank Wayland-Smith described in his journal as "a strong prejudice" against such an effort. So when Noyes urged at an evening meeting that Theodore, for the second time in five years, be readmitted to the Community, he promised he would never again arbitrarily appoint him as leader. Theodore would be an ordinary, rank-and-file member, and any influence he might gain would have to be earned by good faith and good works. Even after his graceless performance as the Community's leader, he was still widely admired and liked. "The Rubicon is passed," a young woman at Oneida wrote to a friend at Wallingford. "Theodore is again our brother, and there was a unanimous vote in favor of his acceptance. Father's face shone as he said fervently, 'I thank God for this unity.' "

*I*n the summer of 1878, six months after the collapse of Theodore Noyes's unhappy administration, the *American Socialist* proclaimed that not for years had there been "so great a degree of harmony in the Community." The assertion was by way of answer to a series of articles in the *New York Times* suggesting that the Community was falling apart. Unlike most critical accounts of Oneida, the shafts fired by the *Times* were embarrassingly close to the mark. Whatever might appear on the surface, the inner life of the Community was deeply troubled. More and more Oneidans were becoming disenchanted with Bible Communism as it had been practiced for nearly thirty years. The grounds of their unhappiness differed, but they had one thing in common. They no longer felt the unquestioning confidence in the leadership of John Humphrey Noyes that Noyes himself once accurately described as "the true anchor of the Community."

The waning of Noyes's authority was in part a consequence of a profound change over the years in the tone and intensity of religious life at Oneida. The Community's founders had shared, and been united by, the exhilarating conviction that they were a chosen people; having freed themselves from sin, they could look forward to achieving immortality in their own lifetimes. But as the years went by and the kingdom of heaven, which once had seemed so close at hand, failed to arrive, that prospect inevitably dimmed. Stirpiculture, Noyes's audacious plan to unite the world with God by breeding a spiritually superior race of men and women—a design that might take tens or hundreds of generations to work out—was a tacit acknowledgment that the Resurrection was a distant hope, not an imminent reality.

As the kingdom of heaven receded like a mirage, there was a fundamental shift in the way the Oneidans looked at themselves and the world—and at God. Despite Noyes's efforts to sustain the intense religious feeling of former years, the tone of communal life became more secular. As more and more Oneidans went off to college or traveled around the country on business—and as Oneidans came to take for granted the amenities of middle-class life, with servants to wash the clothes and hired hands to muck out the stables—the sense of being set apart from the sinful world outside inevitably diminished, and the spiritual purity of the Community's early days was adulterated by a relaxed worldliness.

Many Oneidans slipped into disbelief. Others fought valiantly against the devil of doubt, and sometimes triumphed. One of these was a woman named Mary Louise Prindle. In a letter to Theodore Noyes encouraging him to fight his way free from the toils of atheism, she described her own hard-won victory over the enemy. "I know what it is," she wrote, "to doubt the existence of God and to struggle day and night for months and years even, with the powers of darkness." But few of her contemporaries—she was thirty-seven—and even fewer of the youngest generation of Oneidans had much stomach for the agonies of spiritual combat. Writing about other religious communities, but plainly with Oneida in mind, Noyes once observed sadly that the younger generation of communitarians were "very apt to assume the faith of the fathers in an easy, superficial way, which yields as they grow up to a fascination with free-thinking. The world does not seem so bad to them as it did to those who fought their way out of it."

In the altered spiritual climate at Oneida, even some older members who had never been tempted by free-thinking now found themselves having doubts about Bible Communism. Among the doubters was Harriet Worden, a strong-minded and highly intelligent woman who had worked closely with Noyes for years as editor of the *Circular*. She had had a child by him, and throughout her life had looked to him as both lover and spiritual guide. Her affection for Noyes and her belief in his God were unwavering. But she had come to question the validity of a system in which the most intimate relations—including the relations between mothers and children—were under external rule, even though the ruler was Noyes. "It is very curious . . ." she wrote to a friend, "that often & often I have wondered to myself . . . if I had chosen the true life; or if after all I was . . . devoting my energies to a mistaken doctrine." She went on to confess that "sometimes my personal ambition has made me picture to myself more scope & liberty outside; and . . . I have pictured a home of harmonious family relations, without the interference of others." But to break away from the Community—"to turn from it to the world for happiness" —was, she wrote, unthinkable: "I have said to myself, *I have chosen* the Community, I *cannot change now*; therefore I must devote my life to making it what I think a community should be."

Not surprisingly, Noyes's insistence on seeing Theodore installed as his successor led many Oneidans for the first time to question his political judgment. This led, in turn, to a questioning of his divine inspiration: if his judgment was so badly flawed that he could not see Theodore's unfitness as a leader, could he really be carrying out the will of God? Some Oneidans, bypassing Noyes, now turned directly to God for spiritual guidance. In a letter to a friend at Oneida, a woman living at Wallingford wrote that she herself was determined to "stick to the good medium"—that is, Noyes—"through which my greatest happiness comes." But she added that one of her close friends "says she goes to God for herself—doesn't need to go to Mr. Noyes." This was, of course, a profoundly subversive notion, for it was only by asserting his divinely ordained right to interpret God's will that Noyes had succeeded, forty years earlier, in rescuing Perfectionism from the moral swamps of anarchy and license.

Noyes's ability to command the loyalty and obedience of his followers was further weakened by the decline in his once powerful appeal as a lover and sexual partner. (Indeed, as it turned out, sex was the principal rock on which the Community foundered.) As noted earlier, Noyes had almost always assigned to himself the sexual initiation of young girls as they reached puberty. That initiation, which entailed the careful training of these adolescents as sexual partners, could extend over a period of months, during which Noyes's pupils, with few exceptions, formed strong attachments to him as a lover, surrogate father, teacher, and spiritual guide. Long after their training had been completed, Noyes's former pupils regularly asked his advice about sexual partners and at times, on his recommendation and in deference to the rule of ascending fellowship, accepted as lovers men they might not otherwise have chosen. Noyes thus had the power to reward and punish his male followers, and Theodore Noyes, who for all his shortcomings as an administrator had a shrewd grasp of sexual politics at Oneida, saw this as the key to effective government of the Community. For the system to work, he wrote years later, it had been essential for his father to secure the complete obedience, in sexual matters, of "the young and attractive women who form the focus toward which all the sexual rays converge." But as Noyes's great sexual magnetism weakened with age—in 1878 he was in his sixty-seventh year—he could no longer command that obedience. Teenage girls were bored and sometimes even repelled by Noyes in his role as "first husband" and saw no reason to subsequently seek or follow his advice concerning their sexual choices. By 1879, as far as the youngest generation of Oneidans of both sexes was concerned, ascending fellowship—and with it the power that it placed in Noyes's hands—was virtually dead. The young, Frank Wayland-Smith wrote in his journal, "are fast breaking away from all sense of moral accountability. They are independent, scorning advice."

✦   ✦   ✦

As Noyes's once unchallenged authority declined, there was mounting criticism of his administration, and an opposition party gradually took form. Its principal leader was James William Towner. Before coming to Oneida, Towner had been a universalist minister, a lawyer, a municipal-court judge, and a captain in the Union army who lost an eye at the battle of Pea Ridge. He had also been a member for some years of the notorious Berlin Heights Society. Located in Ohio, fifty miles west of Cleveland, Berlin Heights was a loose grouping of families whose members practiced free love, switching partners as the spirit (or the flesh) moved them. Sex at Berlin Heights had nothing to do with God and was completely unregulated—resulting, as Noyes and his followers saw it, in moral anarchy and unbridled sensuality. In 1866, announcing that he had repented of his sins as a free-lover, Towner applied for membership at Oneida. But although he and his wife visited the Community in an attempt to persuade the Oneidans that they had gotten the poison of free love out of their systems, the Community was skeptical and the Towners were turned down. In 1873, after several more visits, Towner applied again. Thanks to the teachings of Bible Communism and the inspiration of the Oneida Community, he wrote, he "had become so filled with the idea that only as a means of glorifying God is [sexual] intercourse permissible, that I have come to hate and abominate even the virtues, as well as the vices, if I may so speak, of my former sexual life of passional indulgence, as of the devil himself." This was what the Oneidans wanted to hear, and the following year Towner, his wife and children, and half a dozen relatives, bringing with them a dowry of $14,000, were accepted as members of the Community.

At Oneida, Towner's impressive legal credentials—he was generally referred to as Judge Towner—together with his obvious intelligence and firm grasp of practical affairs, quickly gained him a place high in the Community's political hierarchy. A handsome man in his early fifties, with delicate, aristocratic features and deep-set eyes, he handled the Community's legal business, and in 1878, after Theodore's resignation as leader, Noyes picked him as one of his principal deputies in the management of Oneida's business enterprises.

But within a year Towner was calling for fundamental changes in the government of the Community, with or without Noyes's consent. Noyes, for his part, had come to view Towner as the carrier of a "terrible spiritual disease," whose symptoms included "political strife, envies, jealousies, diotrephiasis, unbelief . . . and all sorts of turbulences and calamities." By 1879 the disease had infected a number of other persons who played a leading role in Community affairs. They included Towner's most influential ally, William Hinds, the managing editor of the *American Socialist.* For years Hinds had been one of Noyes's two closest male confidants among the generation that had grown up in the Community, along with the diarist Frank Wayland-Smith, who was the business manager of the *American Socialist* and, at this time, moderator of the evening meetings at Oneida. Gifted with formidable powers of memory and concentration—at the age of fourteen he had memorized, for one dollar, all forty pages of Noyes's essay on "Salvation from Sin in this World"—Hinds was a graduate of Yale's Sheffield Scientific School and the author of *American Communities,* one of the best accounts ever written of the nineteenth century's experiments, both religious and secular, in communal living.

One of Towner's and Hinds's chief quarrels with Noyes was over his management of complex marriage. They saw no reason why Noyes, or one of the tight inner circle of advisers to whom he now occasionally delegated the task, should monopolize the sexual initiation of young girls. The Townerites further argued that Noyes had no right, in the name of ascending fellowship, to bully young women into rejecting certain men as sexual partners and accepting others. They agreed that the sexual activities of minors should be regulated, but insisted that the "controlling influence" should be exerted by their parents, not by Noyes. Adults should be free to sleep with anyone they liked.

Although this proposal to abolish the rule of ascending fellowship was put forward as a means of liberating the women of the Community from sexual tyranny, it is likely that Towner and his male followers had other motives. As Theodore Noyes suggested years afterward, the challenge to his father's administration of complex marriage was in reality a move to gain free access to the young and sexually most exciting women. Control of their choice of sexual partners, Theodore wrote, "was pictured in the inner recesses of the minds of all persons of real intelligence, as a matter not of committees and councils, but of individuals and men—in short a prize to be contended for."

The Townerites' attacks on Noyes were aimed not only at the system he had devised for regulating the sex lives of his followers. They also wanted to do away with the benevolent theocracy under which the Community had lived for so many years and to replace it with an elected government directly responsible to the membership. This was a transformation that Noyes could hardly have been expected to sanction. While he might have consented to changes in the rules of complex marriage and the ascending fellowship, he could not have accepted complete democracy without tacitly conceding that his divine writ no longer ran. "I have told you more than once," he said to Wayland-Smith, "that I have not been put in my present position by the members of this Community. The real stockholders in our institution are the men and women of the invisible world . . . and it is to them that I am accountable. I am resolved not to relinquish one iota of the authority they have given me."

There was another discordant note in the harmony of which the *American Socialist* had boasted. While the Townerites agreed with Noyes on the great virtue of complex marriage—in Towner's view, it promoted "delicacy, modesty, chastity, and self-denial"—other Oneidans, consisting mainly of women in their twenties and thirties, were arguing that it might be a good thing to give up complex marriage altogether in favor of monogamy. In part this was a result of stirpiculture, which had brought couples into longer, and in some cases far deeper, relationships than had been acceptable in the old days, when virtually no one was having children at Oneida. The Community is "tied up in hard knots consisting of family groups," a diarist observed four years before the Community's breakup, adding that "love"—she meant the shifting partnerships of complex marriage—"is stagnant." Lovers infected with the marriage spirit, who would once have been forcibly immersed in an icy bath of criticism, or even geographically separated, were in these laxer days allowed to drift into long-lasting affairs. "The more bold and ultra" of the younger members, Wayland-Smith wrote, "coolly declare in favor of a monogamic relation," taking the heretical position that "one man is enough for one woman." Some drew encouragement from Theodore Noyes, who had staked out an all-but-exclusive claim to the affections of a young woman named Marion Burnham. (He told an inquirer that he didn't mind her taking other lovers as long as their trysts took place on weekdays between 7:00 A.M. and 3:30 P.M., when he was off at work.) Disenchantment with complex marriage grew rapidly in the early months of 1879, when the mounting opposition to Noyes's leadership prompted fears that the Community was falling apart. To many young women, worried about the future of their children, conventional marriage now had a new and powerful appeal.*

✦   ✦   ✦

Noyes at first seemed bent on ignoring the gathering storm. He did, it is true, urge his followers to try to recapture the spirit of earlier and simpler days at Oneida. As a means to that end he enthusiastically backed the establishment of a family chain-making business, in which he recommended that everyone take part, and which he said would be "an industrial reunion for men, women, and children." But any public airing of the issues dividing the Community was ruled out by

---

* In February 1879 Wayland-Smith wrote Noyes that he had "endeavored to persuade some of my young lady acquaintances against the present monogamic tendency . . . but it is immediately assumed that I am hard up in regard to sexual gratification, and owing I suppose to human nature, there is always a temptation to pinch a man as badly as possible if he is thought to be needy in this respect. Therefore my efforts seemed only to aggravate the difficulty, and I left off."

Noyes, who changed the format of the evening meetings to emphasize entertainment and to limit discussions to matters unlikely to arouse strong feelings. One night the topic was gum-chewing: where and when it was acceptable. On another night it was decided that it was all right for elderly members, and those who were ill, to lie down on the back seats in the gallery at evening meetings, provided they didn't snore. There was a lecture one night on "the universal tendency to spherical forms." An old custom was revived of bringing children to the evening meetings; they were ranged on the stage behind a newly constructed platform on which Noyes sat, with the moderator, Frank Wayland-Smith, on one side, and the evening's designated newspaper reader on the other. "Have we not had enough of law-making and politics on this floor?" Noyes asked. "Is it not time to give the lead to the social element, and go for a glorious mixture of men, women, and children with one another and the angels of God?" At this time, Wayland-Smith noted, Noyes was "jovial, hearty . . . talking with everybody." When a friend told him that some people didn't find the meetings religious enough, Noyes laughed and, referring to an Oneidan known for aggressive piety, said mischievously, "I give them a few spoonfuls of religion from time to time to keep such folks as Mr. Burnham from despair."

But the tranquillity of the evening meetings did not reflect the true state of affairs. A loyal supporter of Noyes, noting with approval that there were now "no miserable discussions, no dreary pauses," wrote sadly to a friend at Wallingford that "the only drawback to our having the most homelike and interesting meetings is the spirit of evil-thinking that is constantly brooding over the Community." Noyes, who for a time either failed to perceive—or chose to ignore—the mounting animosity of his opponents, was rudely jolted when one of Oneida's business managers, Charles Burt, complained to him that Theodore had been squandering large sums of Community money on an unauthorized business venture, the manufacture of malleable iron. Burt angrily accused Noyes of having "prostituted the finances of the Community to the pleasure of his son." Asserting that 75 percent of the Community disapproved of Theodore's new business, Burt told

Noyes that he—Noyes—had no knowledge of how people in the Community really felt. Noyes, after taking some quick soundings, was deeply disturbed. He told Wayland-Smith that he might "have to ask to be dismissed from the Community," adding gloomily, "I don't know but I shall die." When he went on to speak about asking the Community to disband, Wayland-Smith told him he must be suffering from the hypo, or depression, which Noyes had taught his followers to look on as a species of hypochondria. Noyes said no, it was just that he felt unable to cope with the spreading disaffection. The Community wanted—and needed—a new leader, he said, and he would "have to go somewhere else and take with me all who want to live as I do."*

Noyes, who thought better of this scheme—at least for the moment—would no doubt have been even more depressed if he had known of a new accusation circulating in the Community. It was said that in his role as first husband he was more concerned with his own sexual gratification than with the proper spiritual and sexual education of the pubescent girls whom he introduced to sex. "The charge which has been made against you," Wayland-Smith wrote to Noyes after his departure for Canada, "is that of sexual impurity and harmful and

---

* At times, during his final months at Oneida, Noyes evidently comforted himself with the thought that, no matter what happened to the Community to which he had given so much of his life, his place in history was assured. That seems to have been the underlying theme of a conversation he had with Wayland-Smith, which the latter, though long accustomed to Noyes's sometimes Delphic utterances, found "occult, or at least obscure." "This morning," he wrote, "Mr. Noyes came to my room and, sitting down in my rocking chair, said, 'I don't know exactly what I came up here to say, but I felt a ripple here (laying his hand on his chest), and thought I would begin and perhaps I should find what I wanted to say.' " Noyes then asserted, referring to his meeting with William Lloyd Garrison forty years before, that it was through his (Noyes's) mediumship that God had animated the abolitionists, and that his (Noyes's) inspiration had "afterwards [been] distributed so that it became epidemic and brought on the war which freed the negroes." Noyes, Wayland-Smith went on to report, "claims to have been and still be the central and principal medium of this power and that, therefore, he is sure to be at the center of whatever movements are before the country."

demoralizing practices"—practices whose precise nature does not appear in the record. Noyes was warmly defended by, among others, Wayland-Smith, who told the Community (also after Noyes's departure) that, in initiating young girls into sex, Noyes had invariably acted from "a deep philosophical view and not from passion." It was true that in recent years young girls had not always been as entranced with Noyes as a sexual tutor as had their predecessors, and Wayland-Smith noted that there had been a lot of loose talk among the young about Noyes's "alleged sexual eccentricities and excesses." But no one cared—or dared—to confront Noyes with their accusations, which were almost certainly false or highly exaggerated. The charges may, in fact, have largely been projections of their own improper conduct by men who had themselves sexually exploited—or so Noyes later asserted—young girls who had not yet gone through the official rites of passage over which Noyes had traditionally presided.

Although accusations that Noyes had been guilty of sexual misconduct were never publicly discussed before his departure for Canada—and until then were probably unknown to many people at Oneida—they added an ugly undertone to the chorus of criticism now directed at him. The opposition was strengthened by his own increasingly dictatorial manner. "He has grown so positive in all his beliefs that he does not care to hear the ideas of others," Wayland-Smith noted. "When he sits down for a talk he delivers his opinions and almost always rises immediately upon concluding . . . not waiting for any reply." By the spring of 1879 the evening meetings, despite Noyes's determination to insulate them from politics and controversy, grew noisy and rancorous. There was no real discussion of the issues of leadership and power that were splitting and threatening to destroy the Community, but minor matters became occasions for angry partisan quarrels. The civility that in the past had marked even the most heated debates was shattered. In the gallery at evening meetings, instead of elderly people stretched out and drowsing on the benches, members of the opposition now occupied the seats to jeer at Noyes and his supporters. Such rude behavior was not confined to formal meetings. "Open scorn and rebellion were shown in *many* places," an Oneidan recalled. Noyes himself was deeply hurt. At one of the last evening meetings that he attended, he said sadly that "party feeling" had affected daily manners to such an extent that people too often "avert their faces, evidently not liking to look at me, and take some pains not to pass a word with me." He went on, "Even if we hate one another, would it not be better to pass one another pleasantly, and with a smile if we can?" It was unpleasant, he continued, to en- counter people he had been "on very pleasant and familiar terms with, and see it manifest that they had rather not look at me and not sit by me at table. I don't know but that I may be tempted to feel so myself. But I have made up my mind that I will not act so."

✦　　✦　　✦

The pressures that sent Noyes fleeing into exile came from the world outside Oneida as well as from within. For years Oneida had been under intermittent fire from crusaders for moral purity. In the early 1870s, Anthony Comstock, founder of the New York Society for the Suppression of Vice, persuaded Congress to classify as lascivious and obscene all information about birth control, and to forbid its dissem- ination through the mails. In response, the Oneidans eliminated all references to their contraceptive practices from the Community's newspaper and withdrew from general circulation such publications as Noyes's *Essay on Male Continence*. Prudery was on the march in Amer- ica, and it was only a matter of time before the defenders of public decency would train their guns on Oneida. The leader of the attack was John W. Mears, a Presbyterian minister who taught at Hamilton College in nearby Clinton, New York. Launching his campaign in 1873 with an article deploring the "corrupt concubinage" of the Oneidans, Mears seemed particularly annoyed because Oneida was regularly visited not only by "throngs of the curious or indifferent," but "even by Sunday school excursions." Over the next few years, Mears and coalitions of clergymen whom he rallied to the cause reg- ularly denounced Oneida as, among other things, a hotbed of harlotry, a "moral defilement," "this Utopia of obscenity," and a "pernicious institution which rests . . . on a system of organized fanaticism and lust." In general, the local press, struck by the sobriety, industry, and prosperity of the sinners at Oneida, continued to show little sympathy for their critics. As the Fulton *Times* explained, "A foul and corrupt fountain cannot send forth a stream so clean and thrifty, respectable and peaceful."

In the winter of 1879, a group of Episcopal, Presbyterian, and Methodist clergymen convened in Syracuse, mainly at Mears's prompting, to consider what could be done about sex at Oneida. Some fifty clergymen were in attendance, along with William Hinds, who was present as a special correspondent for the two Syracuse dailies, both of which took a dim view of the proceedings. "Damn it, what do they want to do?" the editor of the Syracuse *Standard* asked Hinds. "Damn it, why don't they mind their own business?" Although speakers at the convention vied with one another in the fervor with which they condemned the Community's sexual practices, there was confusion as to what, if anything, could be done to stamp them out. The frustrated delegates adjourned after appointing a committee to look into "all questions of fact and law" relating to the Community and to recommend appropriate action. One suggestion was made by a prominent Syracuse lawyer who attended the convention. His notion was to get the state legislature to amend the statutory definition of disorderly persons by adding the words "all persons living in concupiscence and adultery." But although an attempt was made to get such a change adopted at that spring's session of the legislature, a friendly local legislator assured the Oneidans that there had been no support for the proposition. The press, for its part, generally shared the view of the Syracuse editor who had told Hinds the clergy should keep their noses out of Oneida's affairs. *Puck*, to give just one example, ran a cartoon showing a group of self-righteous ministers pointing at Oneida and declaring, "Oh, dreadful! They dwell in peace and harmony and have no church scandals. They must be wiped out."

Noyes and his followers had long argued persuasively that their sexual arrangements were beyond the reach of the law. As the Utica *Herald* warned the outraged clergymen assembled at Syracuse, "The most careful scrutiny has failed to construct a case which would bring either the individuals or the community within reach of the courts." In the minds of many people who disapproved of the way the Oneidans were said to carry on, the fact that they did so in private, and in obedience to religious conviction, should entitle them to immunity from prosecution. As Theodore Noyes later pointed out, the local district attorneys were friendly, and, in any case, he added dryly, "The Community laid out too much money in the neighborhood to make the idea of driving it away popular."

But in late June 1879, for the first time in almost thirty years, there was a threat of prosecution. TESTIMONY BEING TAKEN, the Syracuse *Standard* trumpeted in a fanfare of headlines, WHICH STAMPS THE ONEIDA COMMUNITY AS FAR WORSE IN THEIR PRACTICES THAN THE POLYGAMISTS OF UTAH. . . . THE ARREST OF NOYES . . . IS TO BE MADE AND HIS TRIAL TO BE PUSHED BY GENTLEMEN—the paper failed to name them—WHO WILL BE PREPARED TO GO TO THE VERY FOUNDATION OF THIS THING. The following night Noyes crept downstairs in his stocking feet and began the panicky flight to Canada from which he was never to return.

◆   ◆   ◆

Noyes always insisted that it was the threat of prosecution and the imminent danger not only to him but to the Community at large that had sent him into exile. "I only know," he wrote, "that indictments, imprisonment, mobs and even deaths were in the air at Oneida when I took my flight to the north."

But on investigation it became clear that there was, in fact, no threat of prosecution. Mears himself told a reporter for the New York *World*, "I doubt if we do much at the law," adding candidly that he didn't know what they could do even if they wanted to. The *World* reporter also interviewed the district attorney of Oneida County. When he suggested that the clergymen hoped to prove that Oneidans abused their women, the district attorney said "he did not think an outside body like the committee of clergymen would be competent to take up such a prosecution and furnish evidence in a matter that did not materially concern them." Noyes alone seems to have sensed that deaths were in the air. If fear of being put on trial and jailed had been the only reason for his clandestine departure for Canada, he could have returned to Oneida when it became apparent that he had nothing to fear from the law. The main reason he chose not to return to Oneida, it seems clear, is that he had found his position there intolerable. Months before the Syracuse *Standard* had printed its sensational (and false) report of imminent prosecution, at a time when Noyes and the Community were taking a relaxed and even humorous view of the abortive crusade mounted by Mears and his clerical lieutenants, Noyes had talked despairingly of giving Oneida up to his opponents and starting a new community with a band of loyal followers. Theodore Noyes, who understood his father well despite the theological gulf that lay between them, later wrote that it was not the fear of legal action but "the sudden, rude, and almost insulting assertion of independence on the part of two or three of his chief critics at Oneida which broke his hold and decided him to leave the Community." Noyes's sister Harriet agreed. "This stir-up outside seems to me only a providence to get you away from inward persecution," she wrote to him a few days after his departure for Canada.

As he had made clear to his followers again and again, Noyes was no constitutionalist when it came to the government of Oneida. He might choose, in obedience to divine instructions, to appoint a viceroy (Theodore) to rule in his name. But he could not accept a replacement as leader of the Community against his and God's will. God had not appointed James Towner as Noyes's successor, and to stay on at Oneida as leader of the loyal opposition would be to admit that he had misunderstood or misrepresented God's instructions. Then, too, apart from considerations of God's will, there was the mundane question of power. From the early days at Putney, Noyes had been convinced—and had convinced his followers—that the successful operation of Bible Communism required their unquestioning obedience to him.

Noyes said glumly some time after taking up residence in Canada that by the summer of 1879, three quarters of the family at Oneida had lost confidence in his leadership. This was an exaggeration, but the risk of being overthrown was a serious one. The prospect was so intolerable to Noyes that he chose never to see Oneida again rather than to acquiesce in any diminution of his authority to rule the Community that had been his life work.

arriet Skinner, writing to a friend at Wallingford a few days after her brother's midnight flight to Canada, said how much she had been moved and comforted by the annual Fourth of July celebration at Oneida. A group of children, dressed in white, had performed a dance, she wrote, and "it made me feel that the Community spirit had its own way here in spite of the dreadful state of things. This division is only a surface affair after all." In a similar vein, after a letter from Noyes had been read to the family at Oneida, one of his supporters wrote him, "I never felt such a gust of a good spirit. . . . There were a good many tears shed in meeting Sunday night, and a new baptism of the Community spirit came in." But, as it turned out, this was wishful thinking. With Noyes's departure, the divisions that threatened to split the Community apart grew deeper and more menacing.

On one side were the stunned and bereaved loyalists. On the twenty-third of June, Pierrepont Noyes recalled, something had happened "so unthinkable, so perturbing, that the very framework of life seemed falling about me. . . . I saw tears in my mother's eyes." Furious at the Townerites for having driven their leader into exile, the loyalists wanted nothing more (or less) than his return in triumph to resume his old position and restore the harmony, tranquillity, and spiritual unity of former years.

To this the oppositionists were adamantly opposed. Emboldened by Noyes's departure, they put their demands in writing. While they said they were ready to recognize Noyes, whether in Canada or back at Oneida, as president of the Community—the title Theodore had held during his brief term as leader—he was to be a constitutional president, accountable to an elected governing council and thus, ultimately, to the Community at large. They further insisted on the abolition of ascending fellowship and the ending of all controls over sexual liaisons except as parents might choose to regulate the sexual conduct of their minor children.

At this time there were the first stirrings of a third party, led by Frank Wayland-Smith and Theodore Noyes. In their view, restoring Noyes to his old throne at Oneida, however desirable, was probably a political impossibility. On this point they differed sharply with the loyalists. At the same time, they differed with the Townerites in arguing that Bible Communism—and, in particular, complex marriage —could be maintained only under Noyes's divinely inspired leadership.

Making this point in a "political letter" addressed to Noyes in Canada, Wayland-Smith reported that complex marriage was "pretty well broken up already." There was a "powerful sentiment in favor of marriage" among the young women at Oneida, he wrote, along with "a noticeable leaning . . . toward long dresses and long hair." Some women were insisting they would never have children except by a husband to whom they were legally married; others were refusing to have anything to do with complex marriage. Wayland-Smith noted ruefully, "This feeling has taken such a hold that some of us find ourselves practically monogamists, or nearly, perforce." At the same time, complex marriage was being undermined from another direction. Such sexual activity as still went on at Oneida was virtually unregulated, and Wayland-Smith argued that Noyes alone had the spiritual authority to prevent a disastrous decline into the state of anarchy and sensualism from which he had rescued the early Perfectionists—and which had prevailed at the free-love community of Berlin Heights, where Judge Towner had once lived. To avoid this catastrophe, Wayland-Smith proposed that the Community transform itself "into a Cooperative Society with familism and private purses"— in other words, abandon both complex marriage and communism. This was, he conceded, a "wild and radical proposition." But he suggested hopefully that before the process was complete, people might come to their senses and "with one accord, repent and resolve to go on in the good old way, under your lead." As a first step, he urged Noyes to "withdraw your sanction from our sexual practices until such a time as your influence and authority shall be restored."

Wayland-Smith soon seized the opportunity to share his views with a wider audience. Acceding to the demands of the Townerites, Noyes nominated an administrative council to manage the Community's affairs in his absence. Its members, whose choice was unanimously approved at an evening meeting in late July, were about evenly divided between loyalists and their opponents, counting Wayland-Smith and Theodore Noyes as loyalists. Meeting several times a week, the council became the forum for a protracted debate on the regulation of sex at Oneida. At one of its early meetings, Wayland-Smith argued that, with Noyes no longer in charge, complex marriage had lost its moral legitimacy. He said he would therefore move that all sexual intercourse at Oneida be indefinitely suspended. The Community was already on a downward slide, he said, and who knew where it would stop? "Shall we step off onto the plane of worldly morality by adopting marriage, or shall we go below it into the condition of . . . free lovers?" To suspend all sexual activity, he added dryly, "would help us to reflect clearly on the matter."*

---

* Theodore Noyes, who seconded Wayland-Smith's motion, offered a criticism of his own of the way the Townerites were proposing to regulate sex at Oneida. In the past, he said, the Community had placed no value on virginity. But this was changing now that young people's sexual conduct was to be regulated by their parents. Several women with young daughters, he told the council, "stoutly assert

Wayland-Smith's motion put the Townerites in an awkward position. If they voted no, they would be formally repudiating the notion that Noyes had been appointed by God to regulate the sexual life of the Community, a step that many of their adherents were still hesitant to take. If they voted yes, they would be tacitly admitting that, in forcing Noyes into exile, they had made a bad mistake, depriving themselves and their followers of a highly valued privilege. Determined to preserve complex marriage, but on their own terms, the Townerites elected to oppose Wayland-Smith's plan. William Hinds, citing the Pentecost and quoting from Noyes's own writings, argued that "communism of the affections" was as much a principle of true Christianity as communism of property—it was not something that could be put into practice only under the supervision of one particular person. But Hinds seemed uncomfortably aware of the bind in which he and his followers had been placed. Disavowing any conscious part in driving Noyes away from Oneida, he said he would be glad to have him back—but as a "constitutional" leader. Before voting on Wayland-Smith's proposal for an indefinite suspension of all sexual activity at Oneida, the council decided to submit the plan to Noyes for his comments.

Noyes was now living with a family of Perfectionists, the Bretts, on a farm near the village of Strathroy, not far from London, Ontario. Although accommodations were primitive at Strathroy—the drinking water, he complained, was "no better than warm slush . . . no possibility of bathing within several miles"—he came to like it there. His hostess, who fed her own family mainly on oatmeal, spoiled their distinguished guest with delicacies like sardines and canned lobster, and Noyes found the family "full of life and merriment . . . always ready for a spree." Noyes sawed and chopped wood for exercise, and walked in the forest, where he shot squirrels, partridge, and pigeons. For adult

---

that they will never allow them to be tampered with in social matters"—that is, they would be forbidden to have sex until they were legally married. As a result, the Community would end up with "a more or less distinct class of virgins . . . upheld by their parents [who] will inevitably assume a position of superiority"—a position obviously incompatible with the ideals of Bible Communism.

companionship he had an old friend and trusted lieutenant, Theodore Pitt, whose presence, Noyes wrote, was "an unspeakable blessing." The two men shared a room at the Bretts' and "there was love between us 'passing the love of women.' " At Oneida, Pitt had been criticized for "picking up young sweethearts" when he was traveling on Community business, and in Canada he was still on the prowl. Noyes later wrote, "When the love of women threatened to get the upper hand"—Noyes gave no details—"I, for one, was dreadfully lonesome and jealous till the danger was past." Noyes, for his part, had by no means lost his love of women, either. He flirted with "a romping girl of fourteen, careless of dress and proprieties . . . [who] soon got hold of my heart and led it through a lively love dance." Later he met a Miss Fannie Still, a woman of aristocratic English parentage, with "very white skin, dark auburn hair," who "carried me away into a delightful romance." He was not carried as far as he had hoped, however. At their second meeting, he wrote her after leaving Strathroy, "I was tipsy with love and could hardly keep my hands off you." At their fourth and last meeting, he recalled, "*You allowed me to kiss you.* I said that I was perfectly satisfied; but I doubt whether I should have been satisfied long if I had stayed in Strathroy."

Noyes had remained in close touch with events at Oneida, and he responded quickly to the council's request for his views on Wayland-Smith's proposal. To the surprise and shock of many people at Oneida, he urged a change in sexual arrangements even more radical, by the standards of Bible Communism, than the mere suspension of sexual relations. Complex marriage, he wrote, should be abandoned entirely. And while he said that, like St. Paul, he favored celibacy over conventional marriage and would recommend it to his followers, he proposed that Oneidans who wanted to get married should be free to do so. This change of course, he said, was in no way a confession of error; complex marriage was still "the true, rational, and final status which we look forward to as loyally as ever." But the time had come to abandon complex marriage for the "sake of avoiding offense" to Mears and his allies. Noyes added his hope that the drastic step he was proposing would "also give new liberty and harmony within the Community."

Some members of the council, however appalled at their leader's proposal that they return to the ways of the world in sexual matters, were prepared to go along simply because they still believed in Noyes's divine inspiration. Others saw the change as an essential shield against persecution—a shield that could, perhaps, be laid aside at some future time. Frank Wayland-Smith pointed out that one Mormon leader had recently been sent to prison for the crime of polygamy and that others were about to be tried for the same offense. This, he warned, would almost certainly lead to a new push against Oneida if the Community persisted in its accustomed sexual ways. Despite some misgivings— Wayland-Smith observed that under the new plan "the sexual desires of the young cannot be so readily gratified, nor their sexual education [be] so good as heretofore"—the council approved the plan, with only Hinds dissenting. A staunch loyalist named Myron Kinsley, who had accompanied Noyes on his flight to Canada and since then had shuttled between Oneida and Strathroy, acting as the exile's chief adviser on Community affairs, wrote Noyes from Oneida that when his proposal was read at an evening meeting "the family cheered and cheered."

Still, not everybody was happy with the plan. Hinds conceded that it might be expedient to suspend complex marriage, but said that he couldn't in good conscience do anything that would open the way for the Community to be invaded by the marriage spirit. Towner said he didn't think marriage and communism could exist together—a position that, as he pointed out, Noyes himself had always held. He said he, for one, wanted "none of the privileges of marriage," adding that celibacy would allow Oncidans "an unusual opportunity for self-sacrifice and continence," which he hoped others besides himself would seize. But when a yes vote was called for, everyone rose to his feet except Hinds. It was agreed that complex marriage would end at 10 A.M. on August 28. As Frank Wayland-Smith wrote in his journal, this left "nearly two days to the family for the accomplishment of sexual 'good-byes.' The people cheered this measure of grace enthu-siastically, and there was great activity during the allotted time. I spent the last hour of it with [his son's] mother.''

◆   ◆   ◆

Noyes's mild plea for "heaven-pleasing celibacy" notwithstanding, most legally unattached Oneidans preferred matrimony. It was settled that marriages must be approved by the administrative council, but this was a formality. If they wished, couples could be married in a simple civil ceremony. In *The Days of My Youth*, Corinna Ackley Noyes describes one such "contract wedding." It was held in the family hall, "and a sad spectacle it was. . . . The scene was set upon a bare stage, the only furnishings a flat-topped desk and four straight-backed wooden chairs." Towner stood at the desk and read the marriage contract, the couple signed, "and the deed was done. There was no kissing of the bride." This Spartan wedding was followed by the wed-ding of a second couple in a ceremony much more to the author's taste. The bride, Lily Hobart, who had been the "dazzling Josephine" in the Community's production of *Pinafore*, "was dressed in a long dress of a beautiful jade green cotton with a slight train [that] set off her lovely figure and beautiful complexion in an entrancing manner. Her hair, though short, was naturally curly and was a mass of ringlets." The marriage was performed by James Herrick. "The Episcopal service was not a word too long," Corinna Noyes writes, "and the giving of the ring and the bridal kiss were the supreme touch of romance. Home-made currant wine and fruit cake were then served to the grown-ups. What a thrilling scene!" That so many Oneidans were choosing marriage—by the end of 1880 there had been thirty-seven weddings—did not bother Noyes, who even undertook to find hus-bands for young women who sought his help. Writing to an old friend at Oneida, who had complained that Oneidans were selfishly ignoring St. Paul's (and Noyes's) pleas for celibacy, Noyes said, "God forbid that I or any other man should sit in judgment on anybody's motives for marrying so long as they are good communists."* Noyes did suggest, however, that people who had known the rich rewards of complex marriage might have a hard time making a go of monogamy. "I have a very strong impression," he wrote, "that where the doors of the heart-chambers have been thrown open as they have been in the Community, they can never be closed again in the way [conventional] marriage requires. We've had a great deal of experience going to show that old love affairs leave behind their embers that are unquenchable."

As more and more Oneidans married, the character of life in the Community took on a different tone. In theory, children might belong to the Community, but now they spent most of their time not in the Children's House, but with their parents. Harriet Skinner noted disapprovingly in a letter to her brother that Augusta Towner, recently married to James Towner's son Arthur, was working hard to change the Community into "an aggregation of little family circles. She has worked till she has got hers and Arthur's rooms contiguous, one of which she fixes up as a sitting-room, where she has her children a good deal. She has an ideal of a cozy family circle, and means it shall be a pattern for all." Cozy domesticity did make headway, but there were holdouts. In a letter to a friend at Wallingford just before she was to be married, a young woman at Oneida wrote that she and her husband were not going to room together. "Alfred and I," she explained "have decided that we are not going to be the kind of married folk who tag around after each other and always eat together. We are going to belong to the old Community."

In *A Lasting Spring*, Jessie Kinsley recalls her deep regret at the

---

* Noyes some years later offered a surprising explanation of why Oneidans had been so bent on matrimony. Under complex marriage, he said, there was "really a condition of great restraint between the sexes. . . . Suppression was far more prominent in our experience than liberty." So when complex marriage was abolished, people were seduced by "the sexual freedom & pleasures which marriage gives." The trouble with this theory is that the Oneidans, in the Community's last days, were not given a choice between complex and conventional marriage. Rather, unless they already had wives or husbands with whom they had joined the Community, their choice was between conventional marriage and abstinence.

abandonment of complex marriage, whose standards "had seemed to us so much better and higher and more unselfish" than the prevailing "worldly standard of marriage and morals." She goes on to speak of "the heartache and the pain that came like a bitter wind across some lives." Her own sister, she writes, could not marry the man she loved, and by whom she had had a stillborn child, "because he now had a living son, and both love and duty led him toward marriage with the later mother." The agonizing uncertainties facing many Oneidans, particularly the young women, is piercingly illuminated by a letter from Beulah Hendee, then living at Wallingford, to Alfred Barron, the man with whom she was in love. She had heard, she wrote, that Alfred was planning to get married, and continued:

> Is it true, dear? Tell me—I did not believe it. I thought you would tell *me* if you had such a plan. . . . Tell me how you feel! I have shown you my heart as much as any woman can. You know how dearly I love you. The terrors of this new situation come upon me with an overwhelming force. What did God mean by bringing us so close to one another's hearts, only to tear us from one another now. . . . Our relations are no longer "complex" but they are dreadfully complicated. *Won't* God show us what is right to do. . . . There is John [Sears]. I don't want to break his dear faithful loving heart—and he wants to marry me. So you know all the feelings of my heart toward you and he knows them too. You are my lover, be my brother too. . . . John makes me *perfectly* free to choose—to follow my heart . . . said he was sure I would want you—but do *you* want me?

The story ended happily—for Hendee and her lover, if not for John Sears and Elizabeth Kellogg, the mother of Alfred Barron's fourteen-year-old daughter, who had hoped that Alfred would marry her. A few days before Christmas, Beulah and Alfred were married in a quiet "contract" ceremony in Harriet Noyes's room at Oneida.

Additional light on the politics of marriage in the last days of the Community is shed by Jessie Kinsley's account of the painful choices she herself faced. Two men were pressing her to marry them, and she was uncertain which (if either) she wanted as a husband. She was very close to Noyes—there was a mystery about her parentage, and she had lately come across evidence suggesting that Noyes might be her father—and she wrote to ask his advice. She told him that she wanted to be married and have children, but that she also wanted her marriage "to be one 'born in heaven.' " Noyes replied, "Do not be afraid that I shall keep you from being married and having a baby. I sincerely hope you will have five or six babies, and for this very reason I wish you to have the very best husband that can be found." He said he had reservations about both of her suitors—one, in particular, had irked Noyes by questioning his divine inspiration—and he urged her to wait. His own candidate for a husband, he wrote to his sister Harriet at Oneida, was his confidant and courier, Myron Kinsley, even though, at forty-three, he was more than twice Jessie's age. Harriet had been hoping to nudge Myron into marrying Noyes's niece Constance, in the hope that this would end her attachment to the Townerite party, but she agreed to her brother's plan. She called Jessie and Myron to her room, where, Jessie recalled, "Mrs. S. put our hands together and said, 'John and I wish you two might learn to love one another.' " They agreed to try, and Jessie went to Wallingford, where Myron, between trips to Canada, was running the Community's spoon factory. According to her account, the two spent a lot of time "talking and reading and walking" until love "came to me with a vehemence of which I had not dreamed."* Not long afterward the

---

* Their engagement was, as Jessie knew it would be, a cruel blow to her sister Annie, who was also in love with Myron Kinsley. In a touching letter of renunciation, Annie wrote, "I have taken care of Myron's clothes and his room, and have cared for him in a great many other ways that, of course, I shall miss in giving them up; but I have prayed God to reconcile me to anything that might take place and I felt that God had kindly answered my prayer when I found (with some surprise) that I felt so good about and ready to fall in with Mr. Noyes's choice. I have had happiness in thinking of giving my care of Myron to you, and of letting you have

couple were married in New Haven. The bride, who wore a long dress, recalled "how strangely it felt about my knees and ankles which were so long accustomed to pantalets."

---

my room right next to him." She went on to speak of the "sorrow, pain and discipline" involved in her struggle, under complex marriage, to learn to love unselfishly. But her efforts had not been in vain, she wrote, for now she found it "easier to yield up a love that is very dear to me than I probably should if I had not had the discipline that I have had."

n a letter to Noyes toward the end of 1879, Frank Wayland-Smith described the situation at Oneida as "a sort of armed truce." There was no way, he said, that the council that was supposed to be governing the Community could enforce moral standards when the "very attitude of one-half the Council in defying the authority of the old administration [has] put an end to all spiritual obedience and subordination." Mutual criticism was as dead as complex marriage, he noted, adding that, according to one young woman, her contemporaries at Oneida were "utterly irreverent" and "have thrown off all regard for Community tastes and fashions." Wayland Smith went on to report that the Towner-Hinds party was holding its own private religious meetings and that the two main parties were so suspicious of one another's motives that, at evening meetings, "Almost everything that may be said or read is suspected of a political significance." Theodore Noyes wrote his father that he agreed with his friend's gloomy appraisal. He noted that Hinds's and Towner's followers had blocked a plan recently put forward by Noyes to carry on with stirpiculture. The opposition party, Theodore wrote, had "a strong hostility to marriage, and beyond that a hostility to the bearing [of] children by the married." He said they seemed determined to make marriage unpopular, with a view to "a possible inauguration of free love after the married have been worried sufficiently."

There were times when the hearts of Noyes's followers leaped at what they thought were signs that the clock could be turned back. After an evening meeting near the end of 1879, at which a letter from Noyes had been read, Myron Kinsley wrote him that many people had spoken "in favor of brotherly love and unity and respect and love for you," including some who had been "on the wrong side. . . . I should not be surprised," he added, "if the Community would invite you back as its head at no distant day without one voice the other way." Harriet Skinner, too, was hopeful: "We all think the good spirit gains here." Referring to Henry Burnham and his wife, both leading members of the opposition party, she reported to Noyes, "The Burnhams were quite gushing. . . . He catched Mrs. Kelly"—a loyal Noyesite— "and hugged and kissed her like old times."

But such moments of reconciliation were fleeting. In a moment of high excitement Henry Burnham might kiss Mrs. Kelly, but relations between the two parties more often resembled open warfare than an armed truce. Augusta Towner, outraged by the exclusion of her new father-in-law James Towner from membership on the administrative council, wrote Noyes to register her disgust with "this evil-speaking and evil eye that Mr. Noyes's 'friends' (?) as they call themselves, have toward Mr. Towner . . . I sometimes think that I would like to tell the so-called 'orthodox party' here that I can no longer consider them to be either Christians or Communists but 'Noyesites,' and a disgrace to the name, at that." Another woman wrote Noyes, "I despise the effort on the part of some vaunting themselves as 'loyalists' to suppress, bully, worry and eliminate individuals of the other party from the Council." Many loyalists, for their part, could not bear the prospect of living in a Community run by Towner and Hinds. "I cannot be led or driven by William Hinds, and he cannot be led or driven by me," one man wrote Noyes. Theodore Noyes, maintaining that he rather liked Towner personally, told Wayland-Smith that he "would like to be able to visit my father or anyone else without asking consent of W. A. Hinds or any of that set. In fact, the close relations of communism are becoming almost intolerable."

Nerves were chronically frayed. Harriet Skinner wrote Noyes that Frank Wayland-Smith and his new bride, Cornelia Worden, were avoiding evening meetings because Hinds and Towner's "pious talk exasperates them so [that] Frank told me that it made him want to scream." James Herrick, a leading loyalist, "was taken away to the asylum at Utica raving about Messrs. Towner and Hinds." (Herrick's mind, Wayland-Smith wrote Noyes, had been "wrecked by the political strifes which rage here, aided by an unfortunate dip into spiritualism.") Many felt dismay, verging on despair, at the harsh and rancorous tone of Community life. Henry Seymour, a founding member of the Community, wrote Noyes, "I hate this scuffling more than I can express and sometimes wish myself into the middle of the next century."

At an evening meeting a Townerite mother complained angrily to the moderator, Erastus Hamilton, that her eight-year-old son had been forbidden—apparently by a loyalist—to use the men's privy. The privy, she insisted, "belonged to the Community and was as much hers as it was his, and . . . she should send her boy there when she pleased." Hamilton replied that it was the *men's* privy, not intended for children. The women's privy, he added, "belongs to the Community but that don't give me the right to go in there." There is no record of how the dispute was resolved. There were also angry arguments over more important matters. Hinds complained that Myron Kinsley and his friends were freezing Towner out of responsible jobs, such as a seat on the finance committee, in favor of incompetent disbelievers like Theodore Noyes. Wayland-Smith, at one of the evening meetings he forced himself to attend, argued that a rule permitting substitutes at council meetings allowed people who were "warlike and ferocious"—he seems to have been referring to Augusta Towner—to sit on the council in place of "mild-spoken, unobjectionable regular members." After a stormy debate the Community overrode protests by Augusta and her father-in-law and voted to narrowly restrict the privilege of substitution. "We shoved Mr. Towner out of the Council last night," Harriet Skinner exulted, "and it seems an inevitable thing that the same power will shove him out of the Community." But Harriet's feeling of triumph was short-lived. Even with the new rules in effect, Augusta contrived to take part as a substitute in most council meetings, where she tangled repeatedly with Erastus Hamilton, the generally acknowledged leader of the loyalists. Hamilton, Harriet Skinner reported to her brother, "is flayed alive at almost every council by Augusta's hatefulness and has to renew his purpose to keep himself in the love of God." Friendships and love affairs were broken up by politics. Mary Louise Prindle, who had had a son by William Hinds, rejected his proposal that they remain on close terms despite their differing political opinions. She reported to Noyes that she had told Hinds she "had loved him and suffered with him and for him," but that if she had foreseen that he would forsake Noyes and deny the faith she had supposed he shared with her, she would never have consented to have a child by him. Hinds, she wrote, "was either a dishonest dupe or completely mesmerized" by Towner—"so awfully smooth externally"—who had "come in at the eleventh hour and introduced rebellion and anarchy into our peaceful home." As Prindle reported their conversation, Hinds said he had lost faith in Noyes's leadership only because Noyes had tried to foist Theodore on the Community. He had added placatingly, Prindle continued, that he had no idea of making Towner the leader of the Community; he was sticking up for him only because there was such an attempt to "push him into a corner." Prindle was not won over.

An angry dispute erupted over the way the Children's House was being run. Noyes had urged the Oneidans, even after the abandonment of complex marriage, to go on treating the children as belonging to the whole Community, rather than to their parents. But this recommendation was not universally accepted. Many children no longer slept at the Children's House; instead, they spent the hours from late afternoon until the next morning with their parents. At a council meeting in the winter of 1880, Augusta Towner complained that she and her nine-year-old son Ruddy were being ostracized because of her complaints that William Kelly, who ran the Children's House, was much too strict. Declaring that for this reason she and other mothers had removed their children entirely from the Children's House, she asked, "Are our children to be looked down on, and an evil eye to be kept on them and us, and we to be considered necessarily having a bad influence?" Other Townerites charged that their children were getting the same treatment as Ruddy and that Kelly, a loyalist, was largely responsible. In reply, Kelly admitted that he didn't want the children under his care to play with those who had been removed. He said such mingling undermined discipline and led to "insubordination" among his charges. One father, speaking in support of Kelly, complained that some children who had been taken out of the Children's House were mixing with "outside" children, and said he didn't want his children playing with them because "they would learn bad words and bad manners and get lice." Augusta retorted that since Ruddy was being ostracized by the Children's House children, she had every right to find outside playmates for him. In the end, after Kelly had been replaced by a quadrumvirate acceptable to both parties, parents who had taken their children out of the Children's House agreed to put them back. But they made it clear that they would no longer abide by the thirty-year-old rule that all children were Community property.

Two months later William Kelly was involved in another and nastier quarrel. James Towner angrily charged that Kelly had slandered him. Kelly, he said, had been falsely telling people that Towner had been collecting evidence that Noyes was guilty of incest and rape, and that Towner intended to use this evidence against Noyes. Confronted by an outraged Towner, Kelly said he had heard the story from so many people that he thought it was probably true. When Towner's written denial was read at a council meeting, Harriet Skinner reported to Noyes, Towner's supporters "railed and blasphemed—they thought Mr. Towner was *so* abused—that there never was a man so innocent and so lied about." A week later Kelly made a grudging apology, saying he should have "made a more thorough examination as to the evidence of these reports before giving them credence or circulation." The truth or falsity of Kelly's accusation was never proven. But there was evidence that some of Towner's followers had said they were ready to assist in the prosecution of Noyes on sexual charges and that they may have spoken to Towner about their intentions. The only result of this ugly quarrel was to convince both sides of the viciousness and depravity of their adversaries. Reflecting on what had happened, the unrepentant Kelly told Erastus Hamilton, "I don't know as anything else would have revealed to me the real diabolical nature of [Towner's] hatred of Mr. Noyes."

✦   ✦   ✦

While Hinds, Towner, and their followers had been strong enough to drive Noyes into exile, they had won a Pyrrhic victory. Their success in ending his tight control of Oneida's sexual life had, with the abolition of complex marriage, brought them less freedom in the choice of sexual partners, not more. And with a majority of the Community prepared to block them at every turn—in a vote on the composition of the administrative council, for example, the Towner-Hinds party had lost by 105 to 49—their hopes of restoring complex marriage on their own (or any) terms were slim indeed. The loyalists, even with their leader in exile, were able to elbow their hated opponents aside when it came to the distribution of jobs and responsibilities in Oneida's business enterprises. In a community in which all were on an equal footing financially, these were the only rewards for industry and competence. Hinds and Towner had wanted a democratic government at Oneida; now that they had it, they found themselves at the mercy of a hostile majority.

But being able to carry votes in the council or at evening meetings was small comfort to the loyalists. To many, the pain of Noyes's loss was all but intolerable. The world they had known and, for the most part, gloried in had been rudely shattered, and the only way it could be put back together would be if Noyes were to return and once again rule them in God's name. As his retreat to Canada had shown, however, he had no stomach for the task of governing a Community in which a large minority were in open and bitter rebellion against his authority. And, as he made plain in a letter to Erastus Hamilton, he had no intention of compromising with his opponents on the matter of his leadership. "The rule that comes by telling the truth and doing my best for all who respect me and letting my natural weight of character rest upon the Community cannot be avoided," he declared loftily. "I shall rule the Community in this way forever, whether present or absent."

But unless the Townerites were to pull up stakes and leave—Frank Wayland-Smith had half seriously suggested offering them a large sum of money to go away—it was apparent that Noyes's still potent influence on events at Oneida would be brought to bear from Canada. Toward the end of 1879 he let it be known that he would like to settle down at Niagara Falls in a big enough house so that members of his family could join him there. In January 1880, seven months after he had silently padded down the stairs of the Mansion House on the first leg of his flight to Canada, the Community voted unanimously to provide him with a house, a horse and carriage, and $150 a month for expenses. A large stone house was found with a fine view of the falls.

Though it was called the Stone Cottage, it actually had seven bedrooms, and there were a large barn and six acres of land partly planted with fruit trees. A committee was formed at Oneida to collect furniture (and some hens) to send to Niagara. Harriet Noyes joined her husband there and was followed by a procession of visitors from Oneida who put in long hours planting a garden, making flower beds, converting a shed into a Turkish bath, and—in the case of Erastus Hamilton, who had been the architect of the Mansion House—papering the dining room. One or two at a time, Noyes's children also came to visit.

✦　　✦　　✦

As the spring of 1880 turned into summer, the face that the Community presented to the visitors who once again arrived by the trainload and thronged the lawns and gardens was virtually unchanged. In the family hall there were public performances of *H.M.S. Pinafore*, with Theodore Noyes as Sir Joseph Porter, K.C.B. The *Journal*, the family's little daily newspaper, reported cheerfully—the *Journal* was seldom anything but cheerful—that *Pinafore* "promotes love and fellowship in our family circle and so proves a good medium of communism." In June, a poster announced a "summer's evening entertainment in our Hall . . . consisting of violin solos, instrumental quartets, vocal solos, duets and quartets concluding with a comedy entitled 'The Secret, or, a Hole in the Wall.' " "The Secret" ran off and on for most of the summer, and was seen by thousands of excursionists.

But behind this festive facade there was pessimism and despair. With Noyes in exile and Bible Communism in ruins, there was more and more talk of abandoning communism entirely and "going joint-stock"—that is, turning the Community's property and businesses over to a corporation whose stock would be parceled out among members of the old Community. The idea, as put forward by Wayland-Smith soon after Noyes's departure for Canada, was passionately opposed by many Oneidans. Some, hoping for a miracle that would bring Noyes back, saw the scheme as dangerous and revolutionary—an intolerable repudiation of the brave new world they and their leader had created. Harriet Worden, who for all her devotion to Noyes was also a close friend of Towner, wrote Noyes that the joint-stock idea was "appalling . . . a dagger [aimed] at the very heart of Bible Communism . . . a godless move . . . all our dearest hopes would perish in the abyss of selfishness . . . earthy, sensual, devilish . . . *joint-stock will be the death blow to Communism forever.*" She added, "Many are trembling with apprehension . . . and fear for the safety of our blessed Communism as it was . . . I say God forbid." Followers of Towner and Hinds saw the joint-stock solution as a scheme to deny them the more democratic and sexually freer communism they hoped to establish at Oneida. But the leaders of the emerging third party—Wayland-Smith, Theodore Noyes, and Edwin Burnham, whose Townerite father had caught and kissed Mrs. Kelly—argued that a joint-stock company was the only intelligent way to deal with the "irreconcilable incompatibility" between the two main contending parties. Under the joint-stock plan, Theodore explained, shareholders could continue to live at Oneida, move away, form a free-love community, form a new community of people wishing to live in conformity with Noyes's teachings—perhaps even go back to complex marriage. Harriet Skinner, accusing her nephew Theodore of political cowardice, wrote Noyes that she had told him that "if he and his party were staunch to you we should have beaten William [Hinds] and Mr. Towner before now." But while the elder Noyes allowed himself at times to hope, as he wrote Erastus Hamilton, that his followers at Oneida could "hold on and draw together into closer and firmer unity of heart till the unsound parts of the Community rot away," he was more tolerant than his sister of Theodore's and Wayland-Smith's apostasy. Although he disagreed with them, he wrote, he respected the honesty of those at Oneida who preferred to do away with communism when there is "no real unity of hearts."

Toward the end of June, Noyes sent a conciliatory message to his opponents in the form of a note from Theodore Pitt. Others at Oneida might be trying to "get rid of the malcontents," Pitt quoted Noyes as saying, but that had never been Noyes's policy. "On the contrary," Pitt wrote, "he believes in working for good order and *the things that make for peace*; and he will work heartily, even with his enemies, to secure these things." This somewhat calmed the troubled waters at Oneida, leading Harriet Skinner to report that "social relations between the parties are very much improved." Many people on both sides were now unhappily convinced that something must be done to head off calamity. With the breakdown of the moral authority once wielded by Noyes that had kept the Community's enterprises humming, laziness was a growing problem. More and more of the hard and dirty jobs were being done by hired labor, and the old vegetable-picking and fruit-canning bees had been abandoned. As Theodore pointed out, hard work had gone out of fashion and the Community was drifting toward bankruptcy. In these circumstances, William Hinds proposed that the two sides try to reach some agreement that would, among other things, protect "our aged members, our invalids, our children, and all classes who might be thrown upon the world without adequate means of support." Specifically, he proposed the appointment of a commission, representing all three parties, and including Noyes if he should choose to serve, to consider how communism might be preserved at Oneida, and, if that should be judged impossible, to decide what form of organization should succeed it. After weeks of bickering over its makeup, the commission was voted into being on July 18 and, at its first meeting, chose Theodore Noyes as chairman and Hinds as secretary. (The elder Noyes had declined to serve, pleading his deafness.)

As it surveyed the social and economic landscape of Community life, the commission saw little but disorder and decay. Reflecting on its first meetings, Frank Wayland-Smith noted in his diary, "We have no government worthy [of] the name." At least half the people at Oneida, he estimated, had lost their faith in Noyes's divinely inspired leadership, the bedrock on which the Community had been built. The Community's business enterprises were overextended and deeply in debt. People were working fewer and fewer hours—or not working at all—because "they see no object in toiling while the earnings and profits are controlled by others." Waste and extravagance—the latter fueled by the greatly increased personal allowances voted into effect for 1880—were mounting dangerously.* Young people, Wayland-Smith went on, "do just as they please. Some of the young men have begun to smoke, drink, and swear, and the children will soon catch the habits from them."

In these depressing circumstances the commission moved quickly to consider two plans for major changes in the Community's economic arrangements. Both were aimed at reenergizing the sluggish business life of the Community by giving members the option of

---

* A local newspaper, the Oneida *Dispatch*, reported: "No more bloomer costumes in public; no more severed hair; but in their places elegant dresses and waving tresses will be the rule. . . . Fashionable hats, costly switches, silk dresses, etc., etc., almost daily go from our village to the Community."

breaking free from the bonds of communism. Under one plan all adults would have to donate some four hours a day of free labor to the Community, but would be paid wages for any additional hours they chose to put in. In addition, at the end of each year, any profits would be divided equally among all members of the Community. This plan was rejected because it would do little or nothing to reconcile the warring parties and provided no mechanism by which those parties, if they wished, could split up and go their separate ways. The second plan called for dividing Community members into two classes. One, the "pure communists," would carry on as before. The other class would continue to enjoy the amenities of communal life at Oneida, but would be paid for their work; as employees rather than members, they would have no voice in the management of Community affairs. A "liberal sum" would be paid to anyone choosing to leave the Community. This plan, too, was rejected, on the ground that introducing class distinctions in a previously classless society "would prove an endless cause of evil-speaking and contention."

The commission then turned to the more radical joint-stock proposal. At first neither the loyalists nor their opponents were ready to go along with a plan that would demolish the "communism of property" that had been—along with complex marriage—the chief distinguishing feature of life at Oneida. But the joint-stock scheme had one very appealing feature. It would allow the contending parties to disengage from the battle and go their separate ways. A plan was already afoot to sell part of the Wallingford property and move the tableware business to Niagara, with its abundant water power. One hundred and eight Community members now signed a statement saying they would be interested in joining Noyes at Niagara, where they could form a new Community—perhaps pooling their resources and continuing to live as communists—and where those who wished would have jobs in the transplanted spoon factory or other Community businesses that might be relocated there. The Townerites, if they wished, might stay at Oneida, living in whatever form of association they saw fit and working in those Community enterprises not moved to Niagara. Exhilarated by these possibilities, the commission sent Myron Kinsley to

Niagara to consult Noyes. Noyes quickly gave the plan his approval, saying he hoped only that it would not be pushed through over the protests of a substantial minority, but would be carried by "a breeze of unanimity."

The joint-stock proposal was now put before the Community. At a series of evening meetings agreement was reached, not always without noisy quarrels, on a number of difficult questions, and Noyes had his wish. On the last day of August the plan was adopted without a dissenting vote, "it being understood," the official reporter noted, "that the few not voting on either side did not object."

By their vote, the Oneidans agreed to turn over all Community property, wherever located, to a new corporation whose shares would be held exclusively by members of the Community. They put off the touchy business of deciding how many shares each person should get—of deciding, for instance, whether a founding member who had contributed capital to the Community treasury should be entitled to a bigger slice of the pie than a member who had arrived at Oneida years later and empty-handed. Members were to try to work out for themselves a plan for distributing the stock, which would go into effect only if nine-tenths of the members of the Community agreed; if no agreement could be reached, the matter would be referred to outside arbitrators. Community members would be entitled to rent living quarters, at cost, in the Mansion House, and to have the benefit, as before, of all Community facilities. Those who chose to work for one of the Community's enterprises would be given preference over outside job-seekers; in the interest of keeping dividends as high as possible, however, wages would be kept low. Lifetime support and care would be provided, in lieu of stock in the new company, to elderly and infirm members who preferred the security of such an arrangement. Parents and guardians would be given an allowance for each child under sixteen.

Over the next two weeks the commission drew up a number of plans for allocating the stock, and these were wrangled over at evening meetings. It was decided that people who had contributed capital would get half of it back, in stock, and that the rest of the shares would be distributed to all adult members in amounts proportionate to the number of years they had lived in the Community. Children would receive no stock, but would be educated at company expense until they reached their sixteenth birthdays, when they would be given a bonus of $200. Despite some grumbling, this plan was eventually agreed to by all but one of the members. The holdout was Sewall Newhouse, who refused to accept his allocation of stock on the ground that, as inventor of the original model for the Community's enormously profitable line of animal traps, he deserved a bigger slice of the pie. Newhouse's objections notwithstanding—five years later the old trap maker swallowed his pride and agreed to take his share after all—the joint-stock plan went into effect. At midnight on December 31, as if dying in its sleep, Bible Communism at Oneida quietly expired. No funeral rites marked its passing. Julia Ackley, who had joined the Community in 1849, noted dryly in her diary on January 3, "A good many have gone to work today that haven't done but a precious little for months and months."

Chapter 25

*D*uring the first year or so after the demise of Bible Communism at Oneida a few people—mainly young men—left to go out in the world and live on their own. Others moved to Niagara to work in the spoon and chain factories that had been moved there from Wallingford and Oneida. Eight or ten former Community members too old to work also went to Canada to live out their lives with Noyes.

But the great majority stayed on in the Mansion House. No longer wrapped in the warm embrace of communism, people who had never bought a spool of thread or a pair of shoelaces now had to learn the meaning of private property and the value of money. Some found the process exhilarating. At Oneida, each adult was allowed to claim $30 worth of the communally owned furniture and other household goods; the leftovers were auctioned off. Pierrepont Noyes suspected that many people "felt, as I did, a certain novel elation in thus wielding, for the first time, the age-old power of money." But the lessons were not easy to learn. Frank Wayland-Smith, who was hired on by the new corporation to run its hardware division, wrote in his diary,

"I bought a fast trotting horse, a stallion, and swapped him for a young mare, didn't like the mare, so sold her; in the course of which operations I lost just $100"—one ninth of his annual salary—"and gained some useful experience." He added that his wife (the former Cornelia Worden) "stood my loss very courageously and helped me to recover my equanimity." In *A Lasting Spring*, Jessie Kinsley, who moved to Niagara with her husband and new baby soon after the breakup, recalled that "I was most unsophisticated and green. Our hired girl, Maggie, was often imagined by strangers to be the mistress, because she wore fine clothes and had assurance. I would always forget to use money which I then handled for the *first time*." An exaggerated emphasis was placed on the sanctity of private property. "It was difficult to borrow a hammer," one man recalled, and it was said that anyone who borrowed even a pin felt duty bound to return it. People who had never before had to worry about the rent or paying for groceries were afflicted, in the words of Pierrepont Noyes, "with an economy complex which persisted as long as they lived." Anxieties about money were felt with particular keenness by the younger single women—at the time of the breakup, there were sixteen of these under the age of forty, twelve of them with children—who worried about what would become of them if the corporation should fail and the dividends stop coming. Company salaries were relatively low, and disparity in pay levels smaller than in the outside world, but many people resented any modification at all of the old system under which there were no salaries and no one was any better off than anyone else. Although the president of the new corporation was paid only $1,200 a year, some Oneidans grumbled that it was entirely too much. One elderly man, whose duties had never been more complicated than keeping an eye on the Community's water supply, offered to take on the job of "presidenting" for ten cents an hour.

In the Mansion House, some forms of Community life persisted. People still took meals together, but not in the old family dining room. On the theory that anyone entitled to goods or services from the Community should pay for exactly what he or she received, the directors of the new company established an à la carte restaurant in the new wing of the Mansion House. Elegantly furnished with polished oak tables, its walls painted in what one patron recalled as "a luxuriant, unspiritual green," the new restaurant offered diners the luxury of attentive waiters and a wide choice of food. Cake and pie, once reserved for festive occasions, were now set out daily on a side table. Old egalitarian principles still to some extent held sway, and the superintendent of the restaurant got the same pay as the president of Oneida Community, Ltd., as the new company was called. For this and other reasons, including a naive pricing system that ignored overhead expenses, the restaurant consistently lost money. A number of residents, wishing to return to the simpler (and cheaper) arrangements of Community days, rented the former family dining room, where plainer fare was offered, and where diners could eat as much as they liked for a fixed weekly sum.

According to Pierrepont Noyes, the decision to get along without the amenities of à la carte dining was made, in part, because of "an aversion to its daily reminder of money." But there was another reason. If a desire for old communal forms persisted at Oneida, so did old communal antagonisms. The people who now sat down to eat in the old family dining room were all dedicated Noyesites, and the move was partly motivated—again, according to Pierrepont Noyes—"by the desire of true believers to separate themselves from spiritual backsliders, and partly, I suspect, because the [restaurant] manager was anti-Noyes." At first the new eating arrangements put into effect by the loyalists were for loyalists only. But when the à la carte restaurant was shut down to save money, the old family dining room was opened to everyone living in the Mansion House, regardless of their views on Noyes's claim to divine inspiration. The loyalists continued, however, to hold their own meetings. These were organized and usually chaired by Erastus Hamilton, Noyes's chief deputy at Oneida, and the leader of the loyalist crusade to stamp out the heresy of à la carte dining.

The old factional bitterness was also evident in quarrels over the management of the Oneida enterprises. The question of who was to get the good jobs was a source of particular bitterness. Because the loyalists at the end had outnumbered the Townerites by at least two to one, and because by and large they had lived much longer in the Community, they had received most of the stock in the new corporation, and Noyes, as their still acknowledged leader, became, in effect, the controlling stockholder. He chose to be generous and, with his blessing, three Townerites, including James Towner, were elected to the board of directors when the new company came into being. But Towner was not reelected the following year, and his party's representation on the board was reduced to two. At the end of 1881 the outlook for the old opposition party at Oneida was not bright. Its members faced not only continued social isolation in the Mansion House, but the prospect of being denied a significant role in running the new corporation.* Accordingly, Towner and some thirty-five of his followers migrated as a group to southern California, settling in the area that was to become Orange County. There they continued to live as a closely knit social group, but if they practiced any form of complex marriage it was a well-kept secret. They became active in ranching, citrus growing, the Unitarian church, and politics (some joined the local socialist party). Towner was chairman of a committee appointed to organize the government of Orange County and became its first Superior Court judge. As the decades passed, old battle scars faded and there was visiting back and forth between Oneida and what was sometimes called the "California colony."

Adjustment to the new order at Oneida was not easy. Although most residents of the Mansion House continued to think of themselves as "Community people," they were no longer sustained, in their contacts with the outside world, by a conviction of moral and spiritual superiority. This made it harder to cope with hostile comments about the immorality of their lives in the old Community. Some were so embarrassed by their former ties that when they were away from Oneida they asked to have their dividends mailed to them in plain envelopes. Community children, now mingling freely with outsiders,

---

* As it turned out, William Hinds was elected to the presidency of Oneida Community, Ltd., in 1904, but he had been on much closer terms with the loyalists and with Noyes himself than Towner and most of his principal allies.

had to learn to put up with the taunt of "Bastard!" Pierrepont Noyes recalls his realization that "while our parents' offense was a thing of the past, we, the improperly born product of the Community system, would be continuing reminders of its unforgivable defiance of Victorian morality." A plan to have stirpicults deny their unconventional parentage was scotched by Noyes, who insisted that in time the children of complex marriage would "keep the record of their pedigree as a diploma of nobility."

✦   ✦   ✦

The first president of the new corporation was Erastus Hamilton. He was not a model chief executive. Steeped in the paternalism of the old Community, he interfered in the personal lives of his subordinates, severely chastising one company executive for buying a house without first consulting him. Company managers complained to Noyes, and in 1885 he forced Hamilton to resign. (This does not seem to have diminished Hamilton's affection for Noyes; he soon built a house for himself in Niagara so that he could be near his old friend and spiritual leader.) Hamilton was succeeded by George Campbell. Welcomed as a pleasant change from the tyrannical Hamilton, he proved hopelessly inept at running a business. To the extent that the trap factory and other enterprises prospered, it was because, in Pierrepont Noyes's judgment, departmental managers "brushed aside his futile attempts at supervision."

In general, despite the incompetence of the principal officers of the new company, lower-level managers, who had successfully run various Community businesses in the old days, managed at least to keep them afloat under the new regime. The company provided jobs for all of the old Community members who wanted them, and there was no decline in living standards at Oneida. Religious standards were another matter, however. While Hamilton, in an effort to resist the rising tide of materialism, had continued to hold evening meetings in the spirit of the old Community, his successor as de facto Community leader,

George Campbell, had different ideas. Outside revivalists were invited to conduct services that included hymns, psalms, and fiery sermons—all of which Noyes had outlawed in the old days.

Conventional Christianity made converts at Oneida, and so did spiritualism—this time without the moderating influence that Noyes had exerted when he himself had been an enthusiastic votary and séances had once before been in fashion at Oneida. By 1883 half a dozen devotees were receiving messages from the spirit world that foretold, among other things, a third Resurrection at which Noyes would be "Christ's chosen one to bring heaven and earth together." This did not seem far off the mark from a Perfectionist standpoint, but when several such communications were reported to Noyes he reacted with annoyance and skepticism. He was angered by the fact that the communicants at Oneida had been "instructed" to keep all messages secret for the moment, even from him—a "breach of harmony," he wrote Hamilton, that "nearly killed Mrs. Skinner & me with her." Noyes saw this secrecy as a scheme by "Hadean" spirits to get a firm grip on the minds of the Oneidans before wiser heads—presumably including Noyes's—could intervene. The truth of spirit messages could never be taken for granted, Noyes said, adding that he himself kept a "pigeon-hole for . . . messages of all kinds which I label, 'Doubtful paper.'" While the doubts expressed by Noyes discouraged some of the spiritualists at Oneida, others continued their quest for new revelations about the coming of God's kingdom.

✦   ✦   ✦

If the old faith had been reduced to embers at Oneida, it glowed somewhat more brightly at Niagara, where Noyes, together with his sister Harriet and such trusted disciples as James Herrick—he had recovered quickly from his nervous breakdown—presided over a constantly shifting family of loyal Perfectionists. Like the giant Antaeus, who drew all his strength from the ground on which he stood, Noyes's presence drew visitors from Oneida, who came in relays, some staying for weeks, to regain a lost or fading conviction of spiritual security.* Noyes's stirpicultural children, and children of other loyalists, came to Niagara for long visits. They attended a school where they were taught Greek by Harriet Skinner, dancing and mathematics by Herrick, and Hebrew by Noyes, who for a while got up at four o'clock in the morning to teach himself the language. ("[He] says he finds it more fascinating than solitaire," a visitor reported.) Many of the managers of the chain and tableware divisions of the company, after the transfer of these businesses to Niagara, built houses within easy reach of the Stone Cottage, where they often went on Sundays with their families to reaffirm their union with Noyes and God.

There was no attempt to create another Oneida Community at Niagara. Noyes did on occasion rail against the "marriage spirit" and for a while refused to let his favorite niece, Tirzah, live at the Stone Cottage with her husband, his old friend Herrick. But many of the loyalists who formed an extended family at Niagara—they included Myron Kinsley and his wife Jessie—had married with Noyes's blessings, and with the exception of his flare-up at Tirzah he did not preach the virtues of Pauline celibacy. As for complex marriage, he asserted in 1883 that "I have kept my freedom of loving any body and every body that comes to my heart, regardless of matrimonialism." But there is no evidence that Noyes made any attempt to exercise this freedom after leaving Strathroy and the bewitching Fannie Still. At Niagara, he devoted himself to reaffirming and interpreting the principles of Perfectionism, not to applying those principles as they had been applied at Oneida.

In *My Father's House*, Pierrepont Noyes recalls in rich detail what life at the Stone Cottage was like in 1885, when as a boy of fourteen he spent a year there. His father, he writes, seemed much older than

---

* Some Oneidans claimed other benefits from their visits to Niagara. Soon after the breakup of the Community, James Herrick collected testimonials from visitors who believed their health had been wonderfully improved. They included a seventy-five-year-old man who had suffered for years from a bladder complaint. The "full and perfect union with the Godhead" that he had achieved at Niagara, he declared, had improved his health to a point where "I am apparently free from disease."

he had three years before, when Pierrepont had first visited Niagara. He now passed much of the time in his room, where he could look out over the falls, either alone or talking with Harriet Skinner or Herrick. His deafness had gotten worse, and at mealtimes he sat silently at the table, smiling at the children and listening intently when Herrick, bending close to his ear, told him what was being talked about or explained why everyone was laughing. Occasionally Noyes would give an informal "home talk," following which he would rise from his place at the end of the long dining table and go to his room. After "a respectful silence," those who remained would discuss points he had raised in his talk. The regular evening meetings that Pierrepont remembered from his earlier visit had been abandoned. Instead, with Noyes's encouragement, the little "family," consisting of eight or ten adults (including visitors) plus an equal number of children, spent their evenings playing games, conducting mind-reading experiments, and taking part in extemporaneous dramatic readings. Noyes himself, on those evenings when no home talk was delivered, often took part in these activities. After he had gone upstairs, people played backgammon or listened while Harriet Noyes read aloud. Now seventy-six years old and rheumatic, she walked with great difficulty and spent much of her time sitting by one of the French windows in the dining room, sewing, knitting, making artificial flowers, and playing solitaire. Three times a day, however, sitting on a special high chair pulled up to the kitchen sink, she washed the dishes. At the Sunday gatherings the adults talked with Noyes and one another while the children played games. Later everyone crowded into the parlor to listen to a talk by Noyes, followed by cookies and lemonade. There lingered, in Pierrepont's memory, "a pleasant aroma of spirituality so humanized as to be inoffensive to a boy."

Each morning from nine o'clock until noon Pierrepont and his brothers and the other boys staying at Niagara—there seem to have been no girls at this time—attended school in a nearby cottage whose second floor had been made into a dormitory for them. The curriculum bore little resemblance to what was being taught in other schools. "We leaped from arithmetic to geometry," Pierrepont Noyes writes. "We worked assiduously at phonography, now called short-hand, so that we might report my father's talks; and we studied Greek, largely, I think, to enable us to translate the Greek New Testament. We read aloud from [Noyes's] book *Home Talks*." The boys also put in some time each day at reincarnations of the old Community bees. Under the relaxed supervision of Herrick, who worked along with them, they hoed potatoes, cleaned sheds, and set out strawberry plants. At other times they were free to go off on their own to explore the countryside, to play lacrosse with local boys, and to flirt with local high-school girls. For adults as well as children the old prohibition against mixing with outsiders no longer stood, and Noyes himself often chatted with local shopkeepers and other neighbors. This showed him, Pierrepont thought, "as willing to come down from the clouds of Mt. Sinai and interest himself in the affairs of worldly men. I think that I just a little resented his descent."

But for all the relaxation of old rules, Pierrepont Noyes recalls, the Stone Cottage was enfolded in a gratifying "atmosphere of holiness. . . . Even the assumption that we were living in full view of and close alliance with the heavenly powers, an assumption which pervaded all activities of the Stone Cottage family, was pleasing to me after the ill-fitting materialism of Oneida."

On his earlier visit to Niagara Pierrepont had been struck by his father's "somewhat unexpected air of spiritual assurance. . . . He seemed a great hero and his lifework an epic." At times, indeed, Noyes was able to persuade himself that his great experiment at Oneida had been a total (or only slightly qualified) success. He explained to his sister Harriet that the Oneida Community was never meant to be permanent. Its aim was simply to test male continence and, he implied, complex marriage as well. Having demonstrated the validity of these practices, the Community had done its work. On another occasion he suggested that while the Community might have been killed off, its spirit was destined to live on in the person of the stirpiculats.

But at times, contemplating the wreckage of the paradise he had brought into being, and his expulsion from Eden, he was wracked by anxiety and deep depression. In 1883 he wrote that for five years he had "suffered dreadfully from fear. . . . I know very well what that aching death at the pit of the stomach is which listens for bad news and haunts one day and night, making sleep impossible." To ease the pain of failure he tried to master the experience of Oneida intellectually—to find what comfort he could in seeking to explain exactly what had gone wrong. At times his explanations sounded like a rejected parent lamenting the ingratitude and shortsightedness of his children. Too many Oneidans had simply not understood what even some outsiders had clearly seen—that, as Harriet Skinner reported his saying shortly before the final breakup, it was "his good luck and inspiration that has made [the Oneida Community] what it is . . . and [this] is the tree on which all productiveness and prosperity . . . has grown." Noyes also blamed the poor material with which he had had to work. "Communism is not for swine, but only for the sons and daughters of God," he declared. "We must have the discernment of God to find his true children if they are already converted, and his power *to keep them converted* through all temptations."

In some moods he wrote off the Oneida years as simply a stage in his own spiritual evolution. In a letter (never published) to the editor of the Utica *Morning Herald*, he said he had no objection to the establishment of new communities like Oneida, but would leave the job to younger men. He himself had graduated from Bible Communism to "Pauline Communism"—that is, he had decided to emulate Paul, whose "heart and faith were large enough" to encompass a form of communism consisting of "a system of mutual help and insurance, among churches widely scattered and living in the ordinary forms of society." In a letter to a Mrs. Yoder, who had asked his advice about founding a new community like Oneida, he emphasized even more strongly his determination to put Bible Communism behind him. Instead of trying to start a new communist community, he wrote, sounding more like a conventional revivalist than his old Perfectionist self, she and other would-be community builders should concentrate on "the personal spiritual experience which admits the living God into your hearts, and makes you sensibly members of Christ." In the same letter Noyes conceded that Oneida had been a failure. He had been unable, he wrote, "to carry Communism through to final visible success amid the temptations and enmities of this evil world." But there was a silver lining. His failure, he wrote, had spurred him on to greater spiritual enterprise: "I need a closer junction with Paul and the Primitive Church," he wrote, adding cryptically, "and this I am getting by the seeming failure of what I have attempted."

In other moods, Noyes hinted that the destruction of the Oneida Community and his own overthrow were the work of the devil. The devil's principal agent, he suggested, had been Charles Weld, an old adversary in the fierce Perfectionist wars of the 1830s. While Weld himself had dropped from sight, Noyes argued, he had continued to wage war on Bible Communism through a subagent, Edward Inslee, who was a relative of Weld's by marriage. Although Noyes had promoted Inslee's stirpicultural union with Tirzah Miller, he had later concluded that Inslee was working to turn the young people at Oneida against his leadership, and had had him expelled. Towner, Noyes wrote, was only the attorney for the dissident party; the Community's "real robber and destroyer" had been "Edward Insleeism." There was an obvious advantage to Noyes in blaming Oneida's failure on a foe —the devil—whom God, not Noyes, was presumably responsible for holding at bay.

Toward the end of 1885, Noyes became bedridden. He died on April 13, 1886. Theodore Noyes had arrived at Stone Cottage a few days earlier, and his father's last word was "Theodore." The funeral was held two days later at Oneida. Noyes was buried in the Community cemetery, with a simple headstone identical to those marking other Community graves. In keeping with Community tradition, there was little weeping. One of the children left behind at the Stone Cottage when the grown-ups departed for Oneida wrote in her diary, "Aunt Harriet and Mother Noyes left in good spirits and I heard Auntie say that it didn't seem a bit like a funeral."

hat remained of the Oneida Community after the death of its founder was a large, idiosyncratic, and unabashedly paternalistic family business. Its managers and upper-level white-collar workers, from the president and directors down to assistant plant superintendents and the salespeople who sold its tableware and other products, were bound together by ties of consanguinity, lifelong friendship, nostalgia for the comforting warmth of life in the old Community, and, in many cases, a desire to carry on, at least in an attenuated form, the Community's spiritual and moral mission. Many old Bible Communists, including those who had shared Noyes's last years at Niagara, continued to live in the Mansion House, either in one of the narrow bedrooms that had been theirs before the breakup or in more spacious apartments made by combining two or three of the former cubicles. Over the years many of the company's managers moved out of the Mansion House. But they seldom moved more than a few hundred yards, building houses on former Community farmland in the new village of Kenwood. For many years Kenwood was an extended-family enclave, or compound, whose residents were, almost without exception, former members of the Oneida Community or their spouses or children. As late as 1935, more than half a century after the death of the old Community, only sixty-three of the one hundred and sixty-seven adults living there were "outsiders," and about half of these were married to descendants of old Oneidans.

The existence of this new Community was, of course, predicated on the ability of Oneida Community, Ltd., to provide its residents with enough money, in the form of salaries and dividends, for a reasonably comfortable life. And in the years immediately after Noyes's death there were disquieting signs that the men who were running the company were not up to the job. Most were getting on in years and not attuned to the changes taking place in the American business world. Spiritualism continued to engross many of the old Community members, among them a majority of the company's directors and principal managers. They included John R. Lord, who became president of the company in 1889, and who was said to seek regular advice from John Noyes, via a medium, on company affairs. The advice seems not to have been helpful, and under Lord the company barely managed to keep its head above water.

Happily for the hundreds of old Oneidans and their families who were dependent on it, the company's fortunes were soon restored by a young, energetic, and highly talented businessman, Pierrepont Noyes. After two years of college he had gone to work in the Niagara tableware factory. But he saw little chance for a rewarding career as long as men like Lord were in charge: When his half-brother, Holton, complained that young men were being driven out of the company, he was told, "We don't need young men." Pierrepont soon quit to go into business for himself in New York City as a wholesaler of silverware and novelties. Helped by an infusion of capital supplied by John Humphrey Noyes's old intimate, James Herrick, who had been fired as the Oneida company's Chicago sales representative because of disparaging remarks he had made about spirit advisers, the business prospered. Unlike Herrick, Pierrepont had been discreet in his opposition to management by medium, and his firm was soon taken on by Oneida Community, Ltd., as a sales agent and jobber for the company's silverware.

In 1894, when he was twenty-three, Pierrepont Noyes became a company director. The appointment was only temporary: One of the antispiritualist minority on the Oneida board, Abram Burt, who had been his surrogate father in the old Community, planned to be away for a few months, and he arranged for Pierrepont to sit in for him during his absence. To Pierrepont's frustration and dismay, he found the company "sinking into a morass of elderly incompetence." But he was convinced that it had enormous possibilities if properly managed. With the backing of Herrick and Theodore Noyes, with whom Pierrepont had been living in New York, he mounted an energetic campaign to throw out Lord and the other spiritualists. The effort succeeded, but just barely. At the shareholders' meeting in 1895 the spiritualist majority on the board of directors was ousted by a margin of just sixteen votes. The new board then elected Theodore Noyes, who had long since outgrown his own earlier interest in spiritualism, as the company's new president.

With Theodore in charge, the company's financial condition quickly improved. But the most significant result of the shareholder rebellion incited by Pierrepont Noyes was that it brought him back into the company. After running the Niagara tableware and chain factories, he was put in charge of the trap business at Oneida, and in 1899, at the age of twenty-nine, he was named general manager of the company. Except for a five year stretch during and just after World War I—he served on the Rhineland Commission, which was responsible for the postwar Allied occupation of Germany—he ran the company in that capacity for the next twenty-seven years.

He persuaded older managers who had, in effect, inherited their jobs from Community days to give way to younger and more vigorous men. Many of these were fellow graduates of the Children's House who, like Pierrepont himself, had decided to strike out on their own, but whom he had persuaded to come to work for the company. Under their management, the company flourished. Noyes convinced the directors that silverware, not traps, should be the company's main line of business. He also persuaded them that they would have to overcome their fear of spending money and lay out huge sums on advertising. The money was well spent: unrestrained by the old Oneida Community's distaste for showiness or sham even in business affairs, Noyes and his colleagues pioneered in introducing advertising that featured drawings of pretty girls and photographs of celebrities like the dancer and fashion arbiter Irene Castle. By 1926, when Noyes turned over the general managership to his son-in-law, Miles Robertson, the trap business and other old Community businesses had been sold or closed down, and Oneida Community, Ltd., had become one of the world's leading manufacturers of silverware.

The Oneidans had prided themselves on being good to their hired hands, and Pierrepont Noyes was determined to carry out this policy. He seems to have regarded this as a sound business policy and, perhaps more important, as a moral obligation. The company not only paid good wages, but was at pains to see that its workers were well housed and otherwise well taken care of. In 1913 the silverware business was moved from Niagara to the new community of Sherrill, which the company had laid out just to the north of the Mansion House. Here, any employee who wanted to build a house could get cheap land from the company and a building bonus of a few hundred dollars. The company partly subsidized a social and athletic club, built a five-hole golf course and a baseball field, contributed money for the building of churches (though very few of the company's managers or their families were church members), put up half the money for a new elementary and a new high school, and assumed half the cost of teachers' salaries. All this made a powerful impression on a union organizer who was dispatched to Sherrill in 1916 to scout the terrain. He reported back that "this company is different from any company you have ever heard of in their treatment of their employees." He said there would be no point in trying to organize a company whose workers were happy, well paid, worked short hours, enjoyed a wide variety of fringe benefits, and were treated "like human beings." Sherrill, moreover, was not run like an ordinary company town. Noyes and other company executives had tried to persuade New York's governor, Charles Seymour Whitman, to designate Sherrill as an autonomous "commune." Whitman reportedly said, "I'll be God-damned if I'll have a commune in the State of New York. I'll help you make it a city." In 1916 Sherrill was incorporated as a city   it was, and is, much the smallest city in the state—governed by an elected commission and a city manager.

Pierrepont Noyes was a shrewd and aggressive businessman. Business, H. G. Wells wrote after a visit to Oneida, "had got hold of him, it possessed him like a passion." But Pierrepont believed the company he headed and the village of Kenwood in which he lived to be more —and better—than simply a money-making enterprise set in a pleasant company town. He saw the company's managers and their families as constituting in some sense a continuation of the old Community. To the young men whom he recruited in the early years of his administration he made it clear that the new company, no matter how it might prosper, would not be a place where they could get rich. (Noyes did persuade the directors to raise the low salaries the company had been paying its managers; this was done so that the new managerial recruits could afford to buy up Oneida Community, Ltd., stock as it came on the market, and thereby keep control of the company within the old Oneida Community family. But salaries still remained substantially below competitive levels until well into the next century.)

What Noyes did hold out to his young proselytes, along with the excitement of building a thriving enterprise in which youth would no longer be a bar to rapid advancement, was a chance to subordinate the business of money-making to a higher moral purpose. Noyes saw the company not as an arena for fierce gladiatorial combat, but as a cooperative enterprise, whose managers' aim must be to provide a good and morally satisfying life for themselves, their families, and the other former Oneidans who were dependent on them. Maria Lockwood Carden, in her excellent history of Oneida Community, Ltd., quotes one of Noyes's young management recruits as saying, "The idea of altruism is not hard to sell to the young." It was clear, however, that this altruist was attracted as much by Pierrepont Noyes's dynamism—and his assurances that the days of stagnation and gerontocracy were at an end—as by his moral aims. "It never would have occurred to me to come back if it hadn't been for [Noyes]," he told Carden. "I'd been indoctrinated with the idea it was a dying institution." While Noyes was a tough competitor in his dealings with the outside world, within the company he managed to keep alive some of the cooperative spirit with which his father had tried, not always successfully, to infuse the business activities of the old Community. Important decisions were made, with rare exceptions, by consensus. And even when disagreements could not be settled in this manner, the desire for unity and reconciliation that had prevailed at Oneida before its time of troubles was still strong. In 1915, after a fierce contest for seats on the board of directors, Jessie Kinsley wrote in her diary, "No doubt there were heart-burnings and disappointments, but for the sake of harmony those were not voiced." Seeing this as evidence of the persistence of old Community ideals, she wrote, "I looked about and saw what I thought was a struggle with *self* marking some countenances."

In 1908 Pierrepont Noyes described the Kenwood community as "one hundred people or more so close to each other that the sorrows or joys of one are the sorrows and joys of all." This was plainly stretching things a bit, but Kenwood was, in fact, a tightly knit community in which certain strains of life before the breakup still sounded, if only faintly. Mutual criticism was dead, and there seem to have been no attempts to revive complex marriage (though a few men continued to practice male continence). And while some former Community members may have looked back nostalgically on the distinctive rhythm and the variety of sexual life at Oneida, in public, at least, people at Kenwood seemed to prefer to pretend that there had never been such a life, or that it had been a misguided result of excessive religious zeal. When Pierrepont Noyes and others praised the Oneida Community's founder, as they did, for example, in celebrating the "High Tide of the Spirit," the great day (February 20) on which, at the age of twenty-three, John Humphrey Noyes had declared himself free from sin, nothing was ever said about complex marriage. Pierrepont Noyes

preferred to stress the fact that the old Community had been "a genuine Christian Society where the teachings of its founders were devoted to the Christian doctrines of unselfishness and consecration."
These, he added, "were enforced in every department of human activity with amazing fidelity and literalness."

Although Kenwood children went away to college, and their parents traveled widely like other prosperous Americans, Kenwood, somewhat isolated geographically and socially, had a distinctive flavor. The
old Oneida Community belief in intellectual self-improvement remained strong. There were lectures on the gold standard, temperance,
European history, Indian Vedanta philosophy, and children's diet. Jessie Kinsley's daughter Edith, on annual visits to the Mansion House
during the years her family was living at Niagara Falls, was taught to
play chess by William Hinds and studied the New Testament with a
former Community member named John Freeman. With John Humphrey Noyes's nephew George Miller she read Montaigne, Balzac, and
Flaubert. There were reading clubs for adults, debating societies for
young people, and evening discussions around the Mansion House
fireplace. Great store was set by intellectual and artistic achievement:
Carden notes that in the half century after John Humphrey Noyes's
death, Kenwood residents published fourteen books. Some of the simplicity and egalitarianism of life in the old Community persisted in
Kenwood, whose residents were, in fact, on a fairly equal footing—
Community descendants who failed to win good management jobs in
the company tended to live somewhere else. Competitive consumption was frowned on. The wife of one high-ranking company executive, much admired for her generosity with time and money in
charitable causes, was affectionately teased for wearing cast-off clothes
collected for the poor. A young woman who married into the Community in the late 1920s was criticized for dressing too fashionably;
she, for her part, found the Kenwood women frowsy.

But by the 1930s Kenwood and the company were beginning to
lose their special character. With fewer and fewer remaining survivors,
the old Community receded into the historical past. And while the
board of directors and the top echelon of management continued to

be dominated by descendants of Oneida Community people—or men, like Miles Robertson, who had married into the Community family— more and more of its managers were outsiders for whom Oneida was simply a big corporation, with an interesting history, which was a good place to work. As the years went by, Pierrepont Noyes seemed increasingly uncertain as to just how the old Community ideals that he cherished could be carried out in the amoral and harshly competitive world of twentieth-century big business. "I have no fear," he wrote hopefully but vaguely in 1926, "but that the new generation will develop in a practical way the principles of the past, and will develop them to a point not glimpsed by us of the older times." Robertson, who succeeded Noyes as president in 1926, made no effort to exercise moral leadership in Kenwood as had his predecessor.

Although descendants of the old Community continued for half a century to dominate the management of the company, their influence was declining. By the late 1960s two-thirds of the directors were outsiders, and an outsider succeeded Pierrepont Noyes's son—also named Pierrepont—when he retired in 1981 as chairman and chief executive officer. Oneida, Ltd., as the company was renamed in 1935, now makes china tableware and industrial wire products as well as its extensive line of sterling silver and silverplate. It is also the world's largest manufacturer of stainless steel knives, forks, and spoons. Sales in 1991 were $446 million, and the company's stock is publicly traded and widely held. While a few Community descendants hold upper-middle management jobs, there are no descendants on the board of directors, and none in the senior executive ranks.

Some descendants of old Community families still live in Kenwood, but the attenuated version of communal life that Pierrepont Noyes tried to sustain has vanished. The Mansion House now furnishes living accommodations to several dozen residents, most of them elderly and many of them either Community descendants or the wives or husbands of descendants. As it has for many years, the company, whose Gothic general offices are situated just across the road, puts up business visitors in the Mansion House, and company meetings, including the annual shareholders' meeting, are held in the old family hall. There is a little store offering books about the Oneida Community, and there are guided tours for visitors that include a tiny Community bedroom that can be glimpsed through a glass partition. The family hall, with its allegorical ceiling paintings, and the cozy upper sitting room, where the children of the Community once danced and sang and tumbled about during the daily children's hour, are little changed from the time when the Community was in its prime.

But the logic and character of life at Oneida were never expressed in distinctive and enduring artifacts. The Oneidans produced no equivalent of Shaker furniture, Shaker painting, or Shaker architecture. Unless one knows enough of the history of the old Community to take in the meaning of the haunting photographs that hang on its walls, a visit to the Mansion House today only faintly evokes the rich and singular society that once flourished there.

By many standards, including those he himself applied in his darker moods, Noyes's ambitious plan for the transformation of the world had been a failure. As the years passed, the kingdom of heaven, which had once seemed so near at hand that Mary Cragin had invited members of the Primitive Church to send representatives to Oneida, promising "to do all that lies in our power to make such visit agreeable," receded into a distant theological future. Death did not die for even the most holy of Noyes's followers, as he had confidently predicted it would. In the treatment of illness, faith gave way to quinine, ice, and bracing bedside criticism. As the flood tide of revivalism ebbed after the wild excitements of the 1830s, Oneidans, like other Americans, were attacked by the spiritual disease of secularism; this lowered their resistance to the mounting assaults on sexual practices at Oneida that helped to bring about the Community's dissolution. During the years of Oneida's greatest spiritual prosperity, Noyes forecast that Oneidans would soon establish other Perfectionist communities by the scores and hundreds. Yet there was never more than one Oneida, and as of

January 1, 1880, Bible Communism was dead. With it died Noyes's hope of breeding a race of spiritually superior beings. And with it died his most daring social experiment, the institution of complex marriage.

But if Oneida left no indelible mark on the world, it was in its own time a striking success, flourishing for more than a generation while other utopian communities quickly withered. One reason was the Oneidans' conviction that, at God's bidding and under divinely inspired leadership, they were enlisted in a crusade to transform not just themselves, but the whole world, and this conviction bound the Community's founders to one another and to Noyes.

Another essential element in Noyes's formula for utopia was, of course, the ruling out of conventional romantic love and conventional matrimony. Complex marriage clearly did not exorcise the demon of sexual jealousy, nor did Noyes succeed in altogether suppressing the longing for the emotional security of ordinary marriage and family life. But complex marriage did make possible that undivided loyalty to the Community (and to Noyes) that was an indispensable condition of the total communism prevailing at Oneida. If conventional marriage had been the rule, even so shrewd and charismatic a leader as Noyes could not have overcome the conflicting and competitive loyalties of family groups.

A final and perhaps the most important element in the Community's remarkable durability—and, at the same time, an explanation of why Oneida was never duplicated—was that it was shaped not only by the religious revivals of the early years of the century, but also by Noyes's compelling leadership and unique personality. By turns ruthless and accommodating, possessing extraordinary personal charm, always able to find divine sanction for new measures he had decided on to fit changing circumstances—as when he abandoned the hope of imminent immortality in favor of achieving perfect holiness more gradually by stirpiculture—he inspired in his followers a sense of having embarked on a thrilling voyage of spiritual and social discovery. Equally important, he used both his spiritual authority and his sexual magnetism to ward off the potentially explosive consequences of complex marriage. The license and anarchy of Berlin Heights and of the early Perfectionists were avoided at Oneida because sex was by and large subordinated—though the linkage was not always clear—to a higher spiritual and moral purpose.

◆　　　◆　　　◆

The Oneida Community lasted and prospered because it offered its members an alternative way of living that most found deeply satisfying. Under the regime of complex marriage individual Oneidans were from time to time emotionally bruised and buffeted, but this was also surely true of people governed by the sexual ways of the world outside. The Oneidans were, moreover, spared such frequent concomitants of conventional matrimony as monotony, satiety, and the devastating recognition that one has chosen the wrong partner. Jessie Kinsley, who had a long and happy marriage to Myron Kinsley after the breakup of the Community, nevertheless looked back nostalgically many years later at "the changing and the steadfast lovers. Some heartache, much happiness." (For older men and women, of course, especially those of elevated spiritual standing, ascending fellowship had the merit of securing them the delights, without guilt, of a succession of youthful sex partners.)

Bible Communism offered particularly rich rewards to women, who were free to accept or reject sexual partners; the sexual subjugation that was the lot of Victorian wives was unknown at Oneida. Furthermore, while the Stirpiculture Committee might restrict a woman's freedom of choice by rejecting her application to have a child by a particular man, thanks to male continence no woman had to become pregnant unless she chose to do so. Male continence also meant prolonged intercourse and the virtual certainty, under the unwritten rules by which men were expected to abide, of achieving orgasm—a pleasure not expected and seldom attained in the usual nineteenth-century marriage. Nor were Bible Communism's benefits to women limited to their sex lives. They might not be the equals of men, but the gap was much narrower than in the outside world. Even in the earlier days of austerity, when the Oneidans did all their own household chores, the greater efficiency of communal housekeeping and child rearing, and the fact that men shared in some of the domestic work, meant less drudgery for women than in a great many conventional families.

All in all, if one could put up with mutual criticism, the lack of privacy, and the enforced religious orthodoxy—these were not small ifs, but everyone was free to leave—life at Oneida could be richly gratifying. One of its principal charms was its variety. In accordance with Noyes's theory that it was dangerous to get into a rut, because the devil then knew where to find you, people constantly changed jobs and diversions, transferring from trap shop to silk mill to printing office, studying Greek one month and astronomy the next, and giving up chess for band music or choral singing. For children, Oneida was like a progressive twentieth-century boarding school, with the additional advantage that there was no homesickness because parents, both natural and surrogate, were at hand for love, comfort, and instruction. Old people could work as much or as little as they wished, were encouraged to act as grandparents to the residents of the Children's House, and when they could no longer care for themselves were cared for by other elderly people. For adults as well as children, too, Oneida had much in common with a progressive school. Single-minded cultivation of talent might be frowned on at Oneida by Noyes and the criticism committees, as demonstrated by the putting away of Frank Wayland-Smith's violin. But all members were encouraged to express themselves, Noyes even proposing that the Community should develop and apply a scientific approach to writing poetry. At Oneida, work, play, learning, sex, and religious meditation were blended and mixed and kneaded to form what Noyes once called "that seething mass of miraculous life." As one looks back, Oneida soars above the plain of nineteenth-century revivalism and utopia building, a monument to the irresistible impulse, inevitably doomed but seldom so nearly realized, to create a new world and people it with new men and women.

The members of the Oneida Community believed they were enlisted in a spiritual adventure of high significance, and they wanted the world to know about it. They welcomed the journalists from Europe and America who visited Oneida, tried to answer their questions, and reflected tolerantly on their often sensational and inaccurate reports. Far more important to anyone wishing to gain a real understanding of the Oneida experiment are the accounts written by the Oneidans themselves and published for the edification and entertainment of Community members and their sympathizers throughout the country. There were thousands of such reports. Many were extremely well written, and they convey in wonderfully rich detail the texture of life at Oneida, with its band music, evening lectures, bag making bees, croquet, dancing on the lawn. These reports dealt, too, with such matters as the care and schooling of children, the technology of trap making, the wages to be paid to hired hands, the ceremonial weighing of Community babies, and the ritual and joys of doing the Community laundry.

I have drawn heavily on these accounts, many of which were printed in the little two-page daily newspaper circulated at Oneida in the late 1860s under the title of *Daily Journal of Oneida Community* and the *O.C. Daily*. (The complete run of these publications is reproduced in *Daily Journal of*

Oneida Community volumes 1–3 and the *O.C. Daily* volumes 4–5, Porcupine Press: Philadelphia, PA, 1975.) Other accounts of daily life at Oneida were published in the (usually) weekly newspaper—it was successively called the *Spiritual Magazine*, the *Free Church Circular*, the *Circular* (or the *Oneida Circular*), and, finally, the *American Socialist*—that was mailed out to Christian Perfectionists throughout the country as a means of expounding—and gaining converts to—what John Humphrey Noyes called Bible Communism.

An extensive collection of excerpts from the *Oneida Circular* and its predecessors, supplemented by some reports carried in the *Daily Journal*, was published in 1970 by Syracuse University Press. Titled *Oneida Community: An Autobiography, 1851–1876*, it was edited by Constance Noyes Robertson, a granddaughter of John Humphrey Noyes, and the daughter of parents both of whom were "stirpiculsts"—products, that is, of Oneida's venture into scientific human breeding. Robertson's book is divided into chapters with titles like "How They Lived and Worked," "Businesses," "Complex Marriage," and "How They Played," and I am deeply indebted to her for this fine anthology of what the Oneidans wrote about themselves.

There are also three excellent memoirs written by former members of the Oneida Community. One is *My Father's House: An Oneida Boyhood* (New York: Holt, Rinehart and Winston, 1965), by Pierrepont B. Noyes. The author, a son of John Humphrey Noyes who grew up to become president of Oneida, Ltd., the big silverware company that rose on the foundations of the old Oneida Community, was born at Oneida in 1870. As a boy he visited his father in exile in Canada, and among this book's many virtues is the author's beautifully rendered portrait of the Community's founder in his last years. Pierrepont Noyes's wife, Corinna Ackley Noyes, another stirpicult, also wrote a memoir, *The Days of My Youth* (Kenwood, New York: Mansion House, 1960). I found her account particularly valuable for its picture of life in the Children's House, and for her wrenching account of the pain suffered by many Oneida mothers (including her own) when they had to yield up their children to the care of the Community—a theme also sounded poignantly by Pierrepont Noyes. Still another memoir, *Old Mansion-House Memories* (Oneida, NY: privately published, 1950), was written by Pierrepont's mother, Harriet Worden. A collection of articles published in 1871–1872 in the *Circular*, of which Worden was then the editor, it provides detailed and lovingly drawn portraits of Oneidans as they went about their daily business in the Community's early years.

I have also relied heavily on George Wallingford Noyes's *John Humphrey Noyes: The Putney Community* (Oneida, NY: author, 1931). Like Pierrepont Noyes, George Wallingford Noyes, a nephew of John Humphrey, was a child of stirpiculture. He spent much of the later part of his life working on a detailed history of Bible Communism and the Oneida experiment. He was unable to complete this work before his death in 1941, but he did publish two installments. The second of these, *The Putney Community*, made up in large part of letters and other documents, is indispensable for an understanding of the Vermont years when John Humphrey Noyes tried out many of the ideas—including complex marriage—on which the Oneida Community was later founded.

The first volume in George Wallingford Noyes's projected series, *Religious Experience of John Humphrey Noyes* (New York: Macmillan, 1923), consists largely of excerpts from John Humphrey Noyes's writings. It serves as a useful complement to John Humphrey Noyes's own detailed and revealing account of the formation of his religious views and the spiritual travails of his early years. That account, published at Oneida in 1849, was titled *Confessions of John Humphrey Noyes, Part I: Confession of Religious Experience: Including a History of Modern Perfectionism* (Part II was never published). Noyes was a prolific writer, whose published works, besides this autobiographical volume, include a number of pamphlets and articles setting forth the basic principles of Bible Communism. The most important of these are *Bible Communism: Defining the Relations of the Sexes in the Kingdom of Heaven*, published in 1849 in the *First Annual Report of the Oneida Association; Male Continence* (Oneida, NY: Office of the *Oneida Circular*, 1872; reprinted in facsimile by AMS Press, New York, 1974); *Essay on Scientific Propagation* (Oneida, NY: Oneida Community, 1875); and *Mutual Criticism* (Oneida, NY: Office of the *American Socialist*, 1876; reprinted in 1976 by AMS Press, New York, as *Handbook of the Oneida Community, 1867 & 1871 [bound with] Mutual Criticism*). The Community also published a collection of Noyes's informal evening talks, which admirably convey the range (and quirkiness) of his views on theology, morality, Bible Communism, and the art of "provoking to love." Originally published at Oneida in 1875, *Home-Talks* has also been reprinted in a facsimile edition (New York: AMS Press, 1975).

Other primary sources on which I have drawn include a large and varied body of unpublished material, including diaries and memoirs. Perhaps the most valuable of these is the frank and copious diary kept by Francis Wayland-Smith, a thoughtful commentator who played the part of what would now be called a participant observer in the events that led to the breakup of the Community in 1880. A journal kept by John Humphrey Noyes in 1881–1885 ("Niagara Journal") describes his flight to Canada and the new life he began there, and records his reflections on the demise of the Community to which he had devoted so much of his life. Jessie Kinsley's "A Memory of Youth" is a sensitive and perceptive account of coming of age at Oneida; most of that account has been published in Jessie Catherine Kinsley, *A Lasting Spring*, edited by Jane Kinsley Rich with the assistance of Nelson M. Blake (Syracuse, NY: Syracuse University Press, 1983). A diary kept from 1867 to 1880 by Tirzah Miller is a valuable source of information on sexual politics and practices at Oneida, including her own sexual relations with her uncle and spiritual guide, John Humphrey Noyes.

I have also made extensive use of letters written by members of the Oneida Community. Oneidans were constantly moving back and forth between Oneida and its Wallingford, Connecticut, satellite—Noyes lived there for years at a time—and they corresponded frequently and at length. More than any other source, their letters illuminate Oneidans' agonizing struggles with the devil of religious disbelief, along with the often painful emotional turbulence that was inseparable from complex marriage—aspects of life at Oneida that seldom got into print in the generally elegiac reports published in the *Circular*. Letters also turned out to be an invaluable source of information about the conflicts—religious, sexual, and political—that eventually destroyed the Community. Letters written to Noyes by his supporters at Oneida after his flight to Canada in 1879 were particularly helpful, notably those in which his sister and close confidante, Harriet Skinner, kept him informed—she was an excellent reporter—on the Community's death throes.

When I began work on *Without Sin* in the late 1970s, these journals and letters were either held by descendants of Community members or were squirreled away, uncataloged, in nooks and crannies of the Mansion House, the Community's old home. All or most of this rich trove, along with other diaries, letters, autobiographical sketches, reminiscences, and miscellaneous unpublished writings by Oneidans, has now been assembled at Syracuse University's George Arents Research Library to form the Oneida Community Collection, whose inventory fills 94 typewritten pages.

That inventory would be even larger if it had not been for an event that descendants of the old Bible Communists who have been concerned with preserving intact the records of the Oneida Community sometimes unhappily refer to as the Burning. All the facts are hard to come by—at any rate, I have not come by them. But it is clear that sometime in the 1940s several Community descendants, who were also executives of Oneida, Ltd., concluded that if the public were to learn the full truth about what Noyes once called the "seething mass of miraculous life" at Oneida, the company's image would be tarnished. Accordingly, they ordered the burning of thousands—quite possibly tens of thousands—of documents bearing on Oneida's history. The Oneidans believed in keeping records of everything they did for the edification of posterity, and among the documents that were destroyed were letters, internal communications, and reports of meetings (including records of mutual criticism sessions), without which no comprehensive history of the Oneida experiment could possibly be written.

These documents, filling a large, specially constructed storage vault, had been assembled by George Wallingford Noyes. His intention was to use them as the basis for a continuation of the series he had begun with *Religious Experience of John Humphrey Noyes* and *The Putney Community*. Happily for other historians, Noyes was well along with his project when he died. He had selected the documents he wanted to use, transcribed them, and arranged them roughly in chronological order. These documents were interspersed with extensive narrative passages of his own composition. This documentary history fortunately escaped incineration, remaining in the possession of the author's daughter, Mrs. Imogen Stone, who very kindly made the collection available to me. Photocopies of the twenty-two hundred typewritten pages of what are referred to in the chapter notes that follow as the G. W. Noyes Papers are included although access has been restricted—in the Oneida Community Collection at Syracuse University.

One of the few writers who have been granted permission to mine this mother lode was Constance Noyes Robertson. In 1972, as a companion volume to her earlier *Oneida Community: An Autobiography, 1851–1876*, she published *The Oneida Community: The Breakup, 1876–1881* (Syracuse, NY: Syracuse University Press). Much of Robertson's detailed account of how and why the Oneida experiment came to an end is based on the G. W. Noyes Papers. But her book has a curious flaw. Again and again, the author (who died in 1985) chose to delete passages from letters and other documents (including the diary of Francis Wayland-Smith) without giving the reader any indication that she had done so. Most of the deleted passages have to do with sexual politics at Oneida, and with charges of improper sexual behavior brought against her grandfather, John Humphrey Noyes. This is a major fault in an otherwise useful documentary narrative of the Community's decline and fall, and it would be good if a way could be found to bring out a new edition with the deletions restored.

The Oneida Community has intrigued generations of historians, theologians, and sociologists, who have produced a very large body of doctoral dissertations, books, and articles; many of the latter have been published in scholarly journals—notably, in recent years, in *Communal Societies*, published by the National Historic Communal Societies Association (offices at the Center for Communal Studies, University of Southern Indiana, Evansville, Indiana).

While I have read much of this material, I have chosen to rely, with a few exceptions, on primary sources. One exception is Robert Allerton Parker's *A Yankee Saint: John Humphrey Noyes and the Oneida Community* (New York: Putnam's, 1935; reprinted in 1972 by Porcupine Press, Philadelphia). Parker does not appear to have had access to some of the documents collected by George Noyes, and his biography is marred by a somewhat bouncy style and descriptive passages that may or may not be grounded in historical fact ("The great black eyes seemed to pierce those of the trembling youth," "Unnamed desires pounded like breakers in his imagination," etc.). But I found his account of Noyes's family background and early years a useful supplement to George Wallingford Noyes's *Religious Experience of John Humphrey Noyes*. Another secondary source on which I have drawn is Maren Lockwood Carden's carefully researched *Oneida: Utopian Community to Modern Corporation* (Baltimore: Johns Hopkins Press, 1969; New York: Harper & Row, 1971), on which I have relied almost exclusively for my account of the evolution of Oneida, Ltd. I am also indebted to Dolores Hayden's *Seven American Utopias: The Architecture of Communitarian Socialism, 1790–1975* (Cambridge, MA: MIT Press, 1976). Her excellent and copiously illustrated chapter on Oneida, "The Architecture of Complex Marriage," helped me greatly to understand the way the Oneidans set about shaping their environment—their gardens and grounds, as well as the communally planned Mansion House in which they lived—to fit in with and facilitate the way of living prescribed by Bible Communism. *Seven American Utopias* also illuminated for me the connection between Perfectionist theology and the Oneidans' passion for inventing things, as well as their fascination with machinery, tools, and other forms of technology.

In the notes that follow I have, in general, indicated for each chapter —or cluster of chapters—the principal sources on which I have drawn, and then listed other sources, keying each citation to the appropriate page of the text.

CHAPTER ONE

Much of this chapter summarizes, or touches on, matters and events discussed (and documented) in later chapters. But a few sources may usefully be given here. My account of Noyes's flight to Canada, and of the reaction at Oneida, are based on Noyes's "Niagara Journal" and the diary of Francis Wayland-Smith. Other sources for this chapter include:

3   ". . . girls were ordinarily introduced to sex, usually by Noyes himself, as soon as they reached puberty": letter from Theodore Noyes to Anita Newcomb McGee, April 15, 1892. An obstetrician named Ely Van de Warker, who visited Oneida in 1877, reported that he had asked a number of women at what age they had entered "communistic marriage." Four said they had been "married" at fourteen, eight at thirteen, and seven at twelve (Van de Warker, "A Gynecological Study of the Oneida Community," *American Journal of Obstetrics*, 17(8), August 1884).

3   "Not all of Noyes's followers were convinced . . .": The question of how serious a threat of prosecution confronted Noyes is explored in Chapter 22.

5   Noyes "standing amid the ruins of his lifework": Robertson, *Oneida Community*, p. 26.

6   "Every trait of my character . . .": Allan Eastlake, *The Oneida Community* (London: George Redway, 1900; reprinted by AMS Press, New York, 1973).

6   Noyes's view of Hawthorne as a glorifier of evil appeared in the *Circular*, April 4, 1864.

6   Noyes as "father and liberator": *O.C. Daily*, December 27, 1867.

7   ". . . we shall find it our special duty to be happy": from a "Table Talk" given at the Community's Brooklyn branch in 1852 and reported in the *Circular* (undated clipping).

7   Noyes's assertion that sexual intercourse should be cultivated as an art is from "Bible Argument," *First Annual Report of the Oneida Association* (Oneida Reserve, New York, Leonard & Company, 1849).

8–9   "In a memoir written for her daughter . . .": the quoted passages with which the chapter ends are from Kinsley, *A Lasting Spring*, pp. 9–10, 67.

CHAPTER TWO

This introductory chapter, ranging over the whole history of the Oneida Community, is drawn from a wide variety of sources:

1 0   "a chaos of confusion, tribulation, and war": G. W. Noyes, *Religious Experience of John Humphrey Noyes*, p. 308.

1 0   The vow of obedience exacted by Noyes is given in G. W. Noyes, *The Putney Community*, p. 206.

1 1   ". . . I am right whether they understand me or not": G. W. Noyes Papers, Vol. 1, pp. 86–87.

1 1   Why Noyes shouldn't be criticized: "Community Politics," the *Circular*, June 25, 1853.

1 1   "Not surprisingly, nine of the fifty-eight 'stirpicults' . . .": Different accounts have given different figures for the total number of stirpicults, and for the number fathered by Noyes. I have relied on the list entered in his diary by Francis Wayland-Smith, excluding from the total a child of Noyes that was stillborn.

1 1   Fanny Leonard "a beautiful plant": from the conclusion of a mutual criticism session in 1849, printed in the *Circular* (new series), Vol. 5, Jan. 4, 1869.

1 1   "I don't care anything about her as a wife . . .": G. W. Noyes Papers, Vol. 1, p. 365.

11 Noyes on the "intoxicating" Mary Cragin: "Social Character of Mrs. C.," the *Spiritual Magazine*, April 5, 1849.

12 Romantic love as "a kind of fatality": *Oneida Circular*, April 27, 1874.

12 Noyes thinking with his eyes closed and "communing with St. Paul": Kinsley, *A Lasting Spring*, p. 32; Corinna Ackley Noyes, *The Days of My Youth*, p. 73.

12 Noyes on being "uncomely": undated clipping headed "Criticism of H.H.S.," probably from the *Circular*.

12 Noyes's "social magnetism," etc.: letter from Theodore R. Noyes to Anita Newcomb McGee, April 15, 1892.

12 "One who had been deeply troubled by doubts . . .": letter from Beulah Hendee to Annie Hatch, Sept. 15, 1878.

12 Herrick on Noyes having "the queen-bee quality" etc.: James B. Herrick, "A Reminiscence of John H. Noyes," the *Quadrangle*, Kenwood, New York, May 1908.

12–13 Noyes's bullying of his mother: George W. Noyes, *The Putney Community*, pp. 27, 93.

13 Noyes on the iniquity of Mills: the *Circular*, Nov. 28, 1864.

13 Noyes on the mirthfulness of God: J. H. Noyes, *Mutual Criticism*, p. 58.

14 Noyes on "the science that underlies all poetry": letter to Alfred Barron, Nov. 12, 1876.

14 "Satan transformed into an angel of light": J. H. Noyes, *Confession of Religious Experience*, p. 42.

14 How Noyes consulted the spiritual world: letter from Theodore R. Noyes to Anita Newcomb McGee, Sept. 13, 1891.

14 Why the devil falsely contends that man's "body is gross and his passions vile": J. H. Noyes, "Ascetism Not Christianity," Home Talk No. 70, *Circular*, Nov. 23, 1851.

14 Noyes on the devil's responsibility for disease: *Daily Journal*, March 29, 1866.

NOTES

1 4   Noyes as a "composite of mysticism and common sense": letter from Theodore R. Noyes to Anita Newcomb McGee, Sept. 13, 1891.

1 5   How Noyes cured his brother-in-law of headaches: the *Spiritual Magazine*, Oct. 15, 1847.

1 5   On healing by doses of bedside criticism: J. H. Noyes, *Mutual Criticism*, pp. 71–79.

1 5   On triumphing over death: the *Spiritual Magazine*, May 15, 1846; J. H. Noyes, "Paul's Prize," report of a Home Talk, n.d.

1 5   Noyes as a violinist: Corinna Ackley Noyes, in *The Days of My Youth*, writes (page 25) that Noyes "hadn't a wisp of musical talent," and that his "distressing, off-key mutterings were tolerated with a smile." Her source was her mother, Alice Ackley, one of the Community's most accomplished singers.

1 5   Studying Hebrew: letter from Mary L. Prindle, Stone Cottage, Niagara Falls, to Charlotte Leonard, Feb. 11, 1883.

1 5   Noyes's spotted vest, etc.: Kinsley, "Memories of Youth," p. 59.

1 6   Noyes's room, where people "sometimes went to him for love": Kinsley, "Memories of Youth," p. 60.

1 6   "the liberty of *unity* . . .": *Home-Talks*, p. 346.

1 6   Noyes's reflections on women's dress: *First Annual Report of the Oneida Association*, p. 41.

1 6   Less talk during sex: Home Talk, Sept. 22, 1852.

1 7   "Let us also be heroes in love . . .": G. W. Noyes Papers, Vol. 1, p. 37.

1 7   Noyes's proposal for public sex in the Community meeting hall: letter from Tirzah Miller to George Washington Noyes, March 28, 1869.

1 7   Noyes on the folly of prudery: G. W. Noyes Papers, Vol. 1, p. 320.

1 7 – 1 8   Why Skinner was a poor lover: *Circular*, Feb. 15, 1869; reprint of a report of a criticism session on April 5, 1849.

1 8   Noyes on the virtues of change: *O. C. Daily*, May 11, 1867. The speaker is William Woolworth, but he is clearly quoting Noyes.

1 8   Revamping the evening meetings: letter from Beulah Hendee to Annie Hatch, March 26, 1879.

C H A P T E R S   T H R E E   A N D   F O U R

The two best accounts of the spiritual storms of Noyes's early years, and of the origins of his unorthodox religious views, are contained in two volumes: Noyes's own *Confession of Religious Experience* and George Wallingford Noyes's *Religious Experience of John Humphrey Noyes*. Chapters Three and Four, which take Noyes through his twenty-fourth year, are based almost entirely on these two works. Other sources on which I have drawn include:

1 9 – 2 0   I have used Parker, *A Yankee Saint*, to supplement G. W. Noyes's account of J. H. Noyes's family background, boyhood, and student years.

2 1   "Such declarations were not uncommon in 1831 . . .": This paragraph is based on Bernard A. Weisberger, *They Gathered at the River: The Story of the Great Revivalists and Their Impact upon Religion in America* (Boston: Little, Brown, 1958). For an understanding of the religious movements from which the Oneida Community sprang, I am also indebted to Whitney R. Cross, *The Burnt-Over Districts: The Social and Intellectual History of Enthusiastic Religion in Western New York 1825–50* (Ithaca, NY: Cornell University Press, 1950).

3 3   ". . . one of his nieces said . . ." : letter from Eliza Ann Walbridge to John Humphrey Noyes, Aug. 22, 1875.

C H A P T E R   F I V E

This chapter, like the two that precede it, is drawn largely from *Confession of Religious Experience* and *Religious Experience of John Humphrey Noyes*, with the addition of G. W. Noyes's *The Putney Community*. Other sources:

4 0   "I shall therefore pass and repass . . .": from the first issue of the *Witness*, Aug. 20, 1837.

4 2   "According to a biographical sketch . . .": "A Community Mother," *Circular*, Sept. 17 and Nov. 5, 1866.

4 4   ". . . no particular love of the sentimental kind . . .": from "Financial Romance," *Circular*, Jan. 18, 1866.

CHAPTERS   SIX   THROUGH   EIGHT

With the exceptions that follow, these chapters are based on *The Putney Community*.

4 6   On marrying Harriet Holton for her money: the English journalist was William Hepworth Dixon; the quotation is from the *Circular*, April 15, 1867, reprinted in J. H. Noyes, *Dixon and His Copyists* (Oneida, NY: Oneida Community, 1874).

4 8   "could carry a virgin in each hand . . .": William Hepworth Dixon, *Spiritual Wives* (Philadelphia: Lippincott, 1868), p. 349.

5 1   On New Harmony and other experiments in communal living: I cannot pretend to have read more than a small portion of the vast body of literature about nineteenth-century utopian communities in America. Among the books I found particularly helpful in placing Oneida in context were *Backwoods Utopias: The Sectarian Origins and the Owenite Phase of Communitarian Socialism in America, 1663–1829*, by Arthur E. Bestor, Jr. (2nd ed., rev. and enlarged, Philadelphia, 1970); *The Communistic Societies of the United States* (New York: Harper & Brothers, 1875), by Charles Nordhoff; *American Communities* (Oneida, NY: Office of the *American Socialist*, 1878), by William Hinds (Hinds was a prominent member of the Oneida Community); and John Humphrey Noyes's *History of American Socialisms* (Philadelphia: J. P. Lippincott & Co., 1870). Dolores Hayden's *Seven American Utopias* has an excellent chapter on Fourier and his American disciples.

5 4   "But Noyes was at pains to point out . . .": The quotations from Noyes in this paragraph are from the *Perfectionist* (Jan. 1, 1844); the *Perfectionist and Democratic Watchman* (Sept. 7, 1844); and the *Spiritual Magazine* (March 15, 1846).

5 8   The "pamphlet published at Oneida" was *Male Continence*.

5 9 "Indeed, every evil passion was very strong in me . . .": Constance Noyes Robertson, *Oneida Community Profiles* (Syracuse, NY: Syracuse University Press, 1877), p. 41.

5 9 "Her only ambition was to be the servant of love . . .": *Circular*, Jan. 11, 1852.

5 9 "Noyes once said . . .": from a report of a criticism session published in the *Spiritual Magazine*, April 15, 1849, as "Social Character of Mrs. C."

5 9 ". . . a passage from a notebook . . .": published in the *Circular*, Dec. 21, 1851.

5 9 Footnote: quotation is from Dixon, *Spiritual Wives*, p. 348.

6 1 "He stands opposing my theory . . .": letter to Harriet Skinner, quoted in Parker, *A Yankee Saint*, pp. 123–124.

7 3 "The little group at Oneida grew rapidly . . .": The account of the Community's first year, which takes up the rest of this chapter, is drawn from the *First Annual Report of the Oneida Association* (Oneida Reserve: Leonard & Co., 1849) and from Harriet Worden, *Old Mansion House Memories*. In characterizing the early members of the Community, I have also relied on a "Family Register," apparently kept by Harriet Noyes, which contains short biographical sketches of everyone who joined the Community through the end of 1848.

CHAPTERS NINE AND TEN

These chapters are largely based on the G. W. Noyes Papers; on Robertson's *Oneida Community: An Autobiography;* on George W. Cragin's unpublished "Reminiscences About Businesses in the Community"; on the *Daily Journal of Oneida Community* and the *O. C. Daily;* and on my own reading of the *Circular*, its predecessors (the *Spiritual Magazine* and the *Free Church Circular*), and its successor (the *American Socialist*)—the Community publications from which Mrs. Robertson's account of life at Oneida is largely constructed. I have also made use of a variety of other (mainly unpublished) material, as follows:

8 0   "He was apparently persuaded . . .": *Third Annual Report of the Oneida Association* (Oneida Reserve, NY: Leonard & Co., 1851); Parker, *A Yankee Saint*, p. 190.

8 2   ". . . it was thought that some could support themselves at Wallingford . . .": Constance Noyes Robertson, *Oneida Community Profiles* (Syracuse, NY: Syracuse University Press, 1977), p. 67.

9 0   ". . . a landscape of unspeakable beauty . . .": *Hand-Book of the Oneida Community No. 2* (Oneida, New York: The Oneida Community, 1871), p. 10.

9 2   ". . . God *wanted* his children to enjoy eating strawberries . . .": Table Talk, Brooklyn, 1852.

9 3   "I know what it is to doubt the existence of God . . .": letter from Mary Louise Prindle to Theodore R. Noyes, July 1, 1878.

9 3   "I hope your love for Beulah . . .": letter to Mr. Olds, July 12, 1865.

9 5   "They entertained themselves . . .": Worden, *Old Mansion-House Memories*, p. 61; *Circular*, Feb. 13, 1865; "Oneida Community Journal" (unpublished), Jan. 31, 1863.

9 5   "A granddaughter of Noyes . . . noted that tableaux were 'great favorites . . .' ": Corinna Ackley Noyes, *The Days of My Youth*, p. 26.

9 6   "But by most accounts he played it terribly . . .": Corinna Ackley Noyes, *The Days of My Youth*, p. 25.

9 6   Footnote on "music and sex . . . closely intertwined": Tirzah Miller, diary, Sept. 22, 1868.

9 7   "Where shall we go to scrape our first lesson . . .": quoted in Worden, *Old Mansion-House Memories*, p. 85.

9 7   "Later there were string quartets . . .": Dr. George Edward Cragin, "Miscellaneous Memories of Community Life" (unpublished).

9 7   "One year four of the Community's best singers . . . always room for everyone who came": Cragin, "Miscellaneous Memories"; *Circular*, March 21, 1864.

9 7   ". . . when people badly needed a diversion . . .": Robertson, *The Oneida Community: The Breakup*, p. 227.

99   ". . . work would 'become sport . . .' ": *First Annual Report of the Oneida Association*, p. 39.

99   "A woman named Jessie Kinsley . . .": Kinsley, "Community Work," unpublished memoir, 1933.

102   "When peas were to be shelled . . .": Worden, *Old Mansion-House Memories*, p. 54.

102   "Like many other Community rites . . .": Cragin, "Miscellaneous Memories."

103   "Ah! our old washing days . . .": Worden, *Old Mansion-House Memories*, p. 29.

104   "The standard reply was a bland assertion . . .": Noyes, "Bible Communism," p. 14.

106–107   "In a letter written in 1867 . . . Harriet Worden recalled . . .": Parker, *A Yankee Saint*, p. 258.

CHAPTERS   ELEVEN   AND   TWELVE

My principal sources for these chapters were *Mutual Criticism, Home-Talks*, Robertson's *Autobiography*, the *Circular*, the *Daily Journal*, the *O.C. Daily*, the G. W. Noyes Papers, and Kinsley, "Memories of Youth." Other sources, in addition to those mentioned in the text, were:

109   "The Oneidans . . . had 'regarded themselves as a peculiar people . . .' ": manuscript of talk (undated) by Francis Wayland-Smith.

109   "A designated leader . . ." The description of the evening meetings in this and the four paragraphs that follow is drawn from Corinna Ackley Noyes, *The Days of My Youth;* Robertson, *Autobiography; Home-Talks;* Kinsley, "Memories of Youth"; the *Circular;* and the *Quadrangle* (Kenwood, NY), June 1908.

113   "An older woman, criticized for being 'incautious . . .' ": "Community Journal," Feb. 9, 1863.

114   "A young woman at Wallingford . . .": report (manuscript) on criticism of Mary Louise Prindle, Feb. 7, 1864.

120   "A woman named Keziah Worden . . . described as 'an active unbeliever . . .' '": letter from George Cragin to Marcus L. Worden, ca. March 1850.

120   "Tryphena Seymour . . .": letter from Harriet Skinner to Marcus L. Worden, Feb. 22, 1849.

120–121   "Joseph Skinner, who had spent . . .": G. W. Noyes Papers, Vol. 2, pp. 112–113.

122   ". . . dramatically improve the health of the confessor": John Humphrey Noyes, *The Berean* (Putney, VT: Office of the *Spiritual Magazine*, 1847), p. 486.

126–127   "Noyes now proposed . . . a doctor 'of our own folks' . . .": "Community Journal," Oct. 3, 1863.

127   ". . . Noyes's brother-in-law John Skinner wrote . . .": the *Spiritual Magazine*, May 15, 1846.

128   "God may yet permit some traveler . . .": the *Spiritual Magazine*, Dec. 15, 1846.

CHAPTER THIRTEEN

In this chapter about the position of women at Oneida, I have again drawn heavily on the *Circular* and its predecessors, the *Spiritual Magazine* and the *Free Church Circular*, as well as on Robertson's *Oneida Community: An Autobiography*. Other sources in the citations that follow include works on which I relied for an understanding of what it was like to be an American woman in the mid-nineteenth century who was *not* a member of the Oneida Community.

130–131   "Christ . . . was determined that men and women should 'love one another burningly . . .' ": *First Annual Report of the Oneida Association*, p. 21.

131   ". . . conventional marriage, in which the wife had virtually no sexual rights . . .": Page Smith, in *Daughters of the Promised Land* (Boston: Little Brown, 1970), notes (p. 139) that "mythology circulated that to deny a man sex was wicked, since it would force him into the sin of fornication." Smith also writes (pp. 138–139), "We find a constant litany

running through the writings of the more daring spokesmen of the women's movement: women must gain control of their own bodies; marriage is a form of legalized prostitution because the husband may lay claim to sexual intercourse at his own will." In 1855, Smith observes (p. 164), Lucy Stone wrote Elizabeth Cady Stanton, "I *very much* wish that a wife's right to her own body should be pushed at our next convention."

1 3 1   ". . . that normal women were incapable of enjoying sex . . .": Mary P. Ryan, *Womanhood in America* (New York: New Viewpoints, 1975), writes (p. 159), "According to most nineteenth-century physiologists, the normal woman had no sex drive per se, only the generosity to submit to intercourse out of love for her husband." She adds (p. 160) that many physicians saw female sexuality as a perversion, a disease that must be rooted out—for example, by clitoridectomy.

1 3 1   ". . . coitus interruptus . . . was the only reasonably reliable alternative to complete abstinence . . .": Daniel S. Smith, in "Family Limitation, Sexual Control, and Domestic Feminism in Victorian America" (*Feminist Studies,* 1, 1973, pp. 40–57), noting the striking decline in the fertility rate of white women from 1800 to 1880, writes that while douches and sponges were also used, coitus interruptus and abstinence were the principal means of preventing conception.

1 3 1   ". . . by falling, consciously or unconsciously, into invalidism": "Who can doubt that, in an age when sex and childbirth involved very real threats to the health and life of women, some women would use the pretext of being 'delicate' as a way . . . of closing the bedroom door while avoiding the guilt consequent upon a more flagrant defiance of their duties"—Ann Douglas Wood, " 'The Fashionable Diseases': Women's Complaints and Their Treatment in Nineteenth-Century America," *Journal of Interdisciplinary History*, 4(1) (Summer 1973), pp. 25–52.

1 3 2   ". . . accidental pregnancies occurred at a rate of fewer than one a year": Anita Newcomb McGee, "An Experiment in Human Stirpiculture," *American Anthropologist*, Oct. 1891.

1 3 2   ". . . a childless woman who was eager to have a baby . . .": Parker, *A Yankee Saint*, p. 260.

1 3 2   ". . . the harmful effects of 'sickly maternal tenderness' . . .": *First Annual Report of the Oneida Association*, p. 7.

132 ". . . fussing excessively over its furnishings and appointments": Mary P. Ryan, in *Womanhood in America*, writes (p. 157), "The model homemaker was charged with creating a shrine of domesticity, a total environment of connubial bliss. . . . A woman . . . was required to adorn the structure with symbols of domesticity—curtains, knickknacks, and flowers."

CHAPTER FOURTEEN

This chapter, about children at Oneida, is based largely on the memoirs of people who grew up in the Community—on Pierrepont Noyes, *My Father's House;* Corinna Ackley Noyes, *The Days of My Youth;* and Jessie Kinsley, "Memories of Youth." I have also relied, as in earlier chapters, on Robertson's *Oneida Community: An Autobiography* and on the *Circular.* Other sources on which I drew:

141 Emerson on mothers and communal living: Raymond Lee Muncy, *Sex and Marriage in Utopian Communities* (Bloomington, IN: Indiana University Press, 1973), p. 14.

141 "Robert Owen and Charles Fourier . . .": A. L. Morton, *The Life and Ideas of Robert Owen* (New York: International Publishers, 1969), pp. 209–210, 214; Muncy, *Sex and Marriage*, pp. 69–70.

143–144 "A contemporary of Corinna and Pierrepont Noyes . . .": William M. Kephart, "Experimental Family Organization: A Historico-Cultural Report on the Oneida Community," *Marriage and Family Living*, 25, August 1963, pp. 261–271.

144 "I feel a certain respect for this tenacious philoprogenitiveness . . .": G. W. Noyes Papers, Vol. 1, pp. 82–83.

151 "Looking back on his childhood . . .": Dr. George E. Cragin, "Miscellaneous Memories of Community Life."

151 "Without exception, he reported . . .": Kephart, "Experimental Family Organization."

C H A P T E R   F I F T E E N

Principal sources for this chapter are *First Annual Report of the Oneida Association;* Robertson, *Oneida Community: An Autobiography;* the *Circular;* Parker, *A Yankee Saint;* and the G. W. Noyes Papers, Vol. 1. Other sources on which I drew:

1 5 4   ". . . composed a treatise to which he gave the title 'Bible Argument . . .' ": the quotations that follow are all from the *First Annual Report.*

1 6 2   ". . . gently removed . . . and deposited in a snowdrift . . .": Jessie Kinsley, "Memories of Youth," p. 31.

1 6 3   Guiteau's denunciation of Noyes and Oneida: Charles E. Rosenberg, *The Trial of Assassin Guiteau* (Chicago: University of Chicago Press, 1966). Guiteau's assertion that young women were "sacrificed to an experience easier imagined than described" is from the New York *Tribune,* Nov. 4, 1881.

1 6 3 – 1 6 4   "But the synod noted sadly . . .": *Oneida Dispatch,* 1874 (undated clipping).

1 6 4   Dixon's visit to Oneida: John Humphrey Noyes, *Dixon and His Copyists* (Oneida, New York: Oneida Community, 1874).

1 6 4   "Among them, to give just two examples . . .": Higginson's report on Oneida was published in the *Woman's Journal* and reprinted in *Male Continence;* Reclus's account of his visit was titled "Études Sociologiques. Visite aux Perfectionistes d'Oneida," and was published in *Société Nouvelle* (Bruxelles, 1885–1886, Année 2, tome 1).

1 6 6   " 'No finer example of quiet industry . . .' ": Utica *Observer,* 1873 (undated clipping).

C H A P T E R   S I X T E E N

Except as indicated, this chapter is based entirely on the documents and extracts from Community publications included in the G. W. Noyes Papers.

1 6 7   Oneidans "beset by 'gales . . .' ": *Circular,* March 7, 1852.

1 7 1   ". . . nine months later she admitted at a meeting of the Brooklyn family . . .": this sentence, and the balance of the paragraph, are taken from "Brooklyn Journal" (manuscript) for Dec. 7, 1849, and Jan. 24 and April 12, 1850.

1 7 3   "A much younger woman . . . recalled Harriet Noyes . . .": Jessie Kinsley, "Memories of Youth," pp. 67–68.

C H A P T E R   S E V E N T E E N

This chapter is based on a wide variety of sources:

1 7 5   ". . . Stephen Pearl Andrews, who grandly proclaimed . . .": Andrews, *Love, Marriage, and Divorce* (New York, 1853), p. 70; quoted in Hal D. Sears, *The Sex Radicals* (Lawrence, KS: Regents Press of Kansas, 1977).

1 7 5   "At Modern Times, according to one account . . .": Madeleine B. Stern, *The Pantarch* (Austin, TX: University of Texas Press, 1968), p. 83.

1 7 5   "Other advocates of perfect sexual freedom included Thomas and Mary Nichols . . .": Taylor Stoehr, *Free Love in America* (New York: AMS Press, 1979), p. 6.

1 7 6   "A gynecologist who visited Oneida . . .": Ely Van de Warker, "A Gynecological Study of the Oneida Community," *American Journal of Obstetrics*, 17, August 1884. In an interview in August 1891 with Anita Newcomb McGee, who was writing an article on stirpiculture at Oneida, Tirzah Miller said that boys learned "early and easily" to avoid ejaculation.

1 7 6   "Noyes's niece, Tirzah Miller . . .": Miller, interview with Anita Newcomb McGee; also, interviews with former Community residents by Hilda Herrick Noyes, cited in Carden, *Oneida: Utopian Community to Modern Corporation*, p. 53.

1 7 7   ". . . only about one accidental pregnancy per year": diary of Francis Wayland-Smith.

1 7 7   "When stirpiculture got under way . . .": diary of Francis Wayland-Smith.

177 "making sexual intercourse a quiet affair . . .": *First Annual Report of the Oneida Association*, p. 33.

177 ". . . to go ahead and have one anyway": Theodore R. Noyes, letter to Anita Newcomb McGee, Sept. 13, 1891.

177 "She tried to make me lose control": quoted in Kephart, "Experimental Family Organization: A Historico-cultural Report on the Oneida Community."

177 "Many physicians believed that male continence was bad for women, too": Stoehr, *Free Love in America*, p. 32; the quotation is from Van de Warker, "A Gynecological Study of the Oneida Community."

178 ". . . although the editors . . . praised his report . . .": their praise was contained in a letter printed as an appendix to *Essay on Scientific Propagation*, along with a reprint of Theodore Noyes's article, originally published in the *Medical Gazette* of Oct. 22, 1870.

178 "Coitus might continue for an hour or more . . .": Havelock Ellis, *Studies in the Psychology of Sex* (New York: Random House, 1936 edition; Vol. 4 of *Sex in Relation to Society*), p. 553. Ellis's source was Noyes Miller, who was four years old in 1849 when he joined the Community, and who lived there until the breakup.

178 ". . . it was customary . . . 'the men prided themselves . . .' ": Hilda Herrick Noyes, interview with R. D. Dickinson, September, 1926; from archives of the Kinsey Institute for Research in Sex, Gender, and Reproduction, Indiana University, Bloomington, IN.

179 ". . . one Oneida man told Hilda Noyes . . .": quoted in W. F. Robie, *The Art of Love* (Boston: Badger 1921), p. 188. Robie does not name his informant, but the context makes it clear that she was Hilda Noyes.

179 ". . . a practice of which Noyes took as dim a view . . .": Noyes believed that the habit of masturbation could become "besotted and ruinous," and that coitus interruptus was "unnatural, filthy and wasteful of life." (*First Annual Report of the Oneida Association*, pp. 31–33).

179 "Of the men and boys . . .": Based on a comparison of the "Family Register" kept by Harriet Noyes with a roster of Community members

as of Jan. 1, 1879, compiled by Francis Wayland-Smith and included in his diary.

1 8 0   "Rules for Sexual Intercourse": Home Talk, Sept. 22, 1852.

1 8 0   "Ordinarily a man would go to his partner's room for sex, but . . . a few rooms were set aside . . .": Carden, *Oneida: Utopian Community to Modern Corporation;* also, Anita Newcomb McGee, notes on interviews at Kenwood, NY, 1891.

1 8 1   "Thus, teenage boys . . .": Van de Warker, "A Gynecological Study of the Oneida Community"; his findings on this point were endorsed—in marginal notes on her copy of Van de Warker's article—by Anita Newcomb McGee, presumably on the strength of interviews she conducted at Oneida in 1891.

1 8 1   ". . . by Noyes himself or . . . by one of his most trusted associates": Theodore R. Noyes, letter to Anita Newcomb McGee, April 15, 1892.

1 8 1   "they will not get into bondage to one another . . .": Van de Warker, "A Gynecological Study." The author of the statement was Victor Cragin Noyes (*Circular*, Dec. 2, 1867).

1 8 2   "William Mills . . . appealed in vain to Harriet Skinner . . .": *Circular*, Jan. 9, 1865.

1 8 3   "In 1861, when members were asked . . .": *Circular*, Feb. 28, 1861.

1 8 3   "At an evening meeting in 1861 . . .": *Circular*, Sept. 12, 1861.

1 8 3   "All I wanted to know . . .": undated record of criticism of Tirzah Miller.

1 8 4   "One might as well think of loving some particular tune . . .": *Home-Talks*, p. 150.

1 8 4   ". . . a young woman who had been one of his [Cragin's] admirers recalled . . .": Jessie Kinsley, "Memories of Youth," p. 90.

1 8 4 – 1 8 5   "A young man named John Sears . . .": letter to Beulah Hendee, Jan. 17, 1879.

185 ". . . what one Community elder referred to . . .": *O.C. Daily*, Jan. 28, 1867.

185 "One reason, he wrote in 1892 . . .": letter to Anita Newcomb McGee, April 15, 1892.

186 "At a criticism session in 1849 . . .": report published in the *Circular*, Jan. 4, 1869.

186 "But whatever Stephen Leonard's true feelings . . . there is evidence . . .": for example, see Allan Estlake, *The Oneida Community* (London: George Redway, 1900; reprinted by AMS Press, New York, 1973), pp. 74–77.

186 "Seymour I hope you will not make too much . . .": Sarah Knowles Nash to her husband, Seymour Nash, June 19, 1859 (Nash Family Papers, Stanford University Libraries, Stanford, CA).

187 "The fulfillment of complex marriage . . .": Kinsley, "Memories of Youth," pp. 79–80.

187 "Oneidans even had a special song . . .": Raymond Lee Muncy, *Sex and Marriage in Utopian Communities*, pp. 172–173.

187 "A letter written by a thirty-four-year-old woman . . .": Annie Hatch to Beulah Hendee, Dec. 12, 1876.

188 "Pierrepont Noyes . . . remembered 'our grown folks' . . .": *My Father's House*, p. 131.

CHAPTER EIGHTEEN

For an understanding of the evolution of John Humphrey Noyes's theology and his shifting views of the Oneida Community's mission, which are the subjects of this chapter, I am indebted to May Louise Sobel, *An Experiment in Perfectionism: the Religious Life of the Putney and Oneida Communities* (Ph.D. thesis, Boston University, 1968). Except for sources cited in the text, and in the notes that follow, this chapter is based on the G. W. Noyes Papers and on the files of the *Circular*.

196 "As one member wrote after the Community's demise . . .": Henry J. Seymour, "The Oneida Community: a Dialogue," p. 23.

199   "The Oneidans . . . had already taken up science . . .": this paragraph is drawn largely from Chapter 6, "Education," of Constance Noyes Robertson's *Oneida Community: An Autobiography.*

CHAPTER NINETEEN

Except for the sources in the list that follows, this chapter is based on the G. W. Noyes Papers; John Humphrey Noyes, *Scientific Propagation;* Hilda Herrick Noyes and George Wallingford Noyes, "The Oneida Community Experiment in Stirpiculture," Scientific Papers of the Second International Congress of Eugenics, 1921; *Eugenics, Genetics and the Family* Vol. 1, pp. 374–386 (Baltimore: Williams & Wilkins Co., 1923); and Parker, *A Yankee Saint.*

204   "The standard procedure . . .": this paragraph is based in part on Anita Newcomb McGee, "An Experiment in Human Stirpiculture," *American Anthropologist,* October 1891.

205   "Great Giver of the righteous seed . . .": all three stanzas of the song are contained in an unsigned paper I came across in the Mansion House, bearing the same date as Charlotte Leonard's letter; Leonard sent her mother only the final stanza, in a slightly different form from the version I have given here.

205   "One 'martyr to science' named Mary Jones . . .": this paragraph is based on the diary of Victor Hawley, 1876–1877 (typescript).

206   "But as George Bernard Shaw . . . later pointed out . . .": Muncy, *Sex and Marriage in Utopian Communities,* p. 189.

207   ". . . apparently believing that the time was not right for an assault on . . . 'the last citadel of social falsehood . . .' ": letter from George Washington Noyes to Harriet Skinner, Sept. 13, 1869.

207   "He said to combine with me would be intensifying . . .": diary of Tirzah Miller, Jan. 25, 1874.

207   "But other considerations often weighed heavily": this paragraph is based on the G. W. Noyes Papers; Hilda Herrick Noyes and George Wallingford Noyes, "The Oneida Community Experiment in Stirpiculture"; the *O.C. Daily;* and the diary of Francis Wayland-Smith.

208   Footnote: *O.C. Daily*, June 12 and 20, 1867.

209   "As it turned out, Inslee was a cruel disappointment . . .": letter from John Humphrey Noyes to Harriet Skinner, undated, 1881.

209   "In another case a young woman named Leonora Hatch . . .": this paragraph is based on the diary of Francis Wayland-Smith (p. 321) and a letter from Tirzah Miller to John Humphrey Noyes, June 3, 1882.

210   Footnote: letter from F. W. Frankland to Anita Newcomb McGee, May 15, 1891.

CHAPTERS TWENTY AND TWENTY-ONE

Except as indicated in the text or in the notes that follow, these chapters are based on the G. W. Noyes Papers and the diary of Francis Wayland-Smith.

214   ". . . telling his father that he could no longer endure being ostracized . . .": undated letter to John Skinner, as summarized in a memorandum by Hope Allen, August 5, 1942.

216   ". . . when he had an idea he would 'hold still and consult . . .' ": letter from Theodore Noyes to A. N. McGee, Sept. 13, 1891.

216   ". . . in the 'dark room' in the north garret . . .": Jessie Kinsley, *A Lasting Spring*, p. 42.

221   "Another cause, Theodore later wrote . . .": letter to A. N. McGee, Sept. 13, 1891.

224   "As a member of the Community remembered Theodore   ": Pierrepont Noyes, *My Father's House*, p. 160.

224   "A graduate of the Children's House recalled . . .": Pierrepont Noyes, *My Father's House*, p. 161.

230   " 'Mr. Noyes's mind,' a diarist noted . . .": Constance Noyes Robertson, *The Breakup*, p. 67. The diarist was Cornelia Worden.

231   " 'The Rubicon is passed,' a young woman at Oneida wrote . . .": Beulah Hendee to Annie Hatch, Aug. 5, 1878.

CHAPTER TWENTY-TWO

Much of this chapter is derived from the G. W. Noyes Papers and the diary of Francis Wayland-Smith. But I have drawn much more heavily than in the immediately preceding chapters on a wide variety of other sources.

232   "the true anchor of the Community": letter to Mary Louise Prindle, June 18, 1878.

233–234   ". . . Noyes once observed sadly . . .": letter to William A. Hinds, Aug. 17, 1876.

234   " 'It is very curious . . .' she wrote to a friend . . .": letter to James W. Towner, Dec. 8, 1876.

235   ". . . Theodore Noyes . . . saw this as the key to effective government": letter to Anita Newcomb McGee, April 15, 1892.

236   "Its principal leader was James William Towner": this paragraph is based on Spencer C. Olin, Jr., "The Oneida Community and the Instability of Charismatic Authority," *Journal of American History,* 67(2), Sept. 1980; Olin, "Bible Communism and the Origins of Orange County," *California History,* 58(3), Fall 1979; Robert S. Fogarty, "Nineteenth Century Utopian," *The Pacific Historian,* 16(3), Fall 1972; William F. Vartorella, "Free Love War Waged in Ohio," *Echoes,* 13(6), June 1974 Ohio Historical Society; Taylor Stoehr, *Free Love in America;* and Parker, *A Yankee Saint.*

237   "Noyes . . . had come to view Towner . . .": letter to Abel Easton, June 18, 1879.

237   ". . . Towner's most influential ally, William Hinds . . .": this sketch of Hinds is taken mainly from an article in the *Quadrangle,* Kenwood, NY, June 1910.

238   "As Theodore Noyes suggested years afterward . . .": letter to Anita Newcomb McGee, Sept. 13, 1891.

238   ". . . in Towner's view, it promoted 'delicacy . . .' ": Stoehr, *Free Love in America,* p. 37.

238–239   "The Community is 'tied up in hard knots . . .' a diarist observed . . .": diary of Harriet Worden, Jan. 14, 1876.

240 ". . . Noyes laughed and . . . said mischievously . . .": letter from W.N.M. to Noyes, Jan. 6, 1879.

240 "A loyal supporter of Noyes . . . wrote sadly . . .": Beulah Hendee to Annie Hatch, March 26, 1879.

242 "Open scorn and rebellion . . .": Kinsley, *A Silent Spring*, p. 60.

243 "The pressures that sent Noyes fleeing into exile came from the world outside . . .": this paragraph is based on Parker, *A Yankee Saint*, pp. 267–270.

244 ". . . a group of Episcopal, Presbyterian, and Methodist clergymen convened . . .": this paragraph is based on Robertson, *The Breakup*, Chapter 5, "Crusade of the Clergy."

244 "*Puck* . . . ran a cartoon . . .": reproduced in Parker, *A Yankee Saint*, p. 280.

245 "As Theodore Noyes later pointed out . . .": letter to Anita Newcomb McGee, Sept. 13, 1891.

245 " 'I only know,' he wrote, 'that indictments . . . were in the air . . .' ": Noyes, "Niagara Journal."

245 "Mears himself told a reporter . . .": Robertson, *The Breakup*, p. 118.

245 "The *World* reporter also interviewed . . .": report from Francis Wayland-Smith to John Humphrey Noyes, June 26, 1879; quoted in Robertson, *The Breakup*, pp. 116–117.

246 "Theodore Noyes . . . later wrote . . .": letter to Anita Newcomb McGee, Sept. 13, 1891.

246 "Noyes's sister Harriet agreed": quoted in Robertson, *The Breakup*, p. 116.

CHAPTERS TWENTY-THREE AND
TWENTY-FOUR

Except as otherwise indicated in the text or in the notes that follow, these chapters are based on the G. W. Noyes Papers, the diary of Francis Wayland-Smith, and John Humphrey Noyes's "Niagara Journal."

248 ". . . Pierrepont Noyes recalled . . .": *My Father's House*, p. 18.

255 "In a letter to a friend at Wallingford . . .": Beulah Hendee to Annie (Hatch?), Dec. 19, 1879.

271 ". . . five years later the old trapmaker . . .": Parker, *A Yankee Saint*, pp. 289–290.

CHAPTER TWENTY-FIVE

This chapter is mainly based on Pierrepont Noyes, *My Father's House;* Maren Lockwood Carden, *Oneida: Utopian Community to Modern Corporation;* and John Humphrey Noyes, "Niagara Journal." In addition to those cited in the text, I also made use of the following sources:

275 ". . . Towner and some . . . of his followers migrated . . .": this sentence and the balance of the paragraph are based on Spencer C. Olin, Jr., "The Oneida Community and the Instability of Charismatic Authority"; and Olin, "Bible Communism and the Origins of Orange County."

276 "keep the record of their pedigree as a diploma of nobility": from "letter essays" sent to Tirzah Miller and dated Aug. 20, 21, and 23, 1881.

278 ". . . Noyes, who for a while got up at four o'clock . . . to teach himself the language": letter from Mary Louise Prindle to Charlotte Leonard, Feb. 7, 1883. Prindle was also the visitor quoted in the next sentence.

278 "As for complex marriage, he asserted . . .": Noyes, "The Charitable and Hopeful View of the Social State of the Community," Sept. 1, 1883.

280 "He explained to his sister Harriet . . .": letter to E. H. Hamilton, Sept. 2, 1880.

280–281 "In 1883 he wrote that for five years . . .": letter to Harriet Skinner, May 26, 1883.

281 ". . . as Harriet Skinner reported his saying shortly before the final breakup . . .": letter to E. H. Hamilton, Sept. 2, 1880.

281 "Noyes also blamed the poor material . . .": Noyes, "Niagara Journal."

282 ". . . he had later concluded that Inslee . . .": letter to Harriet Skinner, 1881 (undated).

EPILOGUE

Except for the concluding section beginning on page 293, this chapter is based almost entirely on Carden, *Oneida: Utopian Community to Modern Corporation*. I have also drawn, to a much lesser extent, on Walter D. Edmonds, *The First Hundred Years, 1848–1948* (Oneida, NY: Oneida Ltd., 1948). The quotation from Jessie Kinsley on page 293 is from Kinsley, *A Lasting Spring*, p. 41.

Index